D0359123

the small
GARDEN

designing and planting outdoor living space

the small GARDEN

designing and planting outdoor living space

consultant: Susan Berry

PUBLISHED BY

SALAMANDER BOOKS LIMITED

LONDON

A SALAMANDER BOOK

Published by Salamander Books
Limited,
8, Blenheim Court, Brewery Road,
London N7 9NY,
United Kingdom

1 3 5 7 9 8 6 4 2

© Salamander Books Ltd, 2001

A member of the Chrysalis Group plc

ISBN 1 84065 281 0

All rights reserved. No part of
this book may be reproduced,
stored in a retrieval system or
transmitted in any form or by any
means, electronic, mechanical,
photocopying, recording or
otherwise, without the prior
permission of Salamander Books.

All correspondence concerning
the content of this volume should
be addressed to Salamander Books.

Some of the material featured in
this book has appeared in previous
publications.

CREDITS

Consultant: Susan Berry
Commissioning editor: Will Steeds
Editor: Joanna Smith
Designer: Debbie Mole
Artworks: Sally Launder, Ian Smith
and Debbie Roberts
Text: Susan Berry, Richard Bird,
Peter Blackburne-Maze, John
Feltwell, Carol Gubler, Nicholas
Hall, Jenny Hendy, Ann James,
Mike Lawrence, Sue Phillips,
Yvonne Rees, Wilma Rittershausen,
Rosemary Titterington

Colour reproduction: Media Print
(UK), Ltd.
Printed in Taiwan

HALF TITLE: *Vivid flowers and bold
plants displayed in clay pots around a
small patio garden.*
TITLE: *Colourful and useful herbs
surround a potted bay tree.*
ABOVE: *Geraniums, ornamental grasses
(Hordeum) and other perennials spill
over a gravel path.*

CONTENTS

Introduction   6

CHAPTER 1
CHOOSING A STYLE   10
Design options   12
Formal garden style   20
Basements & courtyards   24
Alleys & narrow spaces   28
Roof gardens   32
Balconies & terraces   36
Garden rooms   40

CHAPTER 2
GARDEN SURFACES   44
Paving   46
Paths & steps   48
Laying slabs on sand   50
Laying slabs on mortar   52
Planting in paving   54
Bricks & pavers   56
Laying pavers   58
Patterns with pavers   60
Pebbles & cobbles   62
Laying gravel   64
Wooden surfaces   66
Decking   68
Soft surfaces   72

CHAPTER 3
GARDEN FEATURES   74
Walls & fences   76
A living boundary   80
Trellis   82
Other vertical features   84
Pergolas   86

Erecting a pergola   88
Obelisks   90
A honeysuckle pole   92
Rustic supports   94
Garden furniture   96
Building a seat   100
Cold frames   102
Water features   104
Installing a pond   108
Installing a water pump   110
Garden ornaments   112
Decorative details   114
Awnings & umbrellas   116
Lighting   118
Containers   120
Decorating containers   122
Making a window box   124

CHAPTER 4
PLANT FEATURES   126
Planting the small garden   128
Planted screens   130
Feature plants   134
Architectural plants   136
Grasses   138
Annuals & bedding plants   140
Planting for sun   142
Shrubs for sun   144
Planting for shade   146
Plants for containers   150
Hanging baskets   154
Bulbs in containers   156
Speedy topiary   158
Moisture-loving plants   162
A barrel water feature   164

A bog garden in a tub   166
Plants for scent   168
Edible plants   172
A formal herb garden   176
Salad crops on a small scale   178
Growing tomatoes   180
Growing strawberries   182

CHAPTER 5
GARDEN TECHNIQUES   184
Soils & mulches   186
Making garden compost   188
Routine tasks   190
Planting   192
Sowing seeds   194
Taking cuttings   196
Dividing plants   198
Layering   199
Pruning   200
Lawn care   206
Pests & diseases   207

CHAPTER 6
SMALL GARDEN PLANTS   208
Trees   210
Shrubs   214
Climbers   220
Roses   224
Perennials   226
Bedding plants   234
Moisture-loving plants   238
Bulbs   242
Ferns, grasses & bamboos   246
Index   250
Acknowledgements   256

INTRODUCTION

BELOW: *York stone pavers, interplanted with creepers to soften their formality, provide an attractive surface for this small patio, while large-leaved foliage plants and a raised water feature add architectural interest.*

TO SOME PEOPLE a small garden is a positive benefit, as it requires less time and effort to keep it well-stocked and tidy. But to frustrated large-scale gardeners a small garden is a problem of logistics – how can you possibly fit in all your favourite plants and express your creativity in a small space? In both cases the solution starts with good design. Small gardens are not just large gardens in miniature. They need very different ingredients and a major shift in emphasis. Attention to detail is the key. When it comes to planting, every available space counts, so plants must be perfect – in quality, behaviour and the contribution they make to the garden. You might prefer to use a few larger plants in strategic positions or many more smaller plants for a more varied effect. And to pack in maximum interest, you will need to make use of vertical space as well as the floor of the garden. Certain techniques are particularly valuable in a small space. For example, there are intensive and decorative ways to grow vegetables, fruit and herbs so that you no longer want to hide them away at the end of the garden. This book aims to show you how to plan and create the small garden of your dreams that is tailor-made for your needs.

One of the key things to consider when you are designing and planting a small space is what your needs actually are, and the amount of time and attention you will be able to lavish on

the garden. If you are constantly away on holiday or on business, it would be a grave mistake to create a garden that needs a lot of attention. Far better, in these circumstances, to opt for a low-maintenance garden with easy-to-care-for shrubs and ground cover, and some good-quality hard surfacing so that the garden looks as good on your return as it did on your departure.

Do not be put off by hostile conditions when planning your small garden – high walls, limited space, poor soil or whatever. Plants can be found that will scale most walls, either on their own or with the help of simple supports, or you can fit brackets to the walls and suspend a number of pots from them. Attractive containers, large or small, in natural materials – stone,

RIGHT: *Note how well the architectural forms have been balanced in this courtyard garden. The irregular rectangles of York stone, banded by pebbles, make a sympathetic surface, while the planting, confined to the house walls and to large containers, creates a soft living frame to the setting.*

terracotta or metal – can be used to house plants if the garden has already been paved over, or if the soil is very bad quality. Plants can be used to screen unsightly views, giving you both much-needed privacy and shelter for your more choice plants, and yourselves, from the elements.

The choice of styles for small spaces is almost limitless, from the neat zen-like efficiency of an Oriental garden, in which natural materials and neatly formed shrubs predominate, to a rampant wilderness of vigorous plants, competing with each other for the available space and light. Scale is not the most important element in success, but using what space you have well is essential. As already mentioned, make the most of what you have by covering the vertical surfaces with plants and ensuring you have a good variety of plants for all seasons since, especially if you live in a town, your garden may be your only opportunity to observe these subtle changes throughout the months, keeping you in touch with the natural world.

If you enjoy contact with nature, try to make the most of it by making your small space a refuge for birds and insects – you will be surprised by how many different kinds even a small garden can attract. A small pond or water feature provides you with an enormous bonus, not only in the range of plants you can grow, but also in the way it attracts insects, birds and dragonflies.

Colour is a great asset in the grey environment of a small city garden, and the plain and simple background of brick, stone and concrete provides an ideal foil for a rich and varied array of flowering plants. If your small garden is in the countryside, you are obliged to plant your garden in harmony with the natural surroundings beyond it and this usually means picking a pastel colour palette, as brighter colours tend to jar with too much greenery. In a city garden you can, if you wish, go for stronger more Mediterranean colours and a generally more exotic look which is well set-off by the buildings around. If you are lucky enough to have brick walls and a reasonable amount of sunlight, you can grow a wide range of sun-loving herbs,

LEFT: *Even a small garden can have a lawn, provided it has a reasonable amount of light. This walled garden contains a mixture of formal and informal elements, with its rectangular box-hedged bed of lavender as the focal point, and the border planting a softer mixture of shrubs and perennials.*

BELOW: *Separated as it is from other gardens, a roof terrace gives you plenty of scope to exercise your imagination. This small roof garden has an Oriental theme, with its pebble and decking surface, its reed screens, low wooden furniture with spare lines, and its classic bamboos.*

with delicious scent and attractive silvery leaves – lavender, rosemary, different kinds of sage, artemisia and senecio are all ideal candidates for an aromatic, silver-leaved planting scheme with a Mediterranean theme.

As anyone knows who has ever walked through the backstreets of European villages and had their eye caught by a single brilliant scarlet pelargonium framed in a small window, even the smallest space can provide a theatrical setting for plants. If you have limited space at your disposal, choosing star performers like pelargoniums, which have brilliant flower colour over a long season and require very little attention, is one of the keys to success.

No matter how inhospitable the space you have at your disposal, you will find plants that will grow in it successfully, although your choice may be limited. A small shady basement, for example, is not the ideal home for plants but there are those that will do very well there – particularly plants that have adapted, say, to life at the bottom of the forest floor where very little light penetrates.

A small garden is not just a space to observe and enjoy nature, it is also a much-needed additional living space, be it a small balcony or verandah, a roof terrace or patio. If the space you have is large enough to use in this way, then make the most of it by turning it into an attrac-

tive outdoor room. Choose furniture that suits the design of the area and fits well into the space, and use canvas umbrellas and colourful cushions, if you wish, to add warmth and verve to the setting and make it feel much more like a living space. Sitting outside in your small garden, enjoying the warm dying light as the sun sinks below the horizon on a balmy summer evening, can provide a wonderful release from the stresses and strains of daily life. A small amount of time spent planning your garden and a little time spent caring for it will be repaid over and over again as you savour its sensual pleasures of scent, colour, life and variety.

CHAPTER 1

CHOOSING A STYLE

YOUR CHOICE of garden style is dictated by the shape, situation and aspect of the plot as much as by personal choice. In this chapter, the principal types of garden are discussed, from small balconies to large outdoor rooms, from narrow shady alleyways that run up the side of the house to purpose-built roof gardens. It includes advice on the different ways to construct, plan and plant these areas so that you make the best use of the aspect and the available light or prevailing conditions. Small gardens can take on many guises; you are not obliged to opt for slick formality – a small jungle-like oasis or even a wild garden are just as welcome as a neatly paved rectangle of patio. Make sure, however, that your choice reflects your lifestyle, and can be maintained with ease in the time you have available.

LEFT: *This simply planted, walled garden has used vertical surfaces for climbers, with a small water feature as a focal point in the gravelled patio area. Mound-forming plants soften the hard surfaces.*

RIGHT: *Attractive York stone paving and an abundance of containers, with topiary, daisies, pelargoniums and patio roses, make this small backyard a delightful oasis.*

DESIGN OPTIONS
FOR THE SAME SPACE

WHEN DESIGNING YOUR OWN GARDEN, go about it in the same way as a professional designer. Start by 'interviewing yourself'. How do you want to use the garden? As a low-upkeep, outdoor leisure room or a plant-lover's paradise? Write down the features you regard as essential – perhaps a pond or greenhouse – the kinds of plants you like and any 'must-have' favourites. Even if you think you already know the answers, this helps to concentrate the mind when you start to prepare a design. But unlike the professional, who would probably only show you one finished idea, you can afford to spend time considering your options. So make at least three completely different plans for the same space. Be creative; see how many different ideas you can devise for the space that meet the same specification. You do not have to come up with them all at once. In fact, it is a good idea to think about just one style of garden in a day and develop the idea to the full, as if each one was the actual garden you were going to make. Leave time for your mind to clear before going back to them. Then compare all the designs critically, just as if you were your own 'customer'. Choose the design you like best, the one you think meets your needs and gives you what you want from the garden. One of your originals may turn out to be perfect, but more likely you will see good and bad ideas in all of them. In that case you can try another alternative which combines the best of the earlier tries. After a few alterations, you will get closer to your ideal. Allow yourself enough time and do the design work in winter when you are not pressured to get on with the preparation and planting.

RIGHT: *Formal gardens look symmetrical. The area is often divided into halves or quarters by paths that meet at a central feature, such as a statue. A formal design could occupy an entire garden, or be just a small part of the garden.*

ABOVE: *A geometric design, in which straight-edged features such as paths and formal ponds are set at an angle to the house, disguises the shape of a traditional rectangular plot, and turns it into a very modern abstract-looking garden.*

ABOVE: *Informal gardens can be quite adventurous. You can use coloured tiles and unusual surfaces to make a garden in which the plants are used more like decorations to the various 'designer' touches dotted around the area.*

ABOVE: *Informal gardens have a more relaxed look and, instead of straight lines, use curving paths and lawn edges. Borders are undulating, with trees and shrubs grouped together and plants used in a much more natural-looking way. Even the pond looks like a fairly natural feature of the land.*

RIGHT: *If you have a particular interest, say in water gardening, the whole design can be based around this. Even in a small space, with permanent paving and plumbing, there is still scope for seasonal effects in the border around the edge, so the garden need not look the same all year.*

DESIGN OPTIONS - A GEOMETRIC GARDEN

A MODERN DESIGN for a very regular, rectangular plot does everything in its power to take away the squareness of the shape. The aim is to distract attention from the parallel sides by confusing the eye with powerful diagonals or bold off-set patterns. These can divide the garden into geometric shapes that have much in common with classic formal designs, but with a very different perspective. The end result can be peculiarly striking. However, gardens like this are much harder to design than a formal garden, since there is no readily apparent starting point. The best way to go about the task is to gather up ideas from similar gardens you have visited (take photos to act as reminders later on) or seen in magazines and start trying to put them together to suit your requirements. After a few attempts, you will find it all starts to fall into place. However, this is not the sort of garden you could create without a plan, unlike some types of informal gardens that you can literally leave to grow up around you. And while the shapes seen on a plan of the garden may be easily recognizable as geometric, they do not appear so when planted up, since the planting style is very informal. You need a distinct range of ingredients from which to select. Include one or two bizarrely shaped architectural plants that make living focal points, and carpets of mixed plants to set them off. Use the same formula in reverse, using carpets of architectural features such as cobbles with a group of containers or a piece of abstract sculpture. And use plenty of lines: linear, horizontal features such as railway sleepers set in gravel, and straight-sided raised beds with upright features such as pergolas and arches and plants such as bamboo. These gardens are great fun to plan.

A plan of a geometric garden design

A modern geometric design should stop you looking straight down to the end of the garden, while teasing you with a focal point that your brain tells you to look at. However, to get there, the eye has to zigzag backwards and forwards between parallel lines like a pinball machine.

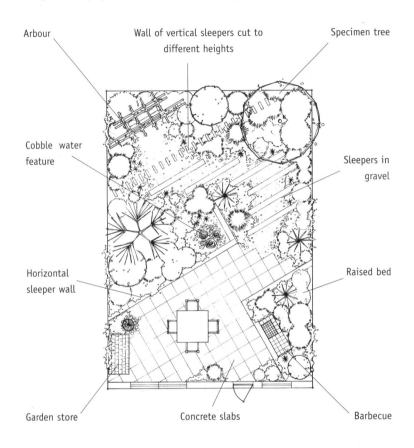

Arbour

Wall of vertical sleepers cut to different heights

Specimen tree

Cobble water feature

Sleepers in gravel

Horizontal sleeper wall

Raised bed

Garden store

Concrete slabs

Barbecue

RIGHT: Old railway sleepers add a variety of form and texture to an area of gravel, without the inconvenience of tending plants growing in it.

Arbour

Do not suddenly introduce a curvy rustic arbour or shaped seat. Keep all the edges straight in order to retain the effect of this distinctive design style. Soften the shape with climbers. Choose something evergreen if possible for year-round effect.

Specimen tree

This specimen tree dominates a complete corner of the design, so make it a good one. Choose a striking, preferably evergreen tree, but one with a non-traditional appearance, such as *Genista aetnensis*. Try a craggy pine, fig tree or perhaps a cryptomeria. Alternatively, train a large shrub into a tree by growing it on a single stem. *Crinodendron hookerianum* or *Clerodendrum trichotomum* var *fargesii* are both possible candidates.

Sleeper wall

Constructing a wall from old railway sleepers is very easy. If they are to stand on soil, simply lay them edgeways on to a bed of dry mortar mix. The cement takes up moisture from the ground and sets slowly. On paving, stand them on to a wet mix. As they are heavy enough to leave just standing in place, you may wish not to use mortar at all so you can redesign the space more easily later on.

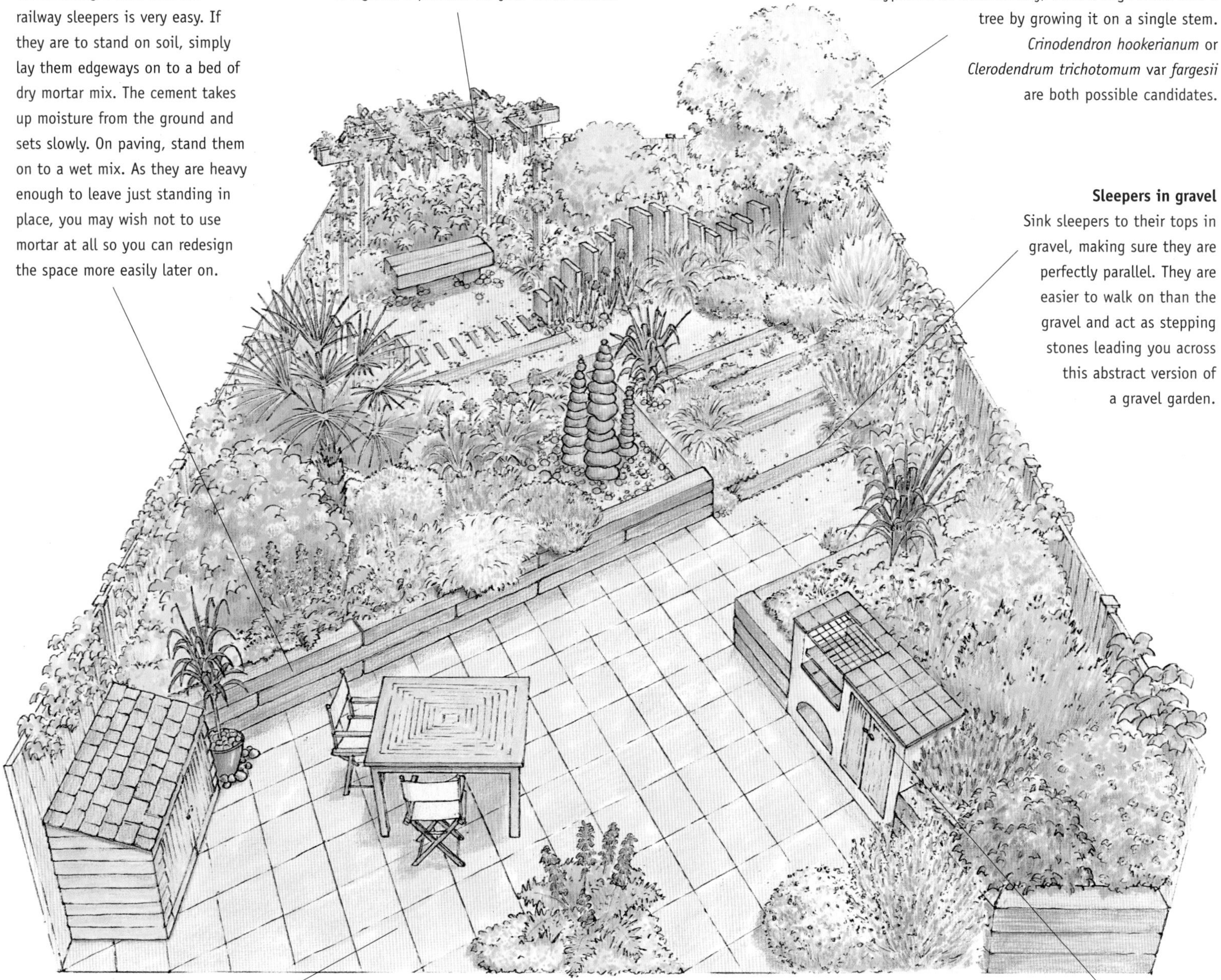

Sleepers in gravel

Sink sleepers to their tops in gravel, making sure they are perfectly parallel. They are easier to walk on than the gravel and act as stepping stones leading you across this abstract version of a gravel garden.

Concrete slabs on the patio

Square, textured concrete slabs complete the modern geometric look, and team up beautifully with the gravel and sleepers. Choose striking, well-designed, modern patio furniture in complementary colours to go with them.

Barbecue

A modern design like this is going to appeal to younger gardeners who will almost certainly want to enjoy high-tech outdoor living. A built-in barbecue with all the trappings is an essential. Include a cupboard in the wall below the cooking surface where barbecue fittings can be kept when not in use.

DESIGN OPTIONS - AN INFORMAL GARDEN

WHEN YOU MENTION INFORMAL GARDENS, most people think of rambling cottage gardens or wild gardens. Both are very informal in style, but informal gardens can also be modern in outlook. The same basic principles apply to all: no straight lines, use of natural materials and plenty of contrasting plant shapes, leaf sizes and textures with harmonious colours. But by using fashionable plants such as grasses or new varieties of perennials, plus stylish furniture and props, you can create a whole new look. To give it a designer edge, base the garden on a series of coordinating shapes instead of letting paths ramble aimlessly, and plant in distinct groups with, perhaps, groups of pebbles in between instead of letting plants merge randomly together cottage-style. Use a wide mixture of plants so that the garden changes as much as possible throughout the seasons and always provides something fresh to enjoy. Vital ingredients should include at least one good small tree, a mixture of flowering shrubs with as much good foliage as possible, perennials, plenty of grasses and scented plants. There is no need to restrict yourself to wild-style flowers or old-fashioned plants; create a modern look using architectural shrubs and perennials with striking shapes: spiky sea hollies, poker-like kniphofia, upright *Sisyrinchium striatum* and flat heads of *Sedum spectabile*. Look for inspired plant associations, such as the flat-topped *Solidago* 'Crown of Rays' with the tiered creamy flowers of *Phygelius* 'Moonraker'. Add enough hardware to balance the planting. Natural materials, such as planed wood and rough timber, cobbles and paving, look good in an informal garden. An informal water feature adds the finishing touch.

A plan of an informal garden design

Curving lines, unfussy plant groupings and a few simple features are the essence of an informal garden. Aim to make a garden that looks as if it just happened naturally; if it runs wild when you are away on holiday, far from looking unkempt on your return, it just looks like romantic disarray.

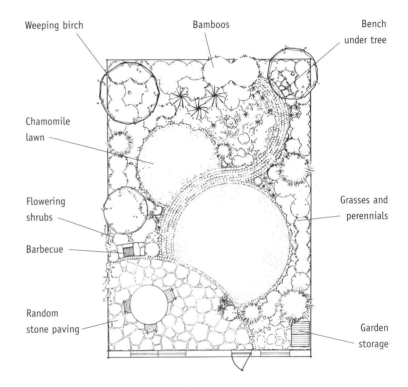

Weeping birch

Bamboos

Bench under tree

Chamomile lawn

Flowering shrubs

Grasses and perennials

Barbecue

Random stone paving

Garden storage

RIGHT: *Perennials are excellent for an informal design. Make the most of those with strong shapes and appealing colours, such as lupins.*

Weeping birch
A weeping birch provides fresh foliage in spring, early summer catkins, yellow autumn foliage and a shining white trunk that stands out well in winter.

Chamomile lawn
Although a chamomile lawn does not take the hard regular wear of grass, it does make a decorative, fragrant feature with stepping stones or a brick surround to walk on.

Flowering shrubs with timber posts
Do not look straight into the back of a border when working at your barbecue. Instead, place three smooth, timber poles among some low, flowering shrubs.

Bamboos
Evergreen bamboos make a good screen. Unlike hedges, they stop growing once they reach maximum height, which in many popular varieties is about 1.8m (6ft). Provide plenty of organic matter so that the soil does not dry out badly in summer.

Water jet
The water from this fountain bubbles over cobblestones and drains back into an underground reservoir, where it is recycled by a submersible pump. It is a safe feature for a garden where small children play.

A bench under a tree
A bench under a tree makes a good focal point from the house, yet when you are sitting on it, you get a completely different view of the garden.

Concrete sett path
Concrete setts make a textured path reminiscent of cobblestones, but because each sett is flat on top it is easier to walk on.

Grasses and perennials
Choose a mixture of flowering grasses and hot red, orange and yellow perennials for the latest look in informal planting.

Random stone paving and concrete sett edging
Use the same type of concrete setts as used for the path to surround other features, such as the patio and chamomile lawn, to add a feeling of continuity.

Three timber posts
This trio of timber posts acts as a visual balance for the three on the left of the garden, and partly screens the garden store.

Garden cupboard
Use a garden 'cupboard' to store essential garden tools, a tiny hover mower for the grass, and barbecue gear when not in use, so there is no need to find room for a walk-in shed.

DESIGN OPTIONS - A FORMAL GARDEN

ALTHOUGH FORMAL GARDENS are normally associated with grand old houses, many of the features that epitomize them adapt well to small-scale use. A formal garden is a surprisingly practical, low-maintenance way of using a small rectangular plot. Formal gardens make good outdoor 'rooms', with hard surfaces underfoot and interesting geometric features (such as the lily pond in the design shown here), where you would normally expect to find a lawn. Since they invariably use a lot of paving, walling, ornaments and upmarket containers and structures, they are relatively expensive to create. (But at least you only have a small area to fill.) However, once everything is in place, they are probably cheaper to keep up than an informal garden, and you certainly do not need much equipment to look after them. This means that you do not need to provide anywhere to keep a mower, or store garden furniture in winter. It is easy to create a formal garden that does not have a lawn.

The benefits of a formal garden design

IF YOU USE STONE benches or classical hardwood seats and tables, they form part of the architecture of the garden and can be left out all year round. To keep the cost of statues, large terracotta urns and so on to a minimum, grow your own topiary and use plenty of hedging and trained, block-shaped evergreens as living walls and sculpture.

A formal garden provides plenty of opportunities for growing plants that are often difficult to fit into a modern or informal setting due to their very symmetrical shapes (such as tulips). Walls or evergreen hedges provide a wonderful backdrop against which to appreciate the shapes of plants such as standard-trained wisteria.

BELOW: *Typical ingredients of a formal garden include paving, arches, containers, geometric beds and ponds, plus raised plinths for statues and containers or as decorative features on their own. Keep the layout as symmetrical as possible.*

A plan of a formal garden design

The thing that sets a formal design apart from any other is the use of straight lines and symmetry to create a classic feel. You could almost design the garden with a geometry set or squared paper. But this style of garden does not suit every house. You can introduce the odd formal feature within an informal garden, but in general, only a formal type of house looks right with a totally formal garden.

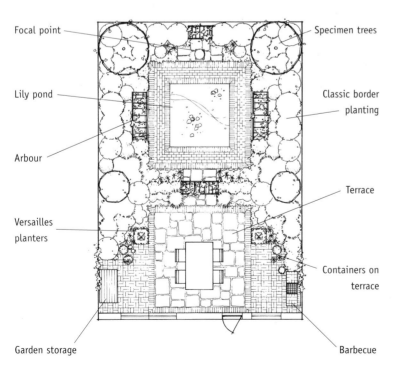

Focal point
Specimen trees
Lily pond
Classic border planting
Arbour
Terrace
Versailles planters
Containers on terrace
Garden storage
Barbecue

Bench beneath rose arbour

Plant scented roses for ambience, or a nearly thornless variety such as 'Zéphirine Drouhin' for comfort. Combine roses with the classic purple-leaved grape vine (*Vitis vinifera* 'Purpurea'). Its foliage sets off the rose flowers well.

Focal point

A formal garden needs something to draw the eye to the end of a view. This is called the focal point, and in a small space a striking urn set back into a niche carved from an evergreen hedge serves the purpose without taking up too much room.

Specimen trees

For the end of the garden, choose a pair of matching specimen trees with a striking shape, such as the weeping form of the Persian ironwood (*Parrotia persica* 'Pendula'), weeping cherries or classic topiary-trained yews or hollies.

Lily pond

Choose a geometric shape for a formal pool; round or square are the most popular kinds, but make it echo the shapes used elsewhere in the garden. Do not try to plant it in a natural way.

Classic border planting

Use evergreen hedging or shrubs at the back of the borders for year-round interest and to outline the structure of the garden. Fill in foreground detail with the smarter spring bulbs, such as lily-flowered tulips and stately herbaceous plants, including acanthus, delphiniums and lilies.

Versailles planters

Use these containers to accommodate topiary shapes or an obelisk planted with clematis.

Paving

Bricks laid in stretcher bond have been used around the pool, and in basketweave bond on either side of the paving outside the patio doors.

Terrace

The terrace is the classical equivalent of the modern patio. You can still have garden furniture and use the area for outdoor entertaining, but keep to classical styles in order not to ruin the effect of the rest of the garden.

Containers on the terrace

Avoid garish modern displays in favour of understated, classical simplicity. Use terracotta or reconstituted stone urns, amphorae or pots with a raised motif.

FORMAL GARDEN STYLE

BELOW: *This stunning formal patio has been designed to echo the surrounding architecture, its key components of gravel, water and evergreen planting all classical formal features.*

VERY SMALL GARDENS are often best laid out in quite a strict formal style, as already mentioned, for several reasons. Firstly, many small gardens are in an urban setting and the architecture of the house forms the backdrop to the garden; a formal style, with its straight lines and neat construction, echoes this built environment that it surrounds. Secondly, the simplicity of a formal arrangement helps to make the most of the limited space.

Formal gardens were originally designed in France in the eighteenth century by garden architects such as André le Nôtre, the aim being to order nature and tame it. The chief attributes were rectangular beds, straight paths and a neat symmetry about the planting. Translated on to a small plot, the French parterre concept can be juggled slightly to create a similarly styled but rather more free design style, with small box hedges, for example, and gravel or brick paths, surrounding small, formally laid out beds. If you are lucky enough to have a reasonable amount of sun, you could grow an interesting range of herbs in the beds between the box hedges. A visit to any good herb garden will give you some good ideas of what to grow, and how to grow it.

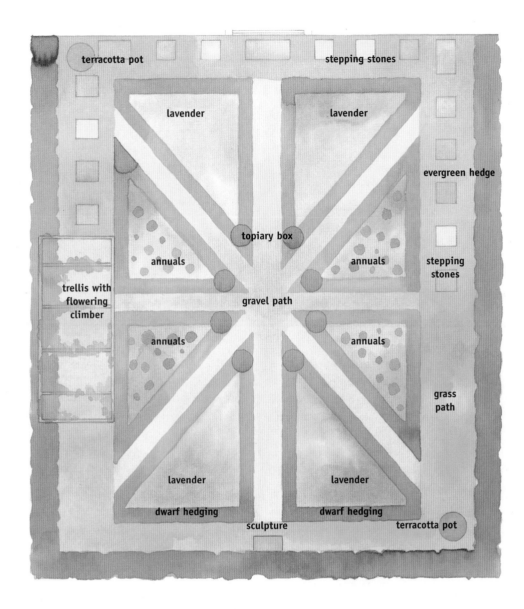

terracotta pot   stepping stones

lavender   lavender

evergreen hedge

topiary box

trellis with flowering climber

annuals   annuals   stepping stones

gravel path

annuals   annuals

grass path

lavender   lavender

dwarf hedging   dwarf hedging

sculpture   terracotta pot

LEFT: *This Union-Jack shaped formal garden is an excellent choice for a small rectangular plot. Low box hedges define the compartments, which can be filled with perennials; herbs are the classic choice, but you could also use massed plantings of one kind of plant to achieve a themed display.*

BELOW: *This star-shaped, box-edged, herb-filled parterre is a good lesson in formal design, the neat little topiary box pyramids at each corner providing an effective punctuation point, while the statue at the far end creating the focus.*

Keeping the colour palette limited and restrained is one of the keys to formal gardening, which tends to make good use of architectural shapes and simple green, gold and white colour themes. Topiary – where slow-growing evergreens are clipped into geometrical shapes – is one of the mainstays of formal gardening, and can be copied in even the smallest garden. Even a windowsill can provide a home for a soldierly row of small terracotta pots, each containing a single clipped box *(Buxus sempervirens)* making a neat, round ball shape.

Repeated plantings, in either ribbon formations or squares, is another hallmark of formal garden style. It makes planning the garden relatively simple, and provided you are prepared to do some simple propagating yourself, you will be able to stock the garden fairly easily and cheaply. Some shrubs, for example, take very easily from cuttings. Rosemary and box both strike very readily from semi-ripe cuttings; simply push them into good compost in a large container, potting them up into individual containers once they have rooted.

As we have seen, water features are often used in formal gardens, often in the form of channels or conduits rather than free-formed pools most of us associate with garden ponds. In a small garden, a rectangular pool or small channel will fit most successfully.

Equally attractive for small formal gardens are pebble pools or splash pools, and spouts or masks mounted on a wall, which pour water into a raised pool. The sound of a splashing fountain or spout is extremely soothing, and makes a wonderful counter-point to the formality of the rest of the garden.

BELOW: *A more relaxed formal design has been used for this patio. Note how the use of symmetry creates the formal effect – matching pairs of pots in this case, or topiary in others, creating the required balance.*

Japanese-style gardens

If you grow a good range of evergreen shrubs, you can create a garden that has a formal core to the design, but with an Oriental flavour to it. Japanese garden design is extremely formal, but in a rather different vein from the symmetrical lines of French formal gardening. In a Japanese garden, the focus is on the shape and form of the plants themselves and their relationship with the space that surrounds them. Rocks, sand, gravel and pebbles all play their part in formal Japanese design, and this can work well in a city landscape, with quiet steely greys and sober greens harmonizing beautifully with the surrounding buildings.

Modern garden designers have poached many of the concepts of the Japanese garden and adapted the style for Western tastes. Although frowned on by purists, it nevertheless represents an attainable and attractive style of gardening. If you like this kind of architectural simplicity, the goal is less rather than more. Choose plants that make a strong architectural statement in their own right, and think carefully about where and how you site them. It is important to make sure that the plants are strong and healthy since attention is more focused upon them. Arrange the garden with

BELOW: *This rectangular water feature, leading to the handsome statue of the lion surmounting the pool beyond, makes a wonderful classical feature. It could be copied on a smaller scale, the grass replaced with gravel or paving.*

certain clear focal points in mind, siting the plants at strategic points in the garden, such as at the end of a path or in front of a window.

statuary and ornament

Statuary and ornament are ideal in a formal garden, and a path or small walkway will often lead towards a single ornament – perhaps a bust on a plinth – sited with care at the end of it. In a small square plot, a large container or a statue may be used as the pivotal point around which a series of four rectangular beds are laid out. Again, as in any formal design, remember that less is more; one decent statue, even if it is reproduction rather than antique, will have far more impact than several of lesser quality. Even a simple ornament can be effective – an old chimney pot, perhaps, or some other architectural relic – provided it is well positioned. An alcove in an end wall, or a trellis arch, could be used as a backdrop for it.

BASEMENTS & COURTYARDS

BELOW: *Two big pots of marguerites mark the division between a narrow alley and the garden. Stargazer lilies, petunias, hydrangeas and pelargoniums create a splash of colour in a shady corner.*

WHEN YOU HAVE a very limited space at your disposal, you will need to think very carefully about how to make best use of it. In a city environment, any small gardening space is bound to be overshadowed by the buildings that surround it, so at least half your energy and effort will be spent on ways to make the best use of shaded areas.

If you have a tall wall bordering your small garden, you will need to get as much light as you can to be reflected into the space. Painting a concrete or brick wall with white paint is the obvious solution. This, in turn, will have a rather dramatic effect on the design, as a plain white backdrop is not normally found in nature, and your design will have to make the most of this rather Mediterranean-style setting.

The best solution is to use the wall to grow climbers on it, either by attaching trellis to the wall or by using wires attached to masonry nails. The climbers you choose will be determined, to a large degree, by the quality of the light and the direction the garden faces, as well as by how dry or damp the area is. Any area with a high wall is normally dry in the shadow of it, so by and large you are likely to need plants that thrive in these conditions, as well as ones that cope with the high alkaline content usually left

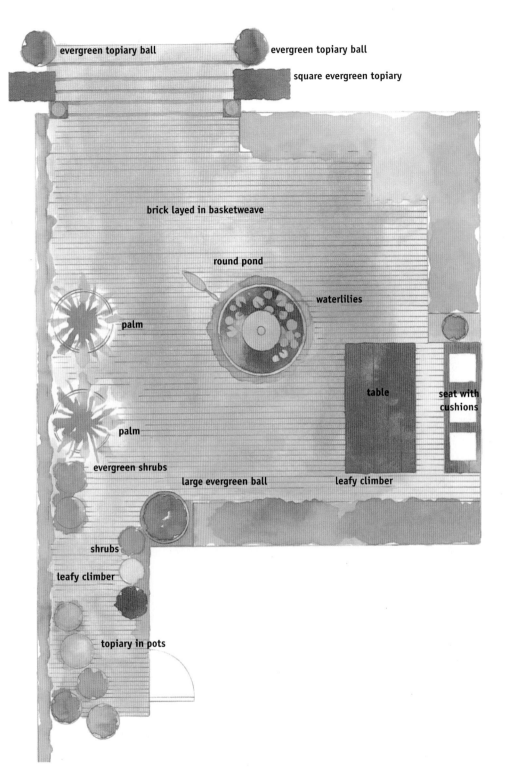

evergreen topiary ball evergreen topiary ball

square evergreen topiary

brick layed in basketweave

round pond

waterlilies

palm

table

seat with cushions

palm

evergreen shrubs

large evergreen ball

leafy climber

shrubs

leafy climber

topiary in pots

RIGHT: *This simple design for a courtyard garden has a central pond as its focal point. The choice of hard surface could be decking, paving, bricks or flagstones. A couple of borders provide the permanent planting, while pots and containers, which can be moved as necessary, provide colour and interest throughout the year.*

BELOW: *This little brick-paved basement garden uses architectural features and foliage plants to make up for the lack of light, in a formalized design.*

behind by quantities of builder's rubble. Clematis will thrive in dry alkaline soil, but does need some light. *C. montana* is one of the toughest species, and will cope with a north- or east-facing wall, covering it in spring with myriad small starry flowers in white or pink, depending on the variety. The flowers are scented as a bonus.

Ivies are the obvious choice for any basement walls, since they will tolerate even quite deep shade, although the variegated forms, particularly those with gold-splashed leaves, such as 'Goldheart', need more light to retain the variegation. *Hydrangea anomala petiolaris* will thrive on a north wall, but is not keen on very dry soil ('hydra' means water), so unless the area

BELOW: *The handsome metal spiral staircase, leading down to the basement patio, makes a feature in its own right. Shade-loving plants, including hostas and ferns, create the backbone of the planting, with ivy clothing the walls.*

is naturally damp or you are prepared to do a lot of watering in dry weather, you might do best to give this one a miss.

Be careful in these kinds of conditions that the soil has enough nutrients in it to keep the plants going, as there may well be very little decaying plant matter going back into the soil to feed it, and it is therefore down to you, the gardener, to supply it in generous amounts. There are plenty of proprietary fertilizers to choose from, and if your plants are failing to grow well, or bloom when they should, inadequate feeding and watering are the most likely causes, apart from lack of light.

In a small plot, apart from covering the vertical surfaces with plants to increase the available growing area, it will pay to group the plants together. You get a commensurably greater effect from three plants grouped together in a single display than you do from ten dotted around in a haphazard way. Also, do not be deceived into thinking that because the space is very small, you must only grow very small plants. One large plant of exceptional beauty in a handsome container is worth 20 of no special merit. If you pick a plant with attractive evergreen foliage, and make sure it is growing well and healthily in a large attractive container, it will form a focus for a small basement or patio. You can surround it with a

LEFT: *The distinguishing features of this small enclosed garden are the choice of surface – natural stone, river-washed pebbles and tiles, laid assymetrically. Screening trellis and a trompe l'oeil arch provide vertical interest, and grouped displays of plants in terracotta pots soften the architectural features.*

BELOW: *Every inch of available space has been used in this narrow basement, with the stairs making a home for colourful containers of busy lizzies, pelargoniums and lobelia The walls can be used to provide colour, not only by using climbing plants, but by hanging wall pots or troughs on them.*

changing display of smaller plants for spring and summer colour if you wish. If the area is overlooked from indoors, try to use the space to give yourself something of particular interest right through the year, picking scented plants, or those that flower in winter, as well as those for summer display, as your small garden is going to be your sole contact with the changing seasons.

Containers are particularly useful, as they allow you to move and change the display as plants come in and out of flower. If you organize your planting carefully, you can group bulbs in a container with smaller plants, thereby giving yourself a display of spring bulbs, followed by perennials in summer, for example. One good choice might be early flowering narcissus with a display of small alliums for summer.

In addition to using any available wall space for growing climbers, you can also hang wall pots (containers with a curved front and straight back) on the walls, and fill them with trailing annuals, such as busy lizzies, trailing pelargoniums, lobelia, diascia and nasturtiums. Ideally, keep the planting colour themed to prevent it looking too bitty and busy. Busy lizzies will cope very well with low light levels and are therefore handy for dark basements.

ALLEYS & NARROW SPACES

RIGHT: *This shady small garden makes excellent use of natural woodland plants, including ferns, pulmonarias and foxgloves, to create a wonderfully dappled secret garden. The use of natural stone for the path is a sympathetic choice.*

BELOW: *This narrow garden makes good use of containers and handsome garden ornaments, including a circular stone table and gothic chairs, sculptures and terracotta pots.*

IN SOME SMALL CITY GARDENS, behind terraced houses, there is a long finger of land that runs alongside the back of the property. All too often, this is an overlooked planting area. This is a great shame if space is limited as it offers great potential for some inspired design solutions.

First of all, consider the surfacing. If it is just concreted over, why not lay ceramic tiles or perhaps wooden decking over it to create a more sympathetic look. Deep red and black quarry tiles are sometimes used in this situation, and provide the key design point for a Victorian-style planting scheme, concentrating on ferns and other evergreens – perhaps formally clipped box balls or pyramids in terracotta pots – as the permanent display, with other container-grown plants brought in to enliven the scheme in spring and summer. *Zantedeschia aethiopica,* the big arum, with its shiny green leaves and brilliant white spathes, will make a good clump and you can divide the plants to increase your stock. They do well in the shady conditions that often prevail, but they will need plenty of humus and a regular and plentiful supply of water. Some spring bulbs – 'Paper White' narcissi in single displays in shallow pots, perhaps, or several small pots of snowdrops – would also look good in this

setting. If there is room, consider putting a narrow table against a wall or fence to act as a permanent display base.

Use the walls to hang wall pots or containers, but try to keep the display with a fairly defined colour palette, and make sure the pots are attractive in their own right, and combine well together. Rather than scatter them over the wall, why not position four or five together in a group, perhaps with a large container nearby with a handsome vine, such as *Vitis coignetiae,* whose large, heart-shaped leaves will make an attractive display for most

of the year, before turning a wonderful glowing russet in autumn. If you decide to give this area a wooden decked surface, then you could also build in some large wooden containers – either square Versailles tubs with neatly clipped geometrically shaped evergreens or low-level window box-style containers. This is particularly useful if the soil in this area has been concreted over. A decked area can have a slightly softer planting scheme, perhaps using more sprawling plants, but again they will have to be able to tolerate a degree of shade. Consider using several different kinds of ivy, perhaps with a *Fatsia japonica* if there is room. Lower-level window boxes could be planted with ferns, hostas and busy lizzies, along with some small ivies.

A sculpture or other garden ornament – such as a single, large, handsome terracotta pot – can provide a focal element at the end of a long passageway, and will look good with an end wall as a backdrop for it. Statues look particularly attractive when half hidden in creepers, either ivy or parthenocissus, for example. Smaller plants that tolerate a degree of shade, such as corydalis, small, tough campanulas and *Viola riviniana* 'Purpurea', are good for softening the edges of paving.

BELOW: *By offsetting the path at an angle, this narrow space is optically widened, its edges softened with creeping plants. Long spaces can be improved by grouping pots together at intervals to divert the eye.*

pathways and entrances

Long, narrow areas can also be found around pathways and entrances and here, especially, it is important to create planting schemes that frame the space attractively and give it some kind of punctuation point. Pairs of pots are ideal for marking the entrance to a house or garden, and they can be either architectural and formal looking, or loosely composed and sprawling. In summer, a pair of large pots of the big regale lily are a wonderful way to mark the entrance to the garden, and the rich perfume is strong enough to drift in through open windows and doors. In autumn, you could replace these with big pots of large white chrysanthemums, and in spring with the glistening, tall, white tulip 'Triumphator'.

In sunnier narrow spaces, you could mark the edges of a walkway with clipped bushes of lavender, santolina or artemisia, all of them fragrant and with silvery foliage. Blue, pink and white flowers go well with silver-grey foliage and salvias, dianthus, *Lychnis coronaria* (in the pink or white form) with soft velvety leaves, or scented tobacco plants in white or deep pink, would all fit in well with this kind of planting scheme. You could also edge sunny paths and walkways with low clipped hedges of box *(Buxus*

RIGHT: *A long alleyway can be transformed into a magical woodland walk with relatively simple design features – in this case a path of offset stepping stones, planted with shrubs, trees and shade-loving perennials.*

sempervirens), which is also aromatic. A large pot of one of the summer daisies, such as *Leucanthemum vulgare,* the ox–eye daisy, which will create a sprawling display, makes a good counterpoint to the neatly clipped hedges, as do some of the flowering climbers, such as violet or white clematis, or white and pale pink climbing roses.

Make sure any doors, gates and other woodwork is painted or stained in sympathetic shades of soft blues, steely greys and bluish greens, so that they present a harmonious picture. Be careful not to include brilliant white tubs or pots in this kind of setting – they make too obvious a statement.

ABOVE: *This little alleyway, with its stepping stones of brick set in bark chippings, the raised beds held with stout wooden planks, and its handsome large-leaved evergreens, makes a delightful, secluded woodland walk.*

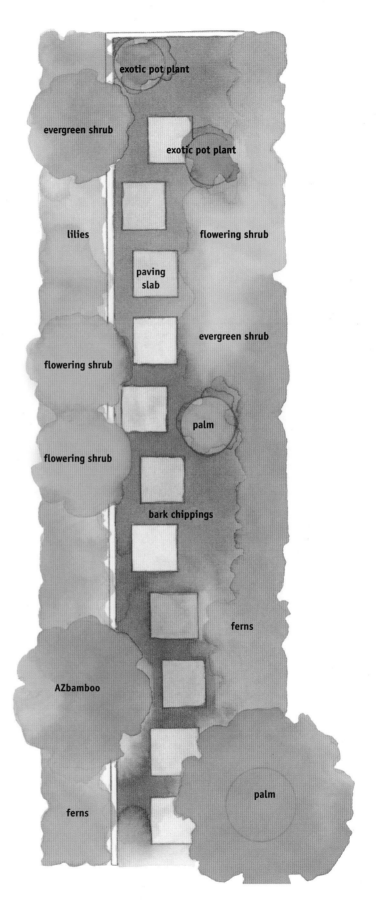

exotic pot plant

evergreen shrub

exotic pot plant

lilies

flowering shrub

paving slab

evergreen shrub

flowering shrub

palm

flowering shrub

bark chippings

ferns

AZbamboo

ferns

palm

ROOF GARDENS

BELOW: *This little roof garden has made sympathetic use of wood with its decked surface and wooden planters. A low-level screen of plants helps to provide shelter without destroying the beauty of the rooftop view.*

MANY NEWLY CONVERTED flats are now boasting small roof gardens, but the problem of creating a private, sheltered and attractive garden on a very exposed site can be daunting to the newcomer to gardening, who may never have grown anything at all before. If the garden is in a windy site, it will not create an inviting place for either plants or people unless you create some shelter from the prevailing winds, both to protect you and the plants, and to give you some very necessary privacy. There is a wide range of ways in which you can do this, but since you will certainly also want to enjoy the view, you will need to find a compromise.

BELOW: *Decking makes an excellent choice of surface for a roof terrace, since the material is natural and sympathetic, and easy to lay on existing foundations. Here the planting has been largely confined to troughs around the perimeter of the terrace, to increase the feeling of space.*

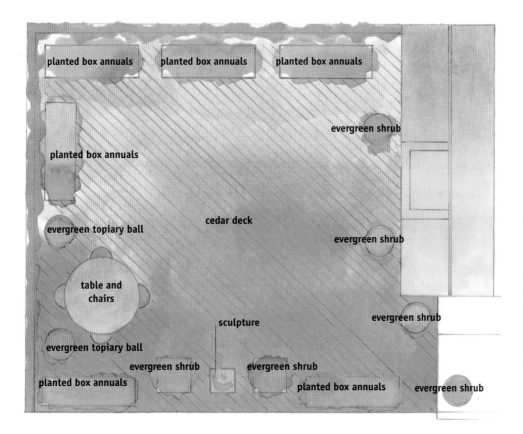

planted box annuals   **planted box annuals**   **planted box annuals**

planted box annuals

evergreen shrub

cedar deck

evergreen topiary ball

evergreen shrub

table and chairs

sculpture

evergreen shrub

evergreen topiary ball

evergreen shrub   **evergreen shrub**

planted box annuals   **planted box annuals**   **evergreen shrub**

BELOW: *Duck-egg blue trellis blends attractively with the natural wooden decked floor of this roof garden. Wooden planters and terracotta pots create a home for sun-loving perennials.*

The best solution is to opt for a mixture of screening and planting that provides a partial rather than a complete screen. The wind will be able to penetrate such a structure to some degree, which will prevent the whole thing acting like a sail and taking off in high winds. Nevertheless, any trellis that you use as a support for plants must be very firmly anchored at the base, and must be reasonably solid in construction.

Remember that the vertical aspect of a roof garden will have to be constructed by you, and without it the garden will look bleak no matter how colourful it is. Aim to include at least a couple of large shrubs in pots or even a couple of small trees, such as bay tree, perhaps, or a weeping cherry or birch. Make sure the screening is covered with a variety of attractive climbers, ideally flowering at different times of year – honeysuckles, clematis, jasmines and roses are all possibilities for the roof terrace. For something more unusual, consider the passion flower (*Passiflora caerulea*) or the kiwi fruit (*Actinidia kolomikta*).

It is essential to get the roof surveyed to check whether its load-bearing capacity is adequate for the garden design you have in mind. Weight is always a problem for roof gardens, as you will have to import soil in which to grow plants, and this is not light. On the whole, the areas around the edge of a roof are the strongest, and this is therefore usually the best place to site any large or heavy containers you wish to include.

Drainage is also a key factor to consider, as rain water and any surplus from watering must be able to soak away without damaging the property. You will need to install adequate drainage, if there is none already, and an

impermeable surface is, of course, a necessity. Over the top of this, you can use a more sympathetic surface such as teak decking, but make sure that you do not pierce any waterproof membranes during construction.

A small pool is always a possibility on a roof garden, provided, again, that the load-bearing timbers are up to coping with the weight. A small half-barrel – perhaps housing a few irises, *Pontederia cordata,* and even a

miniature water lily – makes an ideal little water garden. To fill the pool, and to water the garden which will need frequent attention in hot climates, you must have a handy supply of water, and it is worth getting a tap fitted on the roof to save you time and energy carrying water upstairs.

Some very unusual and exciting roof gardens have been created in some very unprepossessing spaces. Flights of fancy can

be more successful here than on a standard garden plot where the surrounding gardens bring you back to reality with a jolt.

If your roof top is awkwardly shaped and with little space for you to sit out, consider grouping containers together with some interesting mixed planting, wherever the possibility presents itself, to create a mini-jungle. Make sure the displays have a good mixture of foliage and flowering plants of

LEFT: *Tiles make an excellent choice of surface for a roof garden, as they are easy to keep clean and attractive in their own right. Here the planting has concentrated mainly on architectural evergreens, leaving the tiles themselves to make the major colour statement.*

BELOW: *A monochromatic colour scheme, basically white and green, has been chosen for this part-shaded roof garden. Evergreen climbers, foliage plants and topiary provide the planting interest.*

different shapes and sizes. Some good candidates in pots would be *Fatsia japonica, Choisya ternata,* small azaleas (in an acid-based soil mix), a camellia or two, and a couple of climbers, such as a passion flower *(Passiflora caerulea)* and a golden hop *(Humulus lupulus* 'Aurea') as well as a couple of clipped box balls or cones to add formality.

If the space is more rectangular, and open, then you could consider opting for a formal design, such as a Japanese garden, using bamboos in pots, clipped evergreens, mound-forming plants such as the Yakushimanum azaleas, *Viburnum davidii,* and some of the hebes, with gravel for the surface and some simple, low tables and chairs in rough hewn wood, perhaps. A bamboo or reed screen panelling could provide the necessary shelter with a suitably Oriental feel.

Keep the colours fairly subdued so that the eye tends to concentrate most on the architectural shapes, with perhaps just one or two flowering shrubs – such as a large hydrangea – as a focal point.

The whole point of a roof terrace is to allow you to enjoy any good weather, so make sure you leave enough space for at least a couple of chairs, a table and, ideally, a pergola with climbing plants over it to give you some shade.

BALCONIES & TERRACES

BELOW: *A profusion of flowering annuals, growing over every inch of vertical space, gives this small balcony a wonderfully secluded feel. Using the balcony railings on which to hang planters helps to increase the planting space.*

FOR MANY PEOPLE, a small balcony or terrace, perhaps very little more than a windowledge, is the only space available in which to exercise their horticultural talents. However, it is surprising what you can grow in an extremely limited space if you wish to, and how attractive you can make a small balcony or terrace look. Since the area is small, attention is focused on every detail and you will need to make sure that plants are in good condition, and also that the containers are handsome in their own right. Nothing looks worse than a balcony in which a few mismatched, stained plastic pots create a junkyard for a collection of half-dying plants!

First of all examine the space you have available, and look at the structure. Decide what will fit along the base, and what you might grow up the wall behind the balcony or terrace, up any supporting poles, and across or over any railings or fences. Then decide whether the balcony is large enough for you to use, or whether it is to perform simply as a display space for plants. The surface requirements (as for a roof terrace) are such that it must be solid, waterproof and free draining, and able to bear the weight of any pots complete with soil. Even lightweight modern composts are heavy when waterlogged, so do be sure that you have assessed this correctly, and if in any doubt seek professional advice. Another factor on balconies is safety: make sure that none of your

pots and tubs can be blown on to people, buildings or gardens below – even heavy pots can be gusted away in high winds.

You can go for a full-blown cottage look or you can opt for something more restrained and formal. The latter is the best option if you're not a keen gardener, as you can create a handsome-looking planting scheme using evergreens, with

just a few flowers to add colour if you wish. If you keep the planting symmetrical, simple and balanced, framing doorways with pairs of pots, and lining the base of the balcony with a ribbon planting of, say, pansies, tulips, or busy lizzies in a window box, the space will seem larger and better organized. Alternatively, you can amaze the beholder with a veritable

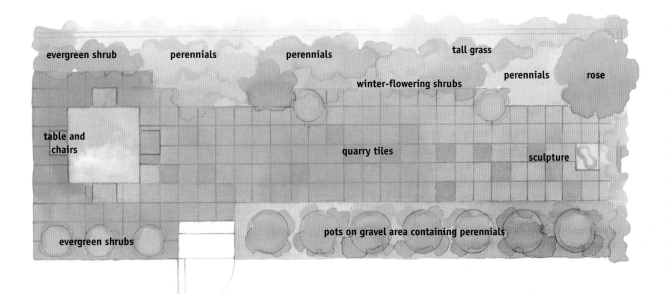

evergreen shrub   perennials   perennials   tall grass

winter-flowering shrubs   perennials   rose

table and chairs

quarry tiles

sculpture

evergreen shrubs

pots on gravel area containing perennials

LEFT: A long narrow balcony has been given an air of privacy with fairly dense planting both along the back wall adjoining the house and at the front of the balcony, using both floor-level planters and troughs attached to the railings. More space has been allowed at one end to accommodate a table and chairs.

hanging garden, created by attaching hanging baskets and wall pots to the walls behind the balcony, fixing window boxes to railings, and using a large range of climbing and trailing plants in addition to perennials and shrubs.

Some singularly wonderful gardens have been created on a horizontal growing space no more than a metre wide and a few metres long, using every bit of wall space and railing that surrounds the area. Trailing pelargoniums are excellent for this purpose, as provided they are given some lightweight trellis they will rapidly clothe a whole wall with a summer-long succession of flowers. Ivies, nasturtiums, diascia and lobelia will all cascade over the edges of hanging baskets, troughs and windowboxes, creating curtains of flowering plants.

In order to maintain a major flowering display over a long period, you will need to water the plants frequently and copiously, and to feed them. To cope with high wall-mounted pots, you will almost certainly need to adapt a garden hose by attaching the last metre or so to a garden cane. It takes very little time for a hanging basket to dry out and for the plants to

RIGHT: Flower power is not always necessary to obtain a richly planted atmosphere. Here foliage plants – principally acers, cornus, euonymus and ivies – have been used to great effect to create a delightfully cool and verdant scheme.

suffer, so if you are opting for this kind of display, make sure that you have the time to keep it in pristine condition – in midsummer, hanging baskets may well need watering twice a day.

On the whole, simple displays using a limited colour theme are the most effective solution for small balconies and terraces, but climbers are ideal, and many will grow in surprisingly small

containers. For example, an ornamental vine will do well in a small wooden barrel, and you can use the same barrel for spring-flowering bulbs – say crocuses or scillas – and, in summer, for a display of sweet peas, which can be encouraged to scramble up the vine.

Making dual use of containers is an excellent solution to limited space, and

LEFT: *This little balcony has a beautifully laid decked surface with planters containing drought-loving plants, such as rosemary, santolina and yuccas. If your balcony is exposed and sunny, as this one is, choose plants that naturally cope in hot dry conditions, otherwise watering will become a chore. Mediterranean plants are among the best choices for this kind of situation.*

successional plantings of this kind are ideal, particularly with bulbs, where the bigger bulbs are planted below the level of smaller ones. For example, you could plant crocuses and snowdrops at one level, daffodils at the next, and summer-flowering lilies and alliums below these. Use metal plant labels to remind yourself what you have planted where.

Try to ensure that you have a few scented plants on a balcony, so that their perfume will waft in through open windows on warm evenings. For example, honeysuckles are wonderfully scented, and cope well with relatively poor soil, and there is even a winter flowering one, *Lonicera* x *purpusii*. A couple of

clematis, such as *C. armandii* and *C. montana*, are scented too, so go for these in preference to the other types. To attract birds and bees to the balcony, train a couple of berrying shrubs, such as pyracantha or cotoneaster, against the wall of the house, perhaps in a neat frame around the window. Large pots of lavender – you could use a neatly clipped pair – will also help attract bees.

No balcony should be without a pot of herbs, and you can grow a few mixed herbs together in one large terracotta pot. Thyme, rosemary, sage, mint and basil are among the best. These days you can buy specially designed herb pots with lots of compartments, so that you can keep those with a tendency to stray, like mint, firmly confined in

their place. Also essential in summer are pelargoniums, which are the easiest to grow of all container plants, requiring almost no attention whatsoever – they suffer only when overwatered. There are many different kinds to grow, some with wonderfully aromatic leaves. It is a good idea to grow a few different types, including upright bushy pelargoniums and the trailing forms mentioned earlier. They are among the easiest of all plants to propagate, and grow rapidly to maturity. If you pinch out the growing tips of young plants, you will get a much more satisfactory bushy plant the following year. However, remember that you cannot overwinter pelargoniums out of doors in colder climates, so make sure there is enough space indoors on windowsills to house your collection once the frosts arrive.

A few small evergreens will help to give year-round structure to any balcony display. Choose either small forms of conifers, such as some of the dwarf forms of chamaecyparis, or else clip box or bay into neat shapes. Young skimmias, with their smooth glossy dark green leaves, are also good and as they are slow growing, it will be some time before they become too large for their surroundings.

GARDEN ROOMS

BELOW: *This small, sunny gravel and stone surfaced garden has an interestingly assymetric design, which helps to create a feeling of space in a small plot.*

ONE OF THE GREATEST joys of possessing a garden is being able to sit in the open air surrounded by both plants and wildlife. The sound of water, birdsong or humming insects can be a great bonus in an urban landscape, and it is worth ensuring, provided your garden is large enough to house a couple of chairs, that you can sit out of doors when the weather allows.

To this end, plan for a small patio or paved area in the part of the garden that gets the most sunshine. This does not necessarily have to be the part closest to the house, although it is obviously convenient if it is, so that you can carry out drinks and food easily. If, though, your garden faces north and the area behind the house is shaded, then why not site the patio at the far end of the garden, perhaps linking it to the house with a specially created and planted walkway? If you pave the patio area with a sympathetic surface – be it decking, paving or bricks – you will have a level, even surface on which to site a table and a few chairs.

The planting around any seating area should serve the following ends: it should screen you so as to give you some privacy, shelter you from any prevailing winds, shield you from any intrusive noise and pollution, and, ideally, offer some shade in very hot

LEFT: *This enclosed small space makes an ideal garden room. A shallow flight of steps leads up to the sitting area, which has been attractively screened with shrubs and trees. Collections of containers flank the flight of steps, and provide themed colour in the summer months.*

BELOW: *A raised deck, whether used to cope with a change of contour or simply as a design feature, helps give a garden interest, especially when it is lushly planted with some handsome architectural plants, such as the Abyssinian banana plant,* Ensete ventricosum, *shown here on the left.*

weather. If at all possible, the plants you choose should provide the bonus of scent, too. A pergola or trellis is ideal, since it will give the benefit of partial shade, plus a support for whatever climbing plants you might wish to grow.

In southern Europe, no small outdoor space is complete without a vine, its large leaves giving wonderful dappled overhead shade in summer. Even in colder countries, vines can be used for the same purpose, although ornamental as opposed to fruiting vines might be more appropriate. *Vitis coignetiae* performs well in most conditions and has handsome large leaves that turn a wonderful ruby red in autumn.

Combine your chosen vine with a scented climber, such as a jasmine, honeysuckle or rose, and perhaps another for flower power, such as one of the large-flowered clematis. They should ramble happily together. Add a couple of large pots to either side of the seating area – which contain hydrangeas, perhaps, or ligularias – and your outdoor room will provide you with a perfect place to relax and enjoy whatever quiet moments you can grab. It will greatly extend your use of the garden if you light it in the evenings. If you do not want to install an electrical supply to the garden, flares or candles can be used instead to good effect.

LEFT: *Gravel is a relatively inexpensive and very relaxed surface to use for an outdoor room and combines well with most architectural forms. The surrounding planting depends on the situation – foliage plants for shade and sun-loving perennials, sprawling over the gravel, in hot spots.*

BELOW: *This delightfully secluded outdoor room, which has been created on a small roof garden, presents a harmonious picture with its emphasis on natural wood for the floor, trellis screens and decking.*

furniture and furnishings

If you don't want to erect and plant up a pergola, then you can opt instead for one of the large new umbrellas. Among the most attractive are the large, natural umbrellas in bleached canvas-weave cotton with wooden supports. They are sturdy, long-lasting and look particularly good with a decked patio surface and attractive well-built teak furniture. Bring the umbrella indoors at the end of the summer season and scrub it well before drying it and folding it away.

Do not be tempted to economize on the furniture or furnishings. They will have to last a long time, and the sturdier and better made they are, the better they will withstand the ravages of the outdoor environment. Ideally, choose all-weather furniture that you can leave out all year round, as most houses and flats have little storage room to spare. The furniture should be scrubbed in the spring with a stiff scrubbing brush and some house-hold detergent, and then rinsed off with clean water before leaving it to dry naturally. A pot scourer will remove any stubborn lichen stains, but take care not to rub so hard that you damage the wood.

If your garden is just too small to accom-modate a full-sized table and chairs, then consider placing a garden bench at a suitable point where you can sit and enjoy some particular delight – whether it is a large container of wonderfully scented summer lilies, or nestling beneath the canopy of an attractive small tree or climber. Benches vary in size and scale, and a tiny iron bench will fit snugly against a wall in even the narrowest of small gardens.

access and views

If you are considering using your garden as an outdoor room, then give some thought to the access. It may be worth your while to alter an existing window to make new access to the garden in the form of French windows, so that not only can you move in and out more easily, but also the scents and sounds of the garden will enter the house when the doors are left open. The view from main living room windows is important, and when planning the garden, you should take account of the main vantage points, framing your design accordingly.

In some town houses, the living room window looks down a long narrow finger of land beside the house, and all too often this becomes a messy storage area rather than a feature of the garden. As this is the gateway to the garden itself, and possibly your only view of it, do plan this area into the garden, even if it is not the principal sitting area. A simple planting scheme at ground level (it is likely to be shady) with an attractive hard surface is all that is required, plus some pots and containers that can be changed as the seasons alter, both at ground level and perhaps fixed to any wall or fence surrounding it.

CHAPTER 2

GARDEN SURFACES

THE MAIN ELEMENTS that really determine the structure and overall appearance of a garden are the horizontal surfaces and hard landscaping – the paths, paving, steps, decking and other surface treatments. The material you choose will greatly affect the style of the garden, whether it is sympathetic natural stone, modern paving slabs laid in a geometric pattern, decking stained in a bright colour or traditional gravel for a softer appearance. This chapter discusses the various choices at your disposal and the different ways in which these elements can be treated, or combined to best effect. It also shows how to go about laying the materials to ensure years of hard wear. Remember that it is the combination of all the choices, and the way they harmonize, that will determine the success of your garden design.

LEFT: *This small roof garden has made excellent use of decking, which has been limed to keep in with the elegant theme. Decking is warm and comfortable to walk on and a practical choice for roofs amd balconies.*

RIGHT: *The muted, aged tone of old bricks gives an old-fashioned feel to a small town garden. Although this surface would take a long time to lay, the effect is stunning.*

PAVING

BELOW: *Large flagstones provide the surface interest in this small parterre-style patio. Clipped box provides the vertical features, and the white-painted cane furniture and the garden gate add a touch of light.*

RIGHT: *This narrow alley garden has employed quarry tiles for the surface, echoing the detailing in the brickwork over the gateway. In a dark setting like this, a bright surface provides a splash of colour and warmth.*

YOUR GARDEN MAY already have some form of paving – all too often rather unattractive expanses of concrete – that you want to replace, or you may decide to create a new patio area outside your back door where you can sit and enjoy the garden at your leisure. It is worth considering carefully the various choices of paving on offer.

natural stone

One of the most beautiful paving materials is natural stone. It has a deceptively soft-looking texture and colour, which blends perfectly with almost any style of planting, from formal to sprawling cottage-style plantings. Its beauty is not without a price, however as it is the most expensive of all forms of surfacing. However, it is definitely a great asset in any garden, if you can afford it.

As with any hard surface, natural stone must be properly laid to ensure it presents an even surface. Normally the ground will have to be dug over, and then the soil tamped down. A footing will be needed of hardcore (broken bits of rubble), over which sand is laid. The stone flags are then laid in the sand, which is also used to fill the gaps between the flags. Naturally the slabs are heavy, and you will probably find it worthwhile to get them professionally laid.

concrete slabs

Cheaper paved surfaces include concrete slabs. These days you can buy concrete flags that imitate real stone ones. Some of the best ones have a slightly warm colouring in imitation sandstone colours, with a slightly rough hewn surface.

When you lay the stones you can choose to butt them up tight together, or to lay them with fairly wide gaps, in which you can plant

some little perennials, such as thymes. These will survive happily when crushed underfoot, and release a wonderful scent in the process. Small paving plants, such as *Acaena buchananii* or *Viola riviniana* 'Purpurea', or even the larger *Alchemilla mollis,* will self-seed happily in the cracks, quickly helping to give new paving an air of permanence. A particularly pretty little self-seeding daisy, *Erigeron karvinskianus,* will provide

clouds of small rose pink to white flowers in summer, spilling over walls and down steps.

Another trick is to lay the slabs like a chequerboard, infilling the spaces with either gravel or a tough grass. Alternatively, you could leave occasional spaces in which to plant a large mound-forming shrub or perennial – the big handsome *Euphorbia characias wulfenii* or a sprawling *Brachyglottis* 'Sunshine' will both relax over paving.

Another choice is to mix stone with other hard-surfacing materials to break up any monotonous appearance that a single surface would give. Bricks could be laid as a course around the paving stones, for example, or large pebbles could be used to fill any irregular shapes that the square format of the stones would naturally leave. Much depends on the size and shape of the space that is being paved, and it is

not a good idea in a very small area to create too bitty a design. A more uniform paving design will help increase the apparent space.

However, that being said, it is often a good idea to use a different paving material for distinctly different areas – for example the long alley down one side of a terraced house could be laid with recycled bricks and the patio area of the garden paved with York stone.

PATHS & STEPS

BELOW: *Steps can be more than just a convenience — wide steps like these provide an opportunity for planting, particularly in pots arranged as these are in an architecturally pleasing formation. Small pots of geraniums are ideal for this purpose.*

ABOVE: *Steps can be attractively softened using creeping plants that flourish in dry, stony soil. Alchemilla mollis and baby's tears (Soleirolia soleirolii) are both good candidates for this situation.*

ALL TOO OFTEN, paths and steps are neglected in small gardens, which is a great shame, as they provide a wonderful opportunity for novel planting ideas. If you are lucky enough to have a flight of steps leading down to a small garden, then make sure you use them to full advantage. If there is enough room, you could put a small container on each step, each containing the same kind and color of plant – for example, chrysanthemums or small terracotta pots of bulbs in spring, geraniums in summer, or even neatly clipped little box balls or pyramids for all-year-round architectural splendor. Alternatively, use the steps as a support for an attractive foliage or flowering climber – the golden-leaved hop *(Humulus lupulus* 'Aureus') or an attractive variegated ivy for example, or even a small-flowered clematis, such as one of the viticella types.

Shallow flights of wider steps can be planted at the sides with sprawling plants, such as some of the spreading forms of cotoneaster, or any of the daisy family. Alternatively, persuade one of the self-seeding perennials, such as the little bellflower *(Campanula portenschlagiana)* to

LEFT: *The effect of a mini tropical jungle can be created quite easily with appropriate planting of large-leaved foliage plants and sympathetic treatment of hard surfaces – here pebbles with a stepping stone path, and timber decking and bridging. Hostas, ligularias and bamboos are good choices for this effect.*

BELOW: *Small changes of contour and direction can be used creatively, as here, to make shallow steps. Mixing surface materials, such as flagstones and bricks, helps to add interest, and is in keeping with the attractive informality of the perennial planting.*

make its home on the steps. These little campanulas are notorious for finding the smallest crack in which to seed themselves. Other good self-seeders for shade are some of the small common ferns, which look wonderful growing alongside brick or stone in a narrow, ribbon-like display.

Paths can be made from a wide range of surfacing materials, including the usual stone and timber, but gravel and wood paths are also attractive, particularly for an Oriental-style garden. You can set round, flat cross-sections of timber into a gravel path, as stepping stones, or use railway sleepers as insets, rather like a railway track, in the gravel.

Be careful when planning steps for a small garden that they are sufficiently wide to be functional if you are going to be carrying equipment, or trays of food, up and down into the garden. The same applies to steps on to a roof terrace, for example. Simple wooden steps can be constructed easily and simply from a couple of thick planks of wood, coated with preservative.

1 *Excavate the site to the required depth. Unless the subsoil is firm, spread and compact a layer of gravel or crushed rock over the site.*

2 *Next, level the subsoil or the crushed rock layer and spread a 7.5cm (3in) thick layer of filling over it. Compact it with a length of fence post.*

3 *Shovel out the bedding sand on top of the compacted filling and rake it out evenly to a depth of 2.5–5cm (1–2in) across the site.*

4 *If you have edge restraints, level the sand so its surface is just less than the thickness of the slab below the top of the edging.*

LAYING SLABS ON SAND

THE QUICKEST WAY TO LAY A GARDEN PATH or patio surface is to bed paving slabs, whether natural or concrete, on a sand bed. The slabs are relatively large, so once you have prepared the site you can quickly cover a sizeable area. First choose your slabs and make a note of their size and thickness. Most slabs are squares or rectangles; square slabs range in size from 23 or 30cm (9 or 12in) up to 60cm (24in) across, while rectangles measure from 45x23cm (18x9in) to 68x45cm (27x18in). The larger slabs are quite heavy and you may need help to handle them. Some ranges of paving also offer interlocking hexagonal slabs, complete with two types of half hexagon for finishing off the edges of the paved area; and slabs with a quadrant cut out in one corner. Four of these placed together create a circular opening to fit round a tree or other feature.

Most slabs are made in shades of buff, red and grey; the surface texture may be smooth, textured, riven to resemble natural split stone, or embossed in imitation of stone setts or paving bricks. Once you have selected your slabs, mark out the site with pegs and stringlines so that you can take measurements and draw up a simple scale plan. This will be invaluable for estimating materials accurately and is a useful laying guide if you want a pattern using slabs of different colours.

5 *The paving should have a slight fall (away from the house if this is adjacent) to help rainwater to run off it. Use a batten and spirit level to check the direction of the fall.*

An edge restraint around the excavated site will prevent sand from leaching out.

6 *Lay four slabs in one corner of the site, setting small wooden spacers between adjacent slabs to ensure an even gap for the pointing. You can remove the spacers as soon as each slab is surrounded by other slabs.*

7 *Lay a batten across the slabs and check the direction of the fall. If necessary, tamp the slabs further into the sand bed using the handle of a club hammer. Check the fall regularly as you work your way across the site.*

BELOW: Natural stone paving complements plants of all sorts and suits any style of garden. Use it for paths, paving and steps. It teams well with other natural hard surfaces such as gravel and cobblestones, bricks and terracotta edging stones.

ABOVE: York stone paving has a rough, craggy look and is the ultimate paving for decorative uses, but do not use it for paths that will be used regularly in the winter as it is very slippery when wet or icy.

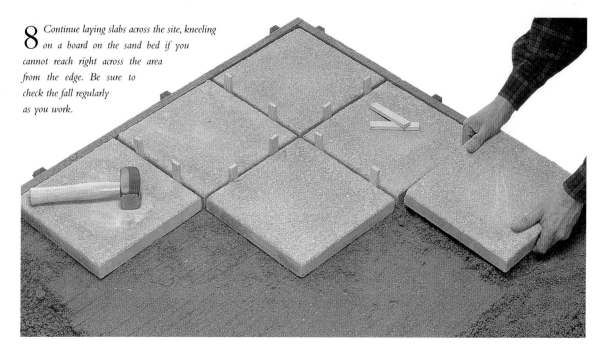

8 Continue laying slabs across the site, kneeling on a board on the sand bed if you cannot reach right across the area from the edge. Be sure to check the fall regularly as you work.

9 Remove the last spacers and spread some fine sand across the surface. Brush it into all the joints with a soft broom, then sweep off the excess.

ABOVE: Paving slabs set in concrete might seem more suitable for a formal garden, but it all depends what sort of slabs are chosen and how they are used. Here, steps and a patio with violas growing in the crevices, make a successful transition into a wildlife garden.

LAYING SLABS ON MORTAR

A PATIO DESIGNED TO SUPPORT nothing heavier than, say, a loaded wheelbarrow and patio furniture, can safely be laid on a sand bed. However, if a patio surface is intended to support a considerable weight it will be necessary to prepare a concrete base on which to lay the paving slabs. Excavate the site to a depth of at least 15cm (6in) – more if the subsoil is unstable – and lay a concrete base a minimum of 10cm (4in) thick. You can use ready-mixed concrete or mix your own with one part of cement to five parts of combined sand and 20mm (¾in) aggregate. Set up wooden shuttering around the area to give the base a neat square edge, tamp the concrete down well, level the surface with a long straightedge laid across the formwork and remove any excess material. Give the base a slight fall across its width, and incorporate full-width vertical expansion joints of hardboard or similar material every 3m (10ft) to prevent the base from cracking. Cover the concrete with plastic against rain or frost, or use damp sacking if it is hot and sunny. Leave to set for at least three days.

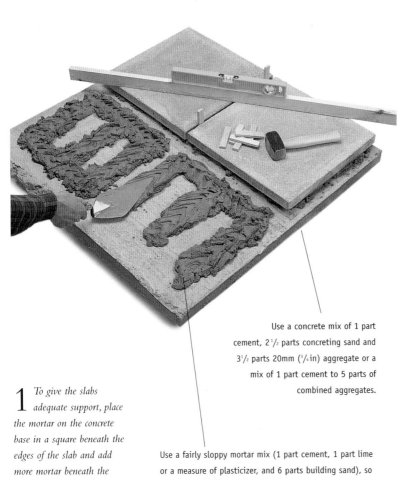

Use a concrete mix of 1 part cement, 2¹/₂ parts concreting sand and 3¹/₂ parts 20mm (³/₄in) aggregate or a mix of 1 part cement to 5 parts of combined aggregates.

1 To give the slabs adequate support, place the mortar on the concrete base in a square beneath the edges of the slab and add more mortar beneath the centre of the slab.

Use a fairly sloppy mortar mix (1 part cement, 1 part lime or a measure of plasticizer, and 6 parts building sand), so that it is easy to spread beneath the slabs.

2 Lower each slab gently on to its mortar bed and tamp it down evenly with the handle of a club hammer to compress the mortar and make the paving slab level with its neighbours.

3 After placing the slab, bedding it down and setting it to the correct fall, insert small wooden spacers between it and its neighbours to ensure an even pointing gap.

A pointing guide

IF THE POINTING MORTAR stains the slab surface as you work, reduce the problem by using a guide made from a plywood offcut. Cut a slot into the plywood to match the joint width and lay the offcut on the slabs. Fill the joints through the slot.

4 *Continue laying the slabs in this way, checking that the surface has the correct fall. Tamp down out-of-line slabs a little more if necessary.*

Use a spirit level and a long straightedge to check level and fall.

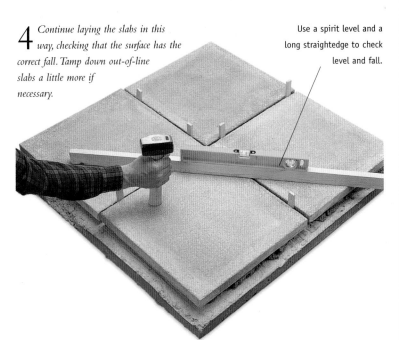

5 *When all the slabs are laid and levelled, remove the wooden spacers and point the joints with a fairly dry mortar mix. Force it well into the joints with the edge of a pointing trowel. Alternatively, brush dry mortar into the cracks between the slabs and water it with a fine rose. This washes in the mortar, wets it enough so it can set and cleans the slabs.*

Mixing mortar

Mortar is used as an adhesive to bond bricks and blocks together when building walls or steps or to bed paving on a solid substrate. A standard mix consists of one part of ordinary Portland cement, one part hydrated lime and six parts of fine sand. You can use masonry cement instead of cement and lime, or replace the lime with a chemical plasticizer.

1 *Measure out dry ingredients by volume on a smooth hard surface. Mix them together, from the edges towards the centre.*

2 *If the sand is at all damp, lumps will form. Break them up as you work, using the edge of the shovel in a chopping motion.*

3 *When the mix is a uniform colour and free from lumps, form a crater in the centre of the heap and add a little water from a watering can or hose.*

4 *Shovel the dry mix into the crater to absorb the water. Turn the mix over and add more water as necessary, but take care not to make the mix too sloppy.*

5 *The mix should hold its shape when formed into smooth ridges. If it is too sloppy, add one small measure of cement and lime and five small measures of sand and mix again.*

6 *Compact the mix into a heap so that it does not dry out too quickly. To test the plasticity of the mortar, take a slice of mortar on to a trowel; it should stick readily to the blade.*

PLANTING IN PAVING

ONE WAY OF LIVENING UP a large area of paving is to make sunken beds by removing occasional slabs and planting in the spaces, or to plant low-growing plants into the cracks between the slabs. You could even combine the two ideas for a bigger, more imaginative planting scheme. Decide where you want to create a bed and stand the plants, still in their pots, on the slab you have decided to remove so that you can judge the effect.

If you are laying a new patio, it is simple to plan for such beds in advance. Instead of laying the usual rubble and concrete base over the whole area, leave the soil clear where your bed is to go. Improve the existing garden soil (assuming it is reasonably good) with organic matter, such as well-rotted garden compost, and pave round it. If you want to take up slabs from an existing paved area, chip away the cement from between the slabs and lever them out with a crowbar. If they are completely bedded into cement, you may not be able to avoid cracking them, and you may need a power hammer to remove them, together with the foundations beneath them, until you reach bare soil. Once the slabs are out, excavate as much rubble as you can from underneath and then refill with good-quality topsoil, enriched with some extra organic matter. You could leave the bed flush with the paving, or make a low raised edge to it using bricks or rope-edged tiles. Plants growing in paving thrive because the surrounding slabs keep their roots cool and prevent evaporation, which means that the soil dries out much more slowly than potting compost in containers. The plants have a bigger root run, too.

ABOVE: Some sempervivum species are about the same size as pebbles, but instead of being smooth and round they have a spiky texture and may be bright red, purple or green. Use an occasional row in soil-filled cracks between paving slabs to contrast with real pebbles, but try to avoid putting them in places that will be walked on.

Removing a slab to make a planting area

1 Lever out the slab – this one is easy as it is loose-laid over soil. Excavate the hole so that there is room to add plenty of good soil or compost.

2 If the existing soil is fairly good, simply add suitable organic matter to improve the texture and help moisture retention around the plants' roots.

3 Put the largest plant in the centre of the new bed. This compact, bushy potentilla will flower all summer. It spreads quickly and could fill the space left by a single slab in one growing season. Clip the plant the following spring after planting to keep it tidy.

4 *Planting compact rock plants in the corners ties in the new bed with rock plants growing in cracks between other paving slabs nearby.*

5 *Plant all four corners for a neat look. Choose plants that contrast in color and shape, and that will eventually spill out over the paving.*

6 *Tuck some gravel around and under the plants for decoration and to improve drainage. Use the same gravel to cover gaps in the rest of the patio.*

Sowing Seeds

SPRINKLE SEEDS of plants such as alyssum or creeping thymes thinly in the cracks between the paving slabs. Do this instead of using ready-grown plants to fill the gaps. Sprinkle a little fine grit over the top, barely burying the seeds, then water well. Keep the area watered until the seedlings grow into small plants. Thin them out – do not replant them. Once they reach a fair size, undisturbed rock plant seedlings are more drought-tolerant than plants that have been moved.

ABOVE: Tip the tiny seeds into your hand and sprinkle the barest pinch of seed very thinly into the crack.

Plants between paving stones

If possible, improve the soil before you lay the slabs, otherwise you will need to lever up some of the slabs around the cracks to work on the soil. If you do lift a slab, replace it carefully in order not to damage any plants. Use an old fork or spoon to make planting holes in confined space.

1 *Choose a mixture of low, mound-forming and compact, low, spreading plants. Plant them in the spaces between slabs.*

2 *Arrange plants of contrasting shapes next to one another. Lift the straggling ends of trailing plants on to the slabs as you plant.*

3 *Plant up several adjacent corners. In time, the plants will almost cover the slabs, so leave walking areas fairly clear.*

4 *Sprinkle pea-sized shingle over the cracks and under the necks of plants. It aids drainage and helps prevent rotting.*

5 *Water plants in well and do not allow them to dry out during the first growing season. After that, they should be able to survive unaided, except in very long, hot, dry spells.*

BRICKS
& PAVERS

OF ALL THE hard-surfacing materials, brick is arguably the most attractive. It wears reasonably well (although not as well as stone), and it has a wonderfully rich warmth and colour, especially as it ages and weathers. It blends with most architectural styles, and with almost any kind of planting scheme, formal or informal. Containers in terracotta are an ideal partner for brick surfaces, the natural soft earth tones of the terracotta picking up the russet colour of the bricks. Try large terracotta pots of hydrangeas or neatly clipped box balls to mark each end of a path, for example.

Similar to bricks, but made of different materials, are granite setts and pavers. Granite setts are usually a steely blue-grey in colour and can look rather severe unless the garden is planted up to alleviate it. Pavers are not made of natural stone but are available in a range of different colours and styles. They are extremely hardwearing. Granite setts and pavers can work very well with modern architecture, where brick, for example, might look rather too rustic. It is important to match the paving surface for the garden with the architectural style and materials of the house. It will give the area unity and help you to feel that the garden flows naturally out from the house itself.

Bricks are, of course, rather more fiddly and time-consuming to lay than paving slabs, but you

can be very inventive in the forms and patterns that the bricks take, using circles, crescents or different rectangular laying patterns, such as herringbone or basketweave. You could, for example, define the sitting area of the garden with a large brick circle, the bricks radiating out like the spokes of a wheel. This design works very well with a low-maintenance shrub and perennial planting surrounding it, in which the plants – big bushes of lavender, rosemary, viburnum and hydrangeas, for example, spill out, softening the edges of the brick area.

LEFT: *Brick paving provides the flooring solution for this small courtyard garden, echoing the brickwork of the surrounding house and walls, which have been painted white to create the maximum reflection of light. Grouping the planting adds to the emphasis.*

BELOW: *A wonderful swirling pattern of bricks and granite setts makes a real feature of the surface of this small Dutch garden. Note how the spokes of the umbrella echo the form of the brickwork.*

laying bricks

Laying bricks, as with paving stones, requires careful preparation of the site if the bricks are not to sink. First you need to ensure that the site is completely level. This is normally done with string and posts. You will then need to prepare the ground, tamp the soil down firmly, lay a good thick hardcore base, about 10cm (4in) deep, with a 5cm (2in) layer of sand on top into which the bricks are set. The bricks should be laid to butt up to each other, and sand can then be brushed into the joints between them. Edges can be created with bricks set on edge, sunk slightly deeper than the adjoining bricks of the main paved area. Alternatively, you can lay the bricks at a 45° angle to create an interesting edge.

bricks with other materials

Bricks are also ideal for edging other paved surfaces, such as stone or granite setts. You can make thin string courses surrounding a whole paved area or around each individual group of stones, to make a chequerboard pattern.

A circular design can be very effective for a small sitting or dining area, either as a full circle or as a half circle. A cheaper variation on the brick and granite sett surface shown right would be to create a gravel circle edged by a double or triple layer of bricks layed side by side.

1 *Place edge restraints – pegged boards or kerbstones – all round the area you intend to pave. Then cover it with sand and level it roughly with a straightedge.*

2 *To get the blocks level with the top of the edge restraints, measure the block thickness and tamp down the sand to this depth, with a slight fall across the area.*

3 *Decide on the laying pattern you intend to follow and start placing the first blocks on the sand bed. For a patio or path, simply tamp the blocks down level with each other using the handle of a hammer.*

4 *Most patterns have a plain border. Here, a single row is laid along each edge. Use a batten and spirit level to check that the second edge is level.*

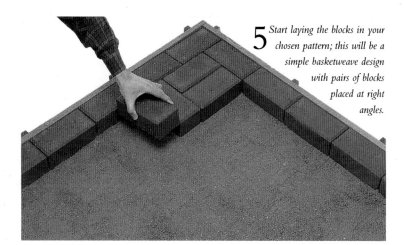

5 *Start laying the blocks in your chosen pattern; this will be a simple basketweave design with pairs of blocks placed at right angles.*

LAYING PAVERS

BLOCK PAVERS ARE RELATIVE NEWCOMERS to the world of garden building, but have rapidly become extremely popular because they are small and easy to handle, are designed to be dry-laid on a sand bed and need no pointing. Unlike other dry-laid paving, they can even withstand the weight of motor vehicles thanks to the way they interlock once laid, so they can be used for all hard surfaces around the garden. They are much harder wearing than standard bricks and are cheaper and easier to handle than granite setts. However, for large areas you must lay the sand bed with a continuous edge restraint to prevent the sand from leaching out. Be sure to use concreting sand for the bedding layer, as building sand is too soft and may stain the blocks.

The blocks are made in a wide range of colours and generally rectangular in shape, measuring 20x10cm (8x4in) and about 6.5cm(2½in) thick. This shape allows you to lay the blocks in a variety of patterns, from a simple stretcher bond arrangement resembling brickwork to herringbone and basketweave designs. You can also lay them diagonally across the area you are paving, filling in the edges with cut-to-size pieces. If the pattern requires many cut blocks, it is well worth hiring a hydraulically operated block splitter that cuts cleanly through the dense aggregate. You can split them with a bolster chisel and a club hammer, but they may not break cleanly. The small size of pavers means they are excellent for creating paving in non-standard shapes. You can make small paved areas anywhere around the garden where they are needed, to support a heavy ornament, for example. Even when loose laid on sand, they make a much firmer foundation than gravel. Pavers are also available in several other shapes including square blocks, bow tie shapes, wedges and wave patterns.

6 *Build up the paving by adding more blocks, working away from the first corner. Check constantly that the pattern is correct as you work.*

7 *After completing a small area, use a straightedge to check that the blocks are level with each other. Then check the fall with your spirit level. Tamp down any pavers that stand proud of the surface.*

8 *When you have completed all the paving, spread some fine sand over the surface and brush it well into all the joints between the blocks. Sweep off the excess sand.*

Rope-twist edging

STRONG RETAINING edges are vital where pavers are bedded on to loose sand, as otherwise rainwater would slowly erode the base away, making a path collapse along its edges. One of the most attractive ways to fix the edges is to use rope-twist tiles. Mark out the position of the path, carefully calculating the width based on the size of the pavers. Then excavate the area to a depth of 10cm (4in). Position the rope tiles along the edge, bedding them into a shallow trough filled with cement to hold them in place. Spread a 4cm (1¹/₂in) layer of sand over the base of the path and lay the pavers in place.

RIGHT: You can use pavers to create attractive dog-leg shapes like this good solid path, which looks equally at home in any type of situation, including a cottage garden, a traditional formal design or a modern contemporary setting.

PATTERNS WITH PAVERS

THE BLOCK PAVER IS IDEAL for creating paths, patios and other paved areas in the garden, because it is light and easy to handle and quick and simple to lay. Most people choose a monochrome effect, laying pavers of just one colour and relying on the way in which they are placed for extra visual interest. However, as pavers are made to a standard size there is no reason why you should not use pavers of different colours to create distinctive patterns, or even mix them with other paving materials or cobbles. Pavers now come in a wide range of shades, from yellow and red to buff and brown and various shades of grey, so you can choose complementary or contrasting effects as you prefer. The only limit to what you can create is your own imagination. One of the simplest options is to use a band of different-coloured pavers along the edges of the area. If you prefer to mix the colours across the whole area, you can simply insert pavers of the second colour regularly or at random. The basketweave pattern – pairs of pavers laid at right angles to the adjoining pair – allows you to create a chequerboard effect, while the popular herringbone pattern can feature zigzagging bands of different-coloured pavers. If you are prepared to cut blocks in half, there is even more scope for creating attractive patterns. Keep an eye open for unusual effects created with block pavers in public spaces; you can then copy any ideas you like in your own garden at home.

Herringbone pattern

1 *A contrasting border is one of the simplest effects you can create with block pavers. Here, the grey border pavers are laid side by side and the infill is added in herringbone style.*

2 *Tamp the pavers into the sand bed, using a wood offcut and a club hammer to set them level with their neighbours. Lift and relay any that sink down or stand proud.*

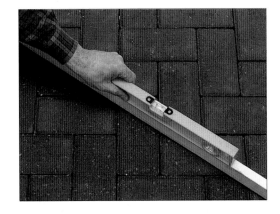

3 *Use a long wooden straightedge and a spirit level to check that there is a slight fall across the paved area. This will ensure that heavy rain can drain freely off the surface of the paving.*

Cutting bricks and pavers

TO CUT A BRICK, mark a line on the brick and score it all round with the tip of a bricklayer's chisel. Place the brick on a bed of sand and drive the chisel with blows from a club hammer to break the brick at the marked position.

To cut a paver, score a cutting line deeply across its face by drawing the corner of a bolster chisel against a straightedge. Place the paver on a sand bed and cut it with a chisel and hammer.

RIGHT: The continuous pattern begins to build up as you work across the area. The cut blocks at the edges of the area maintain the herringbone bond.

Mixing block pavers and paving slabs

Small paving slabs can look particularly attractive when combined with block pavers. Be sure to choose your slabs with care, so that their size coordinates with a whole number of pavers, or you will end up either with unacceptably wide joints or impossibly intricate block trimming.

LEFT: If you are mixing pavers and slabs, choose slabs with sides equal to a whole number of pavers. Experiment with designs on paper. Place extra sand beneath the slabs to keep them level with the pavers.

A squared pattern

LEFT: First work out the pattern you intend to lay on squared paper, so that you can order the right number of each colour. Start building up the pattern from one edge, checking it against your plan as you work.

RIGHT: Half blocks in a contrasting colour have been used to fill in the open centre of a square formed by four full blocks. The repeated motif creates a striking visual effect.

Diagonal zigzag pattern

Mixing pavers of different colours can create even more dramatic effects if you are prepared to work to a diagonal grid rather than a square one. It allows you to create straight lines or zigzags running at an angle to the edge of the paved area, according to the laying pattern you adopt. However, designs of this sort involve a great deal of block cutting at the perimeter of the area, so allow for this when estimating quantities and add some extra pavers to cater for the occasional cutting blunder. Plan the layout and pattern on paper first, so that you can check your progress as you work and avoid costly mistakes.

RIGHT: With the edge restraints and border pavers in place, build up the diagonal pattern. Move a stringline across the area as the pattern extends, and include pavers cut at an angle as necessary to maintain the design.

LEFT: The simple grey zigzag perfectly complements the straight border. Here it is about to be repeated at the near edge of a path. Hire a block splitter to make light work of cutting the angled infill pieces.

Using weathered bricks

RIGHT: The colours and textures of old or recycled bricks vary even within the same brick. To make the most of them, use them very simply for paving, raised beds or a plinth for a garden ornament. Brick colours team well with red flowers.

PEBBLES & COBBLES, EDGES, TILES & SLABS

NATURALLY ROUNDED PEBBLES and larger cobblestones are a good way of introducing varieties of shape and texture to your paving. You can use them to create paths and patios, but they are more commonly used as a visual counterpoint to flat surfaces – perhaps as a border or to highlight a garden feature, such as a sundial or statue. Their advantage over other garden paving materials is their relatively small size, which makes it easy to fit them round curves and irregularly shaped obstacles. However, because of this, they do take much longer to lay than other materials. You can buy pebbles and cobblestones from builders' suppliers and garden centres, in a range of sizes and colours. Small quantities – enough for an individual garden feature – are usually sold in bags, but for larger areas it will be more economical to buy the stones loose by weight. Ask your supplier for advice about coverage, and have large quantities delivered; more than two or three sacks will wreck your vehicle suspension.

Frostproof terracotta pavers, embossed tiles and decorative edging are becoming increasingly popular. They can be used alone or mixed with other paving and edging materials for strong visual contrast. Terracotta pavers and tiles are not as strong as other paving materials, so bed them on a continuous mortar bed for solid support beneath them.

Laying pebbles and cobblestones

It is best to bed pebbles and cobblestones in mortar, especially if they form a surface that will be walked on or are used to line a watercourse or surround a fountain. Within decorative areas they can be laid loose on a sand bed.

1 *To outline a pebble path with a border of pavers, bricks or granite setts, spread a generous mortar bed, set the bricks in place and point neatly between them.*

2 *Place pebbles on the mortar bed, butting them up closely to the border and to each other. Select stones for fit and the colour contrast with their neighbours.*

3 *Use a wood offcut and club hammer to tamp down the pebbles into the mortar bed. It is important to ensure that they cannot subsequently work loose.*

4 *Check that the stones are reasonably level across the surface. If any of them project too far above their neighbours, tamp them down further.*

5 *Water enhances the natural colours and textures of pebbles with dramatic effect. Create this look artificially by coating the finished bed with a clear silicone masonry sealant.*

Laying tiles and edging

Secure terracotta edging strips in place with a strip of mortar along each side. Slope it as shown and check that it is low enough to allow the paving slab to butt up against it. Terracotta rope edging is sold in lengths of about 60cm (24in). Use a strong mortar (1 part cement to 3 or 4 parts sand, plus added plasticizer) to bed the edging in place.

1 *Set the rope edging and corner posts in place. Spread a bed of sloppy mortar over the area to be paved. Place the corner tile first, then add further tiles.*

2 *With a few tiles in place, check that they are level when viewed against the edging. Use a spirit level to ensure that each row is level across the tiled area.*

3 *Here, decorative tiles form a border to plain terracotta pavers, each equivalent in size to four tiles. Place the paver on the mortar bed, tamp it down and check the levels.*

4 *This completed module shows how the edging, tiles and pavers are coordinated in size. The edging length matches three tile widths.*

Mosaic patterns

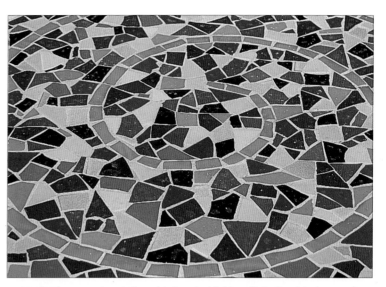

ABOVE: Mosaics are easy to make from almost any hard flat ingredients, though broken ceramic tiles are always popular. Make sure the tiles are frostproof. To make a mosaic work, first fit the pieces together to make the pattern, then transfer them to the site. Push the pieces of tile down into a bed of damp mortar. Use a straightedge and spirit level to check they are even.

Splitting tiles

1 *To cut a paving tile, score a cutting line deeply across its face. Draw the corner of a bolster chisel firmly against a straightedge for increased accuracy.*

2 *Place the paver on a sand bed and cut it with a chisel and hammer. Move the chisel along the line until the paver splits cleanly in half.*

1 Excavate the area over which you want to lay the gravel until you reach solid subsoil. Set out preservative-treated boards around the perimeter of the excavated area and drive in stout corner pegs.

2 Secure the boards to the pegs with galvanized nails. Add more pegs at roughly 1m (3ft) intervals along the boards all round the area to prevent the boards from bowing outwards later on.

3 The best way of discouraging weeds from growing up through a gravel path is to put down a weed-suppressing membrane over the subsoil.

4 To form a firm base for the gravel, cover the membrane with a layer of crushed rock or fine hardcore. You will need at least 5cm (2in) of rock on firm subsoil, and more if the ground is soft.

LAYING GRAVEL

A PATH OR OTHER GRAVEL AREA can be an attractive feature in any garden, especially when used to provide contrast alongside flat paving materials and low-growing plants. Areas of gravel are also a particularly popular feature of Oriental-style gardens. True gravel is available in a range of mixed natural earth shades that look particularly good when wet, while crushed stone, which is rough-edged rather than smooth, is sold in a range of colours from white through reds and greens to grey and black. Although both are attractive and are relatively inexpensive to lay, they do have several practical drawbacks. They need some form of edge restraint to prevent the stones straying on to lawns or into flower beds. They need regular raking and weeding to keep them looking good. They can attract dogs and cats, who find them ideal as an earth closet. And lastly, pushing a laden wheelbarrow along a gravel path is very hard work! However, if you do choose gravel, work out carefully how much material to order. Decorative aggregates are sold in small carry-home bags, weighing from 25–50kg (55–110lbs), and by volume in large canvas slings or in loose loads that are delivered to your door. You will need a bulk delivery for all but the smallest areas. Bear in mind that a cubic metre of gravel weighs about 1.7 tonnes and will cover an area of just over 13sq m to a depth of 7.5cm (3in).

5 Compact the base layer by running a heavy garden roller over it. Fill in any hollows and roll it again until you no longer leave any footprints in the surface. Thorough preparation of the base will pay off at this stage.

6 *Without disturbing the base layer, spread out the gravel or decorative stone. Fill the area up to the level of the perimeter boards.*

7 *Level the gravel. Draw a wooden straightedge along the tops of the boards to identify high spots or hollows. Rake again.*

A gravel path with brick patterns

You can mix gravel with smooth slabs or block pavers to create attractive patterns and contrasts. The blocks also help to keep gravel off lawns and beds. This simple path is cheap and easy to make. Rake the ground to remove any debris, level it and tread it down. Cover the compacted earth with a good layer of moistened sand and flatten it.

1 *Lay a line of bricks from side to side, level with the straight edges – here, pavers set on edge. Make these firm and level, checking them with a straightedge and spirit level.*

2 *Fill the triangular spaces between the bricks with shingle or gravel and tread it down gently. Do not to push the bricks out of line before the shingle or gravel has settled into place.*

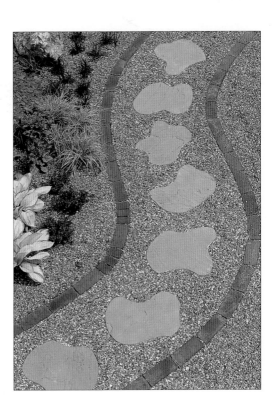

LEFT: In an Oriental-style garden that relies on architectural detail as much as plants for its interest, you can make a plain gravel path into a much more unusual feature by bedding in irregularly shaped stepping stones at intervals. As well as looking attractive, they are comfortable to walk on.

3 *Edge this simple but effective formal path with suitable plants. The path is cheap and easy to make and you only need to cut a few bricks. Gravel is an ideal alternative to grass for narrow paths such as this.*

WOODEN SURFACES

BELOW: *Timber and gravel make excellent partners for an informal path. The effect is softened here by creeping and sprawling plants.*

MORE RECENT IN ORIGIN than stone or bricks as a surface for the garden, decking is widely used in countries that have a natural supply of timber, and is increasingly being adopted as a surface in many gardens by garden designers, who find its flexibility a great asset. It is relatively easy to lay, durable, and easy to maintain, provided you spend the money on a good hardwood, such as teak, for example, which will need nothing more than an annual scrub with a stiff brush and some fungicide. Softwood decking, however, will also need regular treatment with a wood preservative.

Decking produces a wonderfully soft-looking surface, which can be left natural or stained in one of the good new colours now available – slate blue, silvery grey or a soft bottle green all make a good foil for the planting. Stronger colours would be too strident and dominant in most situations.

Decking will cope particularly well with an uneven site, saving you from spending a lot of money levelling it out. You simply adjust the height of the bearing timbers to take in any changes of level. In fact, you can use any changes of level to your advantage to build a tiered or stepped surface, which helps add interest to the garden. If you want to include a water feature

RIGHT: *This little roof garden has been surfaced with diagonally laid decking, painted battleship blue-grey. Wooden decking makes an excellent surface for roof gardens, but take care to ensure that any moisture-proof membrane is not pierced while it is being laid.*

in a small garden, decking is an ideal medium to use, as you can incorporate the pond into the decked area, building the decked surface over part of the pond to form a bridge.

As it is relatively light, decking is also one of the best surfaces for a roof terrace. The main concern here is not to pierce any damp-proof membrane covering the roof terrace in the construction of a new surface, but as the roof-top surface is already flat, you can simply 'float' the decking just above the asphalt on reasonably heavy load-bearing joists. Always check with a building surveyor when planning a roof terrace, or any work to it, to ensure that it will not only bear the weight of whatever you have in mind, but also that any drainage system that exists is adequate for the purpose.

railway sleepers

Another option for a wooden surface is to use recycled railway sleepers, which work well used with another hard surface material, such as stone or gravel. Laid diagonally, these sleepers can form an interesting surface with plenty of texture. Be warned, however, that the timber can become slippery unless scrubbed at least once a year with fungicide. Railway sleepers also make very good surrounds for raised beds, in a simple box-like construction, which would work well with a timber and stone surface pattern.

A raised deck of large railway sleepers could also be used to define a small sitting area at the end, say, of a bricked patio, and looks very good with some of the modern, sturdy all-weather teak garden furniture.

ABOVE: *To relieve a feeling of monotony over a large area, the decking here has been laid on different levels, each change of contour marked with a different direction of the decking. Bold foliage adds to the Oriental feel.*

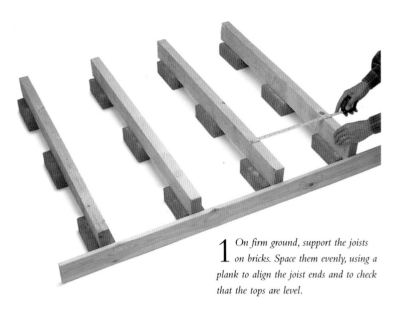

1 *On firm ground, support the joists on bricks. Space them evenly, using a plank to align the joist ends and to check that the tops are level.*

2 *Cut a fascia board to the width of the decking and secure it to the joist ends with galvanized nails. Fix a batten across the tops of the joists at the other end of the deck.*

3 *Cut and position the first plank across the joists so that its front edge projects over the fascia and forms a projecting nosing. Secure it to each joist with two nails.*

DECKING

EITHER HARDWOOD OR SOFTWOOD can be used for wooden decking. The raw material is widely available and softwood costs broadly the same as basic paving. Hardwood will cost more but will last longer and you will not need to treat it regularly with preservative as you will with softwood. Wood is much easier to cut to size than paving slabs or blocks, quickly blends in with its surroundings as it weathers and is more forgiving to walk or sit down on than hard paving. The only disadvantages of wooden decking are that it will need occasional maintenance work and that it can be slippery in wet weather. Make sure that all the sawn joists and planed planks for decking have been pretreated with preservative and apply a preservative stain to the completed structure, paying special attention to cut ends. To keep the decking clear of damp ground and reduce the incidence of rot, set the joists on bricks, ideally with a pad of damp-proof membrane or roofing felt between bricks and joists. Clear the ground beneath the decking, digging out all weed roots, or apply a weedkiller first.

Wooden decking looks particularly good in modern surroundings or teamed with a woodland or Oriental-style garden. To make the most of the timber theme, use wooden containers and furniture and choose plants that suit a timbered background, such as hostas, hardy ferns, camellias, lilies and miniature rhododendrons in wooden tubs. Try the striking shapes of yucca, phormium and Chusan palm with exotic-looking half-hardy plants such as agave, aeonium or abutilon. And for an Oriental feel, go for a few well-shaped, clipped conifers and bonsai shapes in Oriental ceramic pots.

4 *Leave a slight gap between adjacent planks so that rainwater can drain freely. Set a slim batten against the first plank, then position the second plank close against the batten. The temporary batten on the other side holds the joists parallel while you fix the planks in position.*

5 *Secure the plank to each joist, punching two galvanized nails just below the wood surface. A stringline will help to align the nail heads across the decking.*

Finishing touches

ABOVE: Butt-join planks as necessary over the centre line of a joist. Sand the cut ends first to prevent splinters.

ABOVE: Treat the deck with a preservative stain or wood dye to improve its resistance to rot and insect attack.

6 *Set the decking on bricks or blocks bedded in the subsoil so that the joists are held clear of the ground. Hide the supports with pebbles or low-level planting.*

Wooden decking tiles

You can buy small, preassembled wooden decking tiles made from preservative-treated softwood. Some also have a non-slip grooved surface. You can lay them directly on the soil, but it is a good idea to support them on joists to create whatever area of decking you require. Although convenient, these tiles are more expensive than normal decking.

1 *The tiles have closely spaced slats held together by two stapled-on support battens. Start by making up a framework of preservative-treated joists to support the prefabricated tiles.*

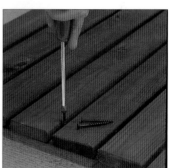

2 *Space the joists to allow the tiles to meet along the centre line of each joist and then lay the individual tiles in the desired pattern.*

3 *Nail the tiles through the slats into the joists beneath. If you prefer invisible fixings, drive screws between the slats through the support battens.*

Decking tiles can cover as large an area as you need.

4 *In this case, all the tiles have been laid with their slats running in the same direction, but you can create different patterns. Try, for example, basketweave pattern, laying the tiles alternately in different directions.*

1 *Use preservative-treated sawn timber for joists. Space them evenly and nail a transverse joist to their ends to hold them in position.*

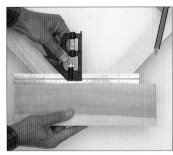

2 *To set planks at a 45° angle to the joists, use a combination square to position the first plank at the corner of the joist framework.*

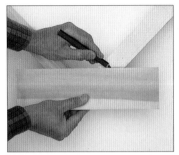

3 *Once you have positioned the first plank accurately, remove the square and mark the plank position with a pencil on the joists below.*

4 *Use the square with its 45° face against the plank edge to mark a guideline for the nails above the centre line of the joist beneath.*

5 *Nail on the first plank. Drive in the nail nearest the corner first, check the alignment of the plank with the pencil lines, and secure it with two more nails.*

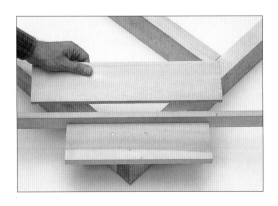

6 *Use a slim batten as a spacing guide to ensure that the gaps between adjacent boards are the same across the decking surface. Place the next plank in position.*

DECKING DESIGNS

SINCE WOOD IS EASY TO CUT to size and shape, you can create any number of decorative designs. Carefully work out the design on paper first, adjusting the spacing between the planks to ensure that a whole number will fit the area you want to cover. You can create chevron and diamond patterns by reversing the direction of the planking on adjacent areas of the decking. Round off cut edges slightly with sandpaper to ensure that they are free from splinters. Provide additional protection for the perimeter of the decking by nailing on edge battens all round.

Wood is a material that allows your inventiveness full rein when it comes to creating walkways and sitting areas in the garden. Set alongside a garden pond or other water feature, it conjures up images of sturdy wooden jetties on a boating lake. Placed among an overflowing border, it creates a natural-looking pathway that blends in with the informality of the planting far more sympathetically than any masonry path can. The structures you create with it can be assembled from small modules put together in your workshop and then arranged – and rearranged – in the garden. However you decide to use it, remember the two essential rules. Firstly, all wood that spends its life in contact with the ground must either be a naturally durable species, or else be thoroughly pretreated with wood preservative to keep rot and insect attack at bay. Secondly, wood can become slippery when wet since moss and algae will grow on its surface, so be prepared to scrub it down once or twice a year to keep it in a safe condition and looking good at all times.

7 *Repeat the procedure with the square and pencil to ensure that the nails securing the second plank are in line with those holding the first one. A combination square (or adjustable try square) is an excellent tool for checking and marking angles.*

8 *Use the spacer batten to position subsequent planks, nailing them to the joists one by one. Punch the nail heads just below the surface of the wood.*

9 *When all the planks are nailed down, place a straightedge over the projecting ends, align it with the outer face of the joist below and mark a cutting line.*

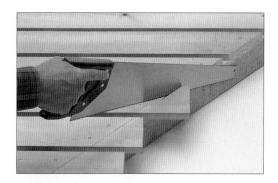

10 *Use a panel saw to cut off the projecting ends of the planks. Saw just on the waste side of the cutting line, taking care to keep the saw blade vertical as you work.*

ABOVE: Raised hardwood decking with a built-in bench surround. The furniture, too, is hardwood so it can safely be left outdoors all year round. From this vantage point, you have a perfect bird's-eye view of a woodland garden.

11 *Sand all the cut ends of the planks to remove splinters. Nail on edging battens for a neat finish and to protect the exposed end grain against rot and damage.*

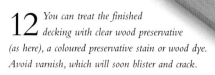

12 *You can treat the finished decking with clear wood preservative (as here), a coloured preservative stain or wood dye. Avoid varnish, which will soon blister and crack.*

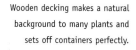

Wooden decking makes a natural background to many plants and sets off containers perfectly.

SOFT SURFACES

GRASS IS THE SURFACE most people automatically choose to cover those parts of the garden where they do not intend to grow flowers and shrubs. It acts rather like a self-regenerating carpet, and makes a natural green backdrop that sets off trees and flowers perfectly. However, to keep grass looking good it needs regular mowing and if it gets heavy wear – for instance from children and dogs playing on it – then feeding and occasional repairs will also be needed. Grass is not always the easy option it is often believed to be. You can make lawn care easier by using paving or gravel in places that get heavy wear, such as the sitting-out area, and by laying hard paths along routes where you frequently walk, say from the back door to the shed or washing line. But in some situations, other forms of soft surface may be more suitable than grass. For instance, under trees, where grass does not thrive due to heavy shade or dry soil, a surface of bark chippings looks pleasing and natural but needs no work to maintain. On a slope that is difficult to mow, ground cover plants grown close together make a dense layer that smothers out weeds, looks good all year round and flowers seasonally. In a hot, dry, sunny spot where grass needs frequent watering, a thyme lawn made of spreading varieties grown through gravel creates a low leafy effect, yet needs no mowing or irrigation; it is also delightfully scented.

ABOVE: A thyme lawn makes a very pretty feature in a decorative 'edible garden'. Plant a mixture of creeping varieties in a random pattern. Well-drained soil and a sunny spot are essential. Dig in plenty of gravel for good drainage.

RIGHT: Bark chippings are the ideal mulch around ground cover plants. Cover the soil immediately after planting to a depth of 5cm (2in). Small chippings are a more effective mulch than large ones and last three years or more.

ABOVE: A living carpet of ajuga with contrasting groups of hosta is a decorative way to clad moist ground in a lightly shady area. Since you cannot walk over the plants, add wooden stepping stones or an informal path of bark chippings if necessary.

The design value of lawns

YOU CAN USE the lawn to link larger features in the garden, or to influence the visual impact of your garden as a whole. A lawn's length, width, shape and position can make the plot appear wider, larger or just more interesting than it actually is. Remember to plan an area of grass from a practical point of view, so that it is fairly easy to maintain. All parts must be accessible to your mower, with no areas narrower than the width of the machine. When you are experimenting with shapes, bear in mind that curves and circles create a softer, informal look, while harder, geometric figures, such as squares and rectangles, appear more formal. Try positioning your shapes on the diagonal or at a slight angle for more interesting and less predictable effects.

BELOW: A good way to make the most of a sloping site is to divide it into two small lawns linked by steps. By making the near lawn short but wide and the top one long and narrower, the garden appears bigger than it really is.

Hard-wearing lawns

HARD WEAR AREAS and gardens used by children and pets need a grass seed mixture with a high proportion of rye-grass, plus drought-resistant varieties, such as crested dog's tail, that will produce a good-quality, resilient turf which recovers quickly. Specialist suppliers can also make you up a mix that will contain clover in whatever percentage you like. Although clover is unacceptable in a smart sward, it is hard-wearing, stays green during drought and can be mown in the same way as a lawn if you do not like the flowers.

ABOVE: A meandering lawn breaks up the straight edges of a regular plot, creating a charmingly informal effect. By making the lawn disappear round a border with tall plants you create the impression that the garden is larger than it is.

Soleirolia among pebbles

Grass will not grow in a very shady area, but helxine (*Soleirolia*) or ivy will thrive. Combine a cobbled surface with these low creeping plants to make an attractive feature. Use this idea between paving stones, as an edging to a path or as unusual ground cover in a problem area.

1 *Prepare the soil well, adding plenty of organic matter. Put in the plants 23–30cm (9–12in) apart. Helxine can become invasive close to lawns or borders.*

2 *Select smooth, evenly sized, coloured cobblestones. Press them into place between the plants. Group them in clusters if you do not want a solid surface.*

3 *Tuck more cobbles around the plants and bed them down firmly. Move any that create large areas of one colour; aim for a mix of speckles and colours.*

4 *Water the whole area to get the plants off to a good start and to firm the stones into place. This is particularly important if you are going to walk on them.*

5 *The end result is a very self-sufficient feature. The cobbles act like a mulch, preventing weed seeds from germinating and keeping the plant roots cool and moist. In a sunny spot, sink cobbles into gravel and plant creeping thymes instead.*

CHAPTER 3

GARDEN FEATURES

IN ADDITION to the plants and the basic structural elements, most gardens are enhanced by a range of special features including pools and fountains, lighting, garden ornaments, garden furniture and vertical screening. The range and choice available to you is enormous, but it is important to decide how to make best use of these features in the confined space of a small garden. This chapter discusses every kind of vertical surface, from walls and fences to trellis and pergolas, different styles and types of furniture to suit every conceivable need and taste, as well as more decorative features, from judiciously placed ornaments to subtle lighting effects. It also shows you how to go about creating garden features of every kind.

LEFT: *This small formal water feature, with its raised pond and fountain spout, enhances a shady corner of a small city garden.*

RIGHT: *A painted bench creates a focus of interest in a small semi-formal garden, with its containers of box and sculptured lawn set among an unusual pink, purple and green planting scheme.*

WALLS & FENCES

LEFT: *A high wall, whether of the house or garden, provides a home for the vigorous* Wisteria floribunda, *with its long racemes of lilac flowers, which appear in late spring.*

RIGHT: *To avoid monotony, the boundary fence for this garden has been given a mixed treatment with a wood panel fence, arranged vertically, topped with square painted trellis. Painting trellis not only helps preserve it, it creates interest while any climbing plants are growing up to cover it.*

THE GARDEN SURROUNDS are extremely important in a small space, where privacy and shelter are essential prerequisites to enjoying your garden. If you are lucky enough to have a walled garden, you can use this as an attractive backdrop for the planting. A few masonry nails and wires will provide adequate support for a range of twining climbers that will offer an enticing display of flowers throughout the year. Clematis, climbing roses, honeysuckles, *Solanum crispum* and jasmines are all ideal candidates, as are some of the wall shrubs, such as *Fremontodendron californicum*, with its showy golden yellow cup-shaped flowers, and *Carpenteria californica*, with its glossy evergreen leaves and sparkling white flowers with a yellow eye.

A low wall can be increased in height by attaching trellis to the upper part, over which you can encourage the climbers to grow. This not only gives you privacy, but with any luck will deter marauding neighbourhood cats.

If the walls around your garden are made of an unattractive material, disguise them firstly by painting them a more appropriate colour – a rich deep green for example – and, secondly, by growing plants over and against them.

fences

Fences in most situations need to be fairly tough as a deterrant to intruders and as a firm support for plants. Make sure that any close-board fences are supported with stout upright timbers at close intervals – normally about every 1.8m (6ft) apart. Again, the height can be extended using trellis, which, unlike closeboard fencing, does not act like a sail in a high wind, and is therefore less likely to blow down.

RIGHT: *This attractive wooden screen, painted a delicate sage green, makes an excellent foil for the handsome Alibaba pot. Painting screens in toning colours is an ideal way to harmonize the surfaces with the planting.*

screens

Screens of any kind are vital for sitting areas, both on a small patio and on an exposed balcony or roof terrace. Bear in mind that if the wind can permeate the screen to some extent it will create less of a problem than a completely weatherproof form. For areas that are exposed to high winds, consider constructing your own trellis from sturdy timber, at least 2.5cm (1in) in section, pretreated with preservative. You can create any pattern you like and you can stain the trellis in any one of a number of appealing natural wood stains, or in a soft pastel shade.

For roof gardens and balconies, you might like to use bamboo or reed screens, popular in Oriental gardens since time immemorial. Similar

LEFT: *Hot tubs – small heated pools sunk into the terrace – have long been popular in warmer climates and can make a wonderfully relaxing addition to a small garden. Such features need to be screened to provide some feeling of privacy. An open timber screen will create an intimate atmosphere without making a solid and imposing boundary that casts heavy shade.*

RIGHT: *Reed or bamboo screens, although not immensely long lasting, provide an excellent solution for temporary screening, being attractive and inexpensive, and sympathetic to both architectural features and planting.*

forms can be found made from willow, hazel or brushwood (see page 81). They will create a soft, natural-looking boundary, perfect for a small garden. Although not as long lasting as trellis, most will last five years. As with trellis, you will need to attach the screens to firmly fixed, sufficiently strong supports.

using trees and shrubs

In a small patio garden, some of the most necessary screening is to hide unattractive views. A judiciously placed, reasonably fast-growing tree can often blot out an eyesore, such as a tall block of flats. A columnar tree, such as *Chamaecyparis lawsoniana*, will work well for this purpose. The golden form 'Ellwoodii' is more attractive than the plain green species.

Even a delicate birch tree, while not completely blanking off an unattractive view, will help to diffuse it, while at the same time allowing quite a lot of light into the garden, which is sometimes a very important requirement in a small-scale garden, which might otherwise become too shaded.

Some plants can make excellent screens for coastal areas, where salty winds can wreak havoc in the garden. Consider using either elaeagnus or grisellinia as an evergreen screen. Both will cope extremely well with pollution

as well as salt spray, and they can be clipped neatly to make a good weatherproof hedge.

Other good screening plants are privet, box and yew. A single large shrub can provide a useful screen for a garden shed in a small patio garden, and low hedges of shrubs such as lavender, rosemary and box can be used to divide and compartmentalize even the most diminutive garden.

Screens can be useful in a small garden to hide any storage, such as a small garden shed, or, if you are ecologically minded, a compost

heap. A large bushy shrub will serve the purpose well – *Elaeagnus* x *ebbingei* makes a good solid evergreen screen, is quite fast growing and has the bonus of scented, but sadly rather inconspicuous flowers which appear in autumn. Alternatively, use trellis and grow evergreen climbers, such as *Hydrangea anomala petiolaris* or one of the more attractive ivies over it. Variegated holly will also make an excellent screen, but most are not very quick growing and will take a while before they begin to serve the purpose you have in mind.

A LIVING BOUNDARY

IN A SMALL GARDEN most people want to make the maximum use of the available space for growing plants, so living boundaries are an appealing option whether they are a full-blown hedge or a flowering climber trained over a wall. However, in a small garden there is the question of how much space the boundary will take up. Hedges often take up a great deal of room, so avoid planting traditional beech, hornbeam or privet which need planting in staggered rows for stability and can be 1m (3ft) wide at the base. Yew can be used in a single row, however, and can be clipped to make a hedge as little as 30–45cm (12–18in) wide.

You can also achieve a hedge-like effect by growing climbers on chain link fencing. This is also a good way to disguise the fencing and cheaper than replacing it with something more attractive. It also makes a living and even flowering boundary that takes up little space in terms of width. Similarly you could plant climbers on a structure of posts and wire netting to make a fast-growing screen for 'instant' privacy and shelter or to hide an eyesore. This has the advantage of stopping at the required height and needing little trimming.

As already mentioned, walls and fences are ideal supports for self-clinging climbers such as ivy and parthenocissus, or you can put in wall nails to support horizontal wires for espalier or fan-trained trees or wall shrubs. Consider growing the climbers on netting or trellis held 10cm (4in) away from the wall which can be removed to allow access to the wall or fence for maintenance.

ABOVE: Privacy and shelter are two vital ingredients for a patio, and where there is no existing wall or hedge to do the job, a trellis screen is the quickest and most decorative way of providing both.

RIGHT: In a wilder style of garden you can make a form of very open weave 'trellis', using rustic sticks woven between stronger stakes driven into the ground.

Thuja occidentalis 'Smaragd'

Thuja plicata 'Zebrina'

Thuja occidentalis 'Holmstrupii'

LEFT: If you want a conifer hedge that is easy to keep at 1–1.2m (3–4ft) tall and does not need endless clipping, then thujas are the best choice. Cheaper hedging thujas are available, but if you only need a few, opt for a named variety so that you can choose the colour or plant shape you prefer.

ABOVE: The variegated ivy *Hedera helix* 'Chrysophylla', here bound and clipped on a section of post-and-rail fence, turns a brilliant shade of yellow in spring when covered in young growth.

RIGHT: Although this is a clinging ivy, it has been wired on to the fence rail to prevent it becoming top heavy and being blown off in the wind. It requires clipping only three times each year.

BELOW: Colour makes a stunning background to a busy border. A large range of water-based timber treatment stains is available to restyle old fences. Blue is effective teamed with orange and purple flowers.

Natural boundries

Natural materials are fast becoming favourites for informal fencing panels, as alternatives to traditional woven timber strips. Natural panels last from five to ten years; less in a very windy site, but longer if the panels are firmly fixed and treated with a suitable preservative. Panels can be used permanently or temporarily to protect new shrubs or while a hedge grows. Many different types are available or you can make a very rustic-looking kind yourself from hazel twigs, bamboo canes or peasticks.

LEFT: Long strands of dried heather stapled together make attractive and long-lasting russet-toned panels. Though more expensive than many forms of fencing panel, these are very robust and make a superb background to plants. Ideal for a natural-look garden or rustic situation.

RIGHT: Bamboo canes or a mixture of canes and straight, slender willow wands, as here, make a striking and unusual fence panel. Sticks can be left natural or treated with water-based stains to colour them. For a novel effect, group canes of different colours together in the same row.

LEFT: Traditional sheep hurdles are made from thick hazel wands bent round stronger stakes. They are available as ready-made panels to fix to stakes hammered into the ground. But you can make your own in situ by bending birch or other flexible twigs around a row of poles 30cm (12in) apart.

TRELLIS

TRELLIS PANELS ARE AVAILABLE in a wide variety of styles and materials. Trellis framework is attractive in its own right and its impact can be accentuated by painting it in different colours. Bright blue, yellow and terracotta water-based wood stains, which double as timber preservatives, are an increasingly popular and fashionable option. Natural wood finish and white paint are traditional choices, the latter conveying a 'classic' style to the garden. You can fix trellis panels to free-standing posts to create simple screens of foliage and flowers, or you can build up arches, arbours, bowers and pergolas to suit your space and budget. In fact, you can buy many such trellis features as self-assembly kits. You can also buy perspective trellis panels to attach to walls. These create the impression of a niche, which is ideal for framing a mirror, statue or urn.

One of the main ways of using trellis panels is to fix them directly to a wall. You can do this simply by drilling through the battens and screwing directly into the brickwork. Do make sure that heavy panels are securely fixed and bear in mind that the climbers will add more weight to the structure. If you are using heavy duty, square-mesh trellis you will need to decide whether to place the horizontal or vertical battens closest to the wall. One way might be better for the plants you use, giving you room to tie in the stems to the framework.

ABOVE: Stylish terracotta wall pots attached at various heights on to a rustic screen made from dried heather stems create a delightful display in which the plants are almost a bonus.

LEFT: Use soft string to tie honeysuckle stems to a trellis panel or a cane. The stems are delicate so take care when handling them and tie knots loosely.

BELOW: Expandable cedar trellis panels need support. Fix them to battens on the wall to create space behind the panels for plant growth.

ABOVE: A wooden trellis panel with the horizontal battens fixed directly to the wall. This leaves the vertical pieces free, but plant growth may be restricted behind the cross pieces.

ABOVE: Turn the panel round and the cross pieces form a series of rungs held away from the wall by the vertical battens. This might give climbers the best chance to develop.

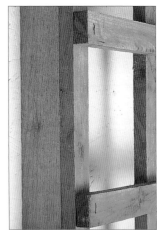

ABOVE: To save deciding which way round to fix the panel, simply space the whole thing away from the wall by fixing it on to a batten down the sides. This gives plants plenty of room.

Making wooden brackets

BELOW: You can make a support that fits over the horizontal lathes of a trellis panel with two pieces of 5x2.5cm (2x1in) planed softwood and a piece of 2.5x2.5cm (1x1in).

ABOVE: Attach a hanging basket bracket to the support and simply hang it on to the trellis. The horizontal lathes are at the front here so the wooden hook fits well.

BELOW: Make a simple wooden bracket with an overhang on the top section and attach a piece of 2.5x2.5cm (1x1in) so that it will hook on to the trellis.

RIGHT: Use one bracket to suspend a hanging basket or two brackets to support a windowbox or any suitable type of trough on top.

Attaching plants to supports

Plant support systems range from small nails or screws driven into the wall to a more permanent system of wires stretched horizontally across the wall at about 30cm (12in) intervals. There are various products for tying plant stems to wire or trellis, from soft green string to plastic and paper ties. Every year, check that plants have not outgrown their ties and loosen or replace them if they are too tight.

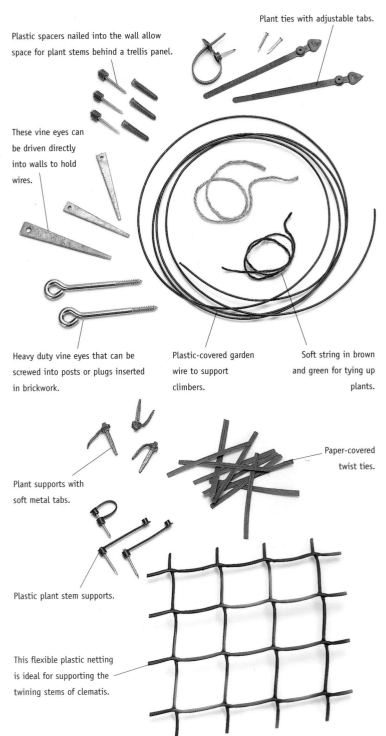

Plant ties with adjustable tabs.

Plastic spacers nailed into the wall allow space for plant stems behind a trellis panel.

These vine eyes can be driven directly into walls to hold wires.

Heavy duty vine eyes that can be screwed into posts or plugs inserted in brickwork.

Plastic-covered garden wire to support climbers.

Soft string in brown and green for tying up plants.

Paper-covered twist ties.

Plant supports with soft metal tabs.

Plastic plant stem supports.

This flexible plastic netting is ideal for supporting the twining stems of clematis.

OTHER VERTICAL FEATURES

WHEN EVERY SINGLE SCRAP of space has to count, you cannot afford to overlook the third dimension. Gardening upwards takes advantage of the space over your garden as well as that inside it. As already discussed, you will want to take advantage of all your walls, fences and outbuildings to grow climbers and wall-trained shrubs, but what about adding extra vertical features deliberately to add extra opportunities for more plants? Arches, pergolas, trellis screens and arbours all act as creative space for climbers. And fashionable willow and rustic twig plant supports or classic iron obelisks add a designer touch to borders.

You can also add to the vertical element in your garden by training climbers up into trees, and have fun converting plants that are normally too big for your garden into something more suitable. For example, you can train wisteria as a standard tree, thus turning a potential problem into a beautiful feature that not only looks good but flowers much sooner and is far easier to prune than the same plant on the side of a house.

Or how about transforming a large shrub into a small, space-saving tree, using much the same technique you would use to train a standard fuchsia. Instead of occupying a space 2.5m (8ft) in all directions, the shrub is now grown on a single stem, much like the bare trunk of a tree. This means you can plant right up to the trunk, freeing valuable space for extra perennials or ground cover plants. And by training large shrubs or trees flat against a wall and keeping them properly pruned, they take up virtually no space at all.

RIGHT: Obelisks are among the smartest ways of raising the interest in borders without using large spreading plants. This one shows off *Clematis* 'Madame Julia Correvon', a late-flowering cultivar. Cut it down hard in early spring to keep it compact.

LEFT: The pewter-purple foliage of *Rosa glauca* always looks particularly good with clematis, such as 'Silver Moon'. Thalictrum flowers at about the same height, making a superb eye level plant association with room for short perennials below.

LEFT: An arch planted with climbing roses makes a good frame for a focal point, adds height to a border and is a good way of getting more plants into the space. Here a rose and euonymus are growing on the same arch.

RIGHT: Training plants on single stems, known as 'standards', leaves space underneath, in this case in a tub, for extra plants; invaluable in a small garden.

BELOW: Climbing roses add vertical colour to brick walls and since the framework of main stems remains permanently in place, you can use it to support annual climbers or clematis that bring a second crop of flowers in new colours or shapes.

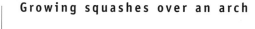

Growing squashes over an arch

1 About six weeks before the last expected frost, fill 9cm (3 ½ in) pots with seed compost. Press one seed into the middle. Water well.

2 Label the pots. Keep them in a propagator, greenhouse or sunny windowsill at 16–21°C (61–70°F). Seedlings soon appear. Keep moist.

3 In a small area, squashes look attractive trained up over an arch in a decorative potager, or grown up strong trellis or along a chain link fence. Support large, heavy fruit with a net. Left to trail on the ground, squashes take up a great deal of space.

Growing morning glory (ipomoea) with a rose

1 Cover the bare stems at the base of some climbing roses by planting annual climbers such as ipomoea close to the base of the plants. Improve the soil first and plant after the last frost.

2 The climber starts flowering within a few weeks, covering the base of the rose in bloom. For best results, choose climbers with contrasting shapes or colours, but not too much foliage.

PERGOLAS

AS WE HAVE SEEN, in any small garden it pays to include some overhead structure to provide both privacy and shade, and a support for climbing or scrambling plants. There is a wide range of such supporting structures to choose from, from the highly ornate to the remarkably simple. How big and how grand you wish to make such a feature is a matter of taste, and also of budget, but even a relatively simple structure can provide a home for a rich array of plants which can be encouraged to scramble and twine themselves over and around both the vertical and the horizontal elements.

For a very basic structure, sink metal or wooden posts well into the ground to give them strength, and tie, screw or nail overhead horizontal posts or rails to them. For a more rustic form you could use strong ropes as the horizontal elements, slotting them through eyes in the upright posts.

Often, some kind of seating is included beneath a pergola as the dappled shade makes such a pleasant environment to sit, especially in warm weather. If you prefer, you can create a smaller structure using one of the garden walls as the back support, so that you have shelter on one side at least. It will make a particularly attractive frame similar to a bower for a bench, and if you grow handsome climbers – ideally those that are scented as well as offering attractive flowers – around it, it will be the perfect place to relax on a summer's day.

arches

Arches can be used in various ways, but are ideal for framing the entrance to a part of the garden. In a small town garden, an arch could mark the transition from an alleyway to the garden proper. If the area is not sunny enough to grow the usual range of flowering climbers, then train ivies or creepers over it instead, which will give it an architectural grandeur. If you wish, you can add further arches and make a small ivy-clad tunnel, clipping the ivy back once a year to keep it under control. An arch will also look good next to the back door, with whatever takes your fancy growing over it.

LEFT: *Trelliswork, here in a sturdy pergola surrounding the seating area of this patio, helps to give privacy and shelter to the plants. Well-designed pergolas are an architectural ornament in their own right, and do not necessarily need to be planted.*

BELOW: *Arches are ideal for framing the entrance to a part of the garden. Here a metal arch, painted a delicate blue-grey, has been used as a support for wisteria, its racemes of delicate mauve flowers drooping attractively from it.*

climbing plants

The aim for most of these structures is to create a canopy of foliage and flowers as quickly as possible. Roses are ideal candidates for pergolas, and most people like to have at least a few with different flowering qualities to receive the full benefit of flowers and scent. The 'Albertine' rose – a vigorous, pretty pale pink rose, and richly scented – is very popular for growing over supports. Other good candidates are the 'English roses' grown by David Austen, and the beautifully scented old-fashioned roses.

Make sure that at least one of the plants you choose has attractive foliage – an ornamental vine would be ideal, as would the pretty golden-leaved hop, *Humulus lupulus* 'Aureus'. Honeysuckle is particularly good because it smells so delicious, and some forms are semi-evergreen, which will ensure that the structure is clad with leaves all year long. Another good subject is the almond-scented *Clematis armandii*, which also has attractive, leathery, elongated, dark green leaves, and the passion flower, with its whorls of evergreen leaves and curious blue and white angular-looking flowers.

ABOVE: *A classical pergola, a small statue on a plinth at the base of each support, makes a focal point in this small city garden. Foliage plants around the base and hanging baskets containing summer annuals soften the outlines and help it to blend with the rest of the garden.*

LEFT: This simple pergola has been embellished with attractive trellis, a great foil on which to display a fine specimen of *Clematis* 'Ville de Lyon', a very fine, free-flowering summer hybrid.

BELOW RIGHT: You can make a living gazebo by training four trees to form a roof. Start with young flexible 'whips' of a compact but decorative tree. After planting, bend the trunks over a frame-work of metal tubes and tie them in place. In time they will 'set'.

Building a pergola

1 Support two of the uprights and lower one of the un-notched side beams into the groove. Decide on the spacing of these uprights before securing them into the ground.

2 When you are happy with the overhang at each end of the side beam, secure it to the uprights with galvanized nails as shown. You may choose to use two nails at each end.

ERECTING A PERGOLA

SELF-ASSEMBLY PERGOLAS are available from garden centres and mail-order suppliers. Following the instructions, you should be able to put one together in just a few hours. The one featured on these pages has four uprights, two side beams, four cross beams and two trellis panels. The wood is treated with a pre-servative stain that will protect it from rotting and will not harm plants growing on it. When you have unpacked the kit and are ready to begin, it is a good idea to have someone to help you and you will also need a hammer, nails, gloves and a stepladder. Wear gloves to prevent splinters and as protection against the preservative stain applied to the wood. If you prefer to build a pergola from scratch, you can buy the wood and cut it to size at home. You will need to stain and preserve the wood as well. Naturally, this is a cheaper option than buying a ready-to-assemble kit. Whichever method you choose, you need to decide where to site the pergola and how to support the uprights. You could sink them in concrete or fix them to metal post holders driven into the ground. This last method requires shorter uprights and, as they are not sunk into the ground, they will not rot. Once the pergola is completely constructed, mark out the bed running along the side or just prepare a square of soil around each of the uprights, ready to take the climbers.

3 *Once the two sides of the pergola are complete, join them together by dropping in one of the four cross beams. Put the end ones 'outside' the uprights for a stable structure.*

4 *With the far end cross beam also in place, space the other two out equally. The width of the pergola is set by the notches in these cross beams.*

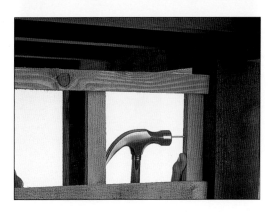

5 *Nail the cross beams to the top of the side beams. Then position and nail the first trellis panel in between the uprights. Raise the panel 15cm (6in) off the ground to protect it from soil moisture and rain splash.*

Climber or rambler?

IT IS IMPORTANT to know whether you have a climbing or rambling rose, as it affects the way they are pruned later. Ask the nursery which kind they are when you buy them.

If in doubt, check the name and habit in a reliable reference book. If you buy a young climber during the dormant winter season, prune it quite hard after planting. This encourages strong new shoots that you tie to the wall or fence. If a new rambler has a few strong, young shoots, keep them, but cut out all the others.

6 *With the second trellis panel in place opposite the first, the pergola is complete. This demonstration sequence has not included the vital task of fixing the uprights securely into the ground.*

LEFT: If you want to grow a large climbing rose such as this 'Paul's Himalayan Musk', use it where it has room to develop and can take over the whole of a pergola.

OBELISKS

CLIMBERS ARE FASHIONABLE and colourful, but if you have a garden without suitable boundaries or pergolas, it can be difficult to find places to grow them. One popular solution is to choose from the wide range of decorative climbing frames suitable for beds, borders and containers. But suit your planting to the type of support. Rustic-looking climbers look better grown on rustic supports. Clematis is ideal for a formal, metal obelisk. For the best effect, plant two or three clematis with differently shaped flowers and colours, for instance a viticella variety, a texensis and a late-flowering, large-flowered hybrid. All three can be hard pruned in spring. Clematis combines well with coloured foliage. *Ampelopsis brevipedunculata* 'Elegans' is specially good, as the cream-, green- and pink-variegated leaves team well with clematis flowers, and the plant is naturally compact but also dies back close to ground level in winter, so will not get overgrown. *Vitis vinifera* 'Purpurea', with its pewter-tinged purple leaves, is another good candidate. Cut back this stronger-growing plant close to the ground each spring.

Planting up a metal obelisk

1 *Prepare the planting site well. Dig a hole about 2.5cm (1in) narrower than the diameter of the base of your obelisk, position the frame and press it down firmly into the ground.*

2 *If you are using a number of different plants, put in the clematis first as it needs to go in deeper than other climbers. Plant everything well inside the base of the obelisk.*

Planting clematis

CLEMATIS PLANTS ARE BEST planted deeply, with the surface of the rootball up to 15cm (6in) below soil level. In this way, large-flowered hybrids, which are susceptible to clematis wilt, are able to regrow from underground buds if the tops of the plants are killed off. But even wilt-resistant species, such as *Clematis viticella* cultivars can regrow if they are damaged when you are hoeing. Before planting, prepare the site well. Remove any weeds and dig in plenty of well-rotted organic matter. When planting clematis, do not break up the rootball unless the plant is badly potbound; instead lower the whole thing carefully into the prepared hole and firm it down gently.

LEFT: Fill the planting hole with a mixture of topsoil and well-rotted organic matter, taking great care not to bruise the stem of the plant.

ABOVE: This *Clematis* 'Jackmanii' looks very attractive grown against an ornamental frame, but will need coiling around an obelisk to stop it outgrowing the support. This also encourages flowering, as the stems are more horizontal.

Perfect partners

Clematis are perfect plants to grow on an obelisk as the airy foliage does not swamp the shape of the frame or smother anything else you plant with it, and the large, symmetrical, rosette-shaped flowers complement the formal effect. By choosing varieties that can be cut back almost to ground level in early spring each year, the obelisk never looks overgrown. If you want to grow earlier flowering clematis, choose naturally more compact varieties, such as *Clematis alpina* cultivars, and leave them virtually unpruned except to tidy the shape back close to the framework of the obelisk shortly after flowering finishes. In this case, avoid mixing them with climbers that need different pruning, as the stems intertwine making the job almost impossible.

3 Add a plant with colourful foliage. If space is short and the soil is deep, rich and fertile, you can safely plant other climbers above the clematis rootball.

4 Fill the gaps between the rootballs with more garden soil, firm gently and water so the soil sinks before you secure the stems to the climbing frame.

RIGHT: 'Arctic Queen' has two flushes of double white flowers. To keep the first flush of flowers, cut back the plant close to the shape of the obelisk after flowering finishes in late summer.

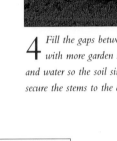

5 Starting near the base of the plant, lean the stems up and around the obelisk and tie them in a loose spiral around it.

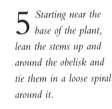

6 Once the tips have been tied in place, the new growths of clematis will hold on to the frame for themselves, by their leaf stalks.

7 Already the base of the obelisk looks well-clothed. Twist the new growth around the frame every week or two, otherwise the new shoots rush straight up to the top and will not flower so well.

ABOVE: Together, *C. texensis* 'Etoile Rose', *C. viticella* 'Etoile Violette' and *C. v.* 'Polish Spirit' make a good display of flowers in complementary colours from mid- to late summer.

1 *Hammer a strong pole into the ground where the climber is to grow, or push it into a large container filled with potting mix. Hammer in a large metal staple.*

2 *Take a slim, flexible willow or hazel wand about 1m (3ft) long. Push it through the hoop and adjust it until both ends protrude the same amount.*

3 *Do the same with another three willow wands. Separate the stems so they open out like the spokes of a wheel, with the staple as its centre. It is helpful to have someone else to hold them roughly in place at this point.*

4 *Holding both ends of one stem, bend them down until they cross about 30cm (12in) below the top of the pole. Tie both ends of the stem to the pole with soft string.*

5 *Bend all the stems in the same way so they form a globe. Do not risk breaking the stems to achieve an ideal shape; the climber will hide any irregularities later.*

A HONEYSUCKLE POLE

CLIMBERS OFFER PLENTY of creative possibilities, and when you garden in a small space it is worth investigating unusual vertical solutions. For example, growing a honeysuckle as a standard allows you to fit a potentially large plant into a small space. Once it has grown and formed a dense ball, the head of the plant will be completely covered with wonderfully scented flowers for three months or more every summer. And even when not in flower, the striking shape of the plant acts as a stylish topiary that would enhance any border. A certain amount of training and pruning will be needed to keep the standard in shape. Simply tie in new shoots to the ball as they grow, and as soon as the plant finishes flowering for the year, trim back excess growth to within 15cm (6in) of the ball. Other climbers with a similar natural growth habit can be trained in this way. Clematis are particularly successful; choose one of the varieties that starts flowering after midsummer, as these can be hard pruned in early spring every year. But do not prune it right back to the ground; instead, just prune all the stems back to within 15–30cm (6–12in) of the top of the support frame. And since clematis cling on to their supports with their leaf stalks, tuck the new growth back into the ball to make a dense solid head to the plant. Do not be tempted to shape the head of the plant by pinching out the tips of the shoots, as honeysuckle and clematis will not flower this way.

6 *Use several rows of soft string, knotted to each wand in turn, all round the middle of the sphere, to space the wands apart. This not only looks good but also gives the stems something to cling on to as the head forms.*

Using wicker supports in the border

Wicker plant supports are fashionable, and whether you buy them or make your own, they are a good way to show off naturally sprawling plants such as trailing nasturtiums, turning them into novel displays in the border. Expect natural wicker, willow or hazel twig structures to last for two or three years; a little longer if you treat them with a plant-friendly wood preservative, although this can be a laborious task.

7 Plant the honeysuckle or clematis close to the base of the pole. Knock it out of its pot, but leave the stems tied to their cane. Water thoroughly and wait for the soil to settle around the roots.

8 Remove the cane. Untangle the stems and, holding two at a time, twist them round the pole in opposite directions. Tie the top of the stems in place with soft string.

1 Press the plant support into level, prepared ground so its legs leave a mark in the soil. Remove it. Knock the plants out of their pots and plant them inside the cage shape.

2 Fill the space well. Two or three pots of well-grown plants should fit underneath a 30–38cm (12–15in) diameter cage. Firm the plants in well and water them thoroughly.

9 Keep the plant well fed and watered. Each time the stems grow another 15cm (6in), tie them back up to the pole. When they are long enough, train some stems around the sphere.

ABOVE: Flowering honeysuckles look equally good growing through hurdles made from hazel twigs and other screens and supports made from natural materials. Be sure to choose a scented variety of honeysuckle.

3 Fit the cage carefully over the top of the plants. Tuck the flowers and foliage inside to avoid damaging them. Then push the legs of the cage firmly down into the soil.

4 The growing plants scramble up and over the wickerwork, forming a loose, rustic-looking mound of flowers and foliage. The bare twigs of the cage contrast well with the soft plant material.

RUSTIC SUPPORTS

Rustic willow plant supports are fun and fashionable. They are readily available from craft stands at flower shows or by mail order direct from craftspeople. A limited range is sometimes available in garden centres, too. The basic material is versatile and easy to work with, so provided you can find a source of suitable willow stems, you can make them yourself, tailoring them to your own designs. The long, slender, one-year-old willow stems (correctly called withies) are sometimes available in winter by mail order from basket makers in willow-growing regions (look for advertisements in craft or gardening magazines). Willow plant supports do not have a long life compared to synthetic materials (perhaps one to three years), but their natural charm is more than compensation – and any imperfections only add to their attraction. They are so quick to make, you could easily replace them every year or two.

WITH CARE, AN UPRIGHT WILLOW support in a patio pot, with two horizontal bands for tall climbing plants, should last for two seasons or more in the garden. It is cheap and easy to make.

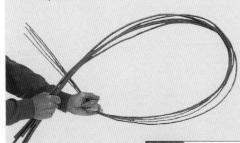

1 Lay short willow wands out flat in a bath of water to soak. Tie up and loop long withies into large circles, so that they fit into a water butt or large bucket.

2 Secure the ends so that they do not spring out, and wedge the hoops into the container. Leave them to soak for 12–24 hours (overnight is fine) immediately before use. It will not do any harm to leave them in the water longer.

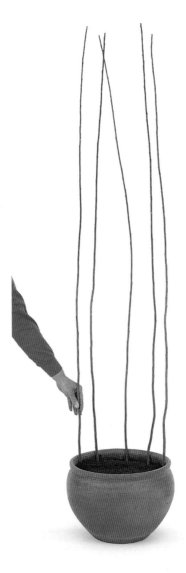

1 Choose a container heavy enough to support a tall structure. Fill it with compost and push an odd number of tall, straight willow wands evenly around the edge to form the uprights of the plant support.

2 Take a prepared willow wand and tie the thick end firmly to one of the uprights above the rim of the pot. Weave the wand in and out between the uprights, keeping the uprights evenly spaced.

3 Once the first wand is in place, press the layers close together to tighten the weave. Tie or tuck in the loose end to secure it. Do not try to weave with the very thin material at the tip of the stem.

4 Weave in a second wand as before. Continually check that the uprights remain evenly spaced; it takes a long time to put things right later on if you overlook this essential monitoring.

5 To neaten the thin end of the withy, hook it round an upright, bend it back in the opposite direction and tuck it into the weave, down the edge of an upright.

6 Only tie in the first withy. Then weave in new stems leaving a long tail inside. When both bands are complete, cut off the excess with strong secateurs.

8 Take a very thin, flexible piece of willow 0.6–1m (2–3ft) long, and push one end of it down between the tops of the stems. If the string is secure, it should be a tight fit.

7 Gather together the tops of the uprights and tie them well with strong string. Do not worry if this looks untidy; it will be hidden by a decorative willow covering later on.

9 Bind the new piece of willow around the string, working neatly from bottom to top. At the top, bend the tip of the willow and push it firmly inside the collar so that it cannot work loose.

Planting sweet peas

1 Annual climbers, such as sweet peas, make a fine show in summer, and will not outgrow the pot. Morning glory or trailing nasturtiums are also good.

2 Sweet peas need help to start them off in the right direction. Tie each stem loosely to an upright, so they are spaced evenly out all round the container.

3 Water the container. Stand it in a sheltered spot with direct sun for most of the day, but not exposed to scorching midday sun.

4 Team the finished container with similar materials, such as rustic hurdles. Slight imperfections are normal and even desirable in craft work; other people never notice them as much as you do.

Sweet peas cling on to suitable supports using their own tendrils.

GARDEN FURNITURE

BELOW: *When positioning a bench in the garden, it pays to consider its setting carefully. A screening arbour of trellis creates a feeling of privacy and seclusion for this traditional-style bench.*

THERE IS, TODAY, no shortage of good garden furniture from which to choose. Manufacturers have created some excellent ranges of outdoor furniture from a variety of natural materials, much of it now imported relatively cheaply from the Far East. Wood is one of the most durable and most sympathetic materials, and there is a wide range of furniture types from which to choose, from classic reproductions to modern designs. Since the furniture has to stay out in all weathers, it pays to buy the best you can afford, as it will undoubtedly last better and longer. For this purpose you need a good-quality hardwood, such as teak, which will cope with all weather conditions. Cheaper softwoods need an annual coat of preservative to prevent them rotting.

Painted metal garden furniture also looks good – the idiom borrowed from the French with their classic dark green circular fretwork tables and round-seated café chairs with bent backs which look good in most small gardens, especially urban ones. Beware opting for white, however, as it gets grimy very quickly. Dark green or slate-blue are better options. There is also a wide range of cast-iron furniture, some in quite ornate designs. Because it is very heavy, it has the virtue that it does not collapse or fall over

easily, but it is difficult to move around the garden, which can be problem if you want to use more than one area for sitting out.

If you do not see what you want in the shops, there is nothing to stop you designing and making your own simple furniture. Plain

benches or tables, for example, are relatively easy to construct, or you could use a hewn log or railway sleepers to make a simple bench. If you are furnishing the garden on a budget, then hunt out bargains in junk shops and unify any disparity in design by painting

BELOW: *Consider the colour of any furniture carefully. White shows any dust or grime very quickly. Dark green paint, used here for this elegant metal table and chairs, is ideal and blends with the planting.*

them in matching, or toning, colours. Even plastic furniture can be painted, and you can transform an old white plastic chair into something perfectly acceptable if the basic shape is attractive. Interesting industrial relics can make attractive patio furniture – the base of an old sewing machine can be topped with a piece of marble to serve as a small table, for example.

If you are planning to eat out of doors, it is worth remembering that you need a rea-sonable amount of space to do so. For a table and chairs for four people, you will need an area at least 1.5m (5ft) across, to allow you room to pull back the chairs from the table. A good solution if you want to eat out of doors in a small garden is a bench, a table and a couple of folding chairs for guests. The slatted French café chairs are ideal for this purpose, as they fold up very small and are easily stackable.

It is important in small spaces, such as balconies, verandahs or roof terraces, to pick furniture that fits well into the available space. Folding furniture certainly comes into its own here, as do benches that fit snugly against a wall, for example. If you are at all handy at carpentry, why not make a small table that is hinged to the back wall of the balcony or terrace, so that you can fold it down when not in use.

LEFT: *Deckchairs are among the cheapest forms of garden furniture, and because they can be stored flat, are ideal for small spaces. Pick plain-coloured canvas or simple striped ones. Try to ensure that both the material and the style are sympathetic to the overall atmosphere of the design of the garden.*

ABOVE: *Steamer chairs look equally at home in an informal cottage-style garden or on the stone flags of a more minimalist design. This handsome pair make an elegant addition to a beautifully paved patio with its richly coloured slate and stone surface.*

lounging furniture

In most small gardens there is not a great deal of space for serious relaxation. However, a few good, carefully-chosen chairs that enable you to put your feet up while enjoying the vista you have created are a great bonus to a more relaxed lifestyle, plus a boon when friends come round.

Among the most attractive lounging chairs are the steamer chairs first developed for luxury cruises and now sold in many good department stores. They have the architectural lines of a standard upright chair with the addition of an elongated leg rest. In natural hardwood, such as teak, and furnished with

RIGHT: *Good-quality, well-designed sturdy garden furniture is not cheap, but it is a worthwhile investment, and functional too. It will last well, and show remarkably little sign of wear and tear. A once-a-year scrub to remove any lichen or grime is all that is required in the way of upkeep.*

attractive boxed cushions in natural fabrics, such as linen and sailcloth, they make a worthy addition to any outdoor room.

The good old-fashioned deckchair is an excellent standby for the small garden. It folds up to take up minimum space and if the fabric used for it is of good quality, it will last extremely well. There is a wide range of suitable furnishing fabrics, and you can easily revamp old deck chairs with any strong sailcloth or canvas fabric.

al fresco eating

For most people, at least half the benefit of a garden is the opportunity to eat and drink out of doors when the weather permits. Once a purely Mediterranean concept, outdoor eating has spread into more temperate climates, with the addition of some all-weather screening from the worst of the elements.

The scale and style of your entertaining out of doors will obviously depend on the space you have available, but for many people a barbecue is a must for the summer months. Such a large range is now manufactured that you are almost certainly spoiled for choice, and you can have anything from a good old-

fashioned scouts' barbecue – a couple of twigs and a pole over an open fire – to a mini-oven, powered with bottled gas.

If you are going to cook out of doors, you should think about it carefully. First of all, it is important to consider all the safety aspects. Do not site the barbecue too close to buildings, fences or plants, particularly precious plants that may suffer from scorch. Think about where the prevailing winds blow from, and do not organize your barbecue so that smoke drifts downwind over your guests. You should also try to ensure that smoke does not drift into the windows of neighbouring flats or houses. Although it involves more fetching

and carrying, a spot away from your house, and your neighbours, would be much wiser.

Some people prefer to build a permanent barbecue area out of bricks at a specific point in the garden, and this is probably very sensible if you have the room to do so. Make sure, however, that you have taken the preceding points into account when planning where to site your barbecue as mistakes will be hard to rectify. Finally, make sure you have some kind of permanent table or sturdy trolley you can use while cooking, keep a fireblanket close by, and keep any flammable or poisonous chemicals out of reach of children and away from naked flames.

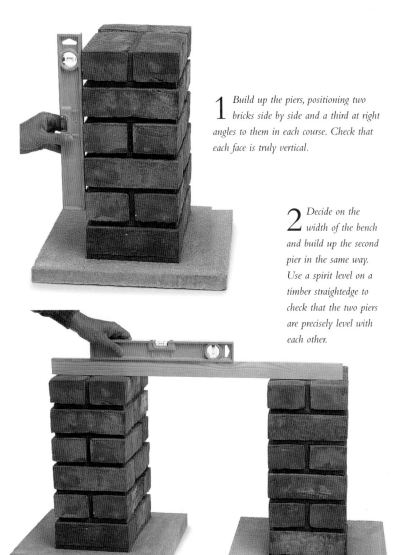

1 *Build up the piers, positioning two bricks side by side and a third at right angles to them in each course. Check that each face is truly vertical.*

2 *Decide on the width of the bench and build up the second pier in the same way. Use a spirit level on a timber straightedge to check that the two piers are precisely level with each other.*

BUILDING A SEAT

MENTION GARDEN SEATS and people think either of traditional wooden chairs and benches or lightweight portable garden furniture. Both can be surprisingly expensive to buy. Portable items have to be set up before use and then stored away under cover when they are no longer required, while traditional pieces (usually left outdoors in all weathers) are becoming an increasingly popular target for thieves. One inexpensive, permanent and thief-proof solution is to build your own seating using bricks, mortar and preservative-treated wood. You can site a seat like this anywhere in the garden, but the best positions will allow you to catch the sun while you rest from your labours and admire the view. This simple bench consists of two piers of brickwork, built without the need for any cut bricks, and a slatted seat that is screwed unobtrusively to the masonry. You can build it directly on any existing paved or concrete surface or set two paving slabs on some well-rammed subsoil to provide a stable base for the masonry. Choose bricks that match those used to build your house if you plan to site the seat close by. If you prefer to build it further down the garden, you could use garden walling blocks to create a seat with a more rustic appearance. The seat can be left with a natural finish (protected by clear preservative), or can be stained or painted if you prefer a coloured finish. The slats allow rainwater to drain away freely, but if you prefer a solid seat, simply close up the gaps between the slats and glue them together with waterproof wood adhesive before screwing the bench top to the supporting framework.

5 *Screw on the first seat slat so that it rests on top of the front edge slat. Use a spacer plank to position the next one correctly. Countersink all screw heads. Add more slats to finish the bench.*

3 *Cut two support blocks from 5cm (2in) square timber, making them slightly longer than the depth of the piers. Fix one to the outside of each pier with screws and wallplugs.*

4 *Cut two seat edge slats to length and attach them to the ends of the seat support blocks. An overhang at either end will help to conceal the support blocks when the seat is complete.*

Stone seats

Stone seats are a permanent part of the garden. They last forever and, if anything, look better as they age due to the natural encrustation of lichens they acquire in an area with clean air. However, if necessary, scrub them annually with a stiff brush and soapy water. Do not use chemicals on stonework.

ABOVE: A stone bench surrounded by pebbles lends a Mediterranean air to a paved area against a color-washed wall. A matching statue or plant container plus some aromatic plants would really strengthen the theme.

6 *Apply two coats of clear preservative to keep rot and insect attack at bay, or use paint or stain if you prefer a colored finish to the natural look.*

Round off the edges of the slats with sandpaper to prevent splinters.

Bed support slabs on a compacted subsoil and sand base.

Making a tree seat

A tree seat turns a bare tree trunk into an attractive garden feature that provides generous seating even in a small garden. Ready-to-assemble tree seats are available in various sizes to match a range of different tree diameters and most are simple to install. Use curved, molded edging stones as a sturdy base for the legs.

1 *Buying a prefabricated tree seat avoids the need for fairly complex carpentry. Treat the seat with a preservative stain before assembling it.*

2 *Cut away the turf, compact the subsoil and lay a bed of sand in the excavation. Put each molded edging stone in place and tamp it down to get it level.*

3 *Stand the first prefabricated seat section in place on its stones, then position the second section. Raise or lower the stones slightly as necessary.*

4 *Thread the bolts through the predrilled holes. Add another washer before fitting the nut so that it does not bite into the wood. Tighten the bolts well.*

5 *Give the seat a new coat of preservative paint when necessary. Wood is ideal for garden use; it is both warm and comfortable to sit on and dries off quickly after rain. Durable hardwoods are more expensive than softwood.*

1 *Cut the planks that will form the front, back and sides of the frame to the desired length. Make angled cutting lines on the two top side boards and cut carefully along them. Keep the saw vertical as you cut.*

COLD FRAMES

A COLD FRAME IS A USEFUL ADDITION to any garden. It is basically a bottomless box with a glazed lid and is used like a miniature greenhouse to grow seeds and cuttings and to acclimatize tender plants that have been raised under cover before they are finally planted out in the garden. It can stand on a hard surface, such as a patio or path – the best idea if you intend to fill it with seed trays and plant pots – or can be placed directly on the soil so that you can plant things in it. You can buy ready-made cold frames, but making your own is a simple and satisfying project that allows you to tailor-make the frame to just the size you want. You can make the cold frame entirely from softwood, or build up the base in brickwork and add a wooden-framed lid. The lid can be glazed with glass, but plastic glazing materials are safer and easier to work with. Hinge it to the base so that you can open it during the day for ventilation and fit a simple catch to the front edge to keep it closed at night; strong winds could lift and damage it otherwise. If you want a larger planting and growing area than a single frame provides, simply add further bays to the basic structure as the need arises. Site the completed frame in a sunny position, ideally sheltered from the prevailing winds, and keep the lid clean to allow the maximum amount of sunlight to reach the plants inside. Cover it on cold nights.

2 *Cut front legs to the height of two full boards, plus the thinner end of the top side board. Drill holes in the boards. Screw the bottom two boards to one leg.*

3 *Interlock the grooved edge of the second full board over the tongue on the first board. Tap it down to close up the joint. Screw the board to the leg as before.*

The legs are cut to length from 5cm (2in) square softwood.

4 *Cut the back legs to match the height of two full boards, plus the thicker end of the top side boards. Continue to build up the box; attach the second set of boards all round with screws.*

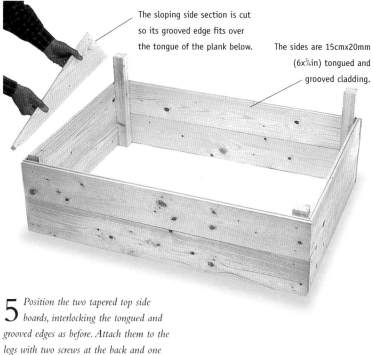

The sloping side section is cut so its grooved edge fits over the tongue of the plank below.

The sides are 15cmx20mm (6x¾in) tongued and grooved cladding.

5 *Position the two tapered top side boards, interlocking the tongued and grooved edges as before. Attach them to the legs with two screws at the back and one screw at the front.*

Use 3.8cm (1½in) countersunk screws.

6 Cut the top back board to match the height of the thicker ends of the tapered top side boards. Cut a board to create a strip the same height as the thinner ends of the top side boards. Screw to the front legs to complete the base.

7 Treat the frame and lid with two coats of preservative stain and leave it to dry with the lid propped open. Check that the brand of wood stain you buy is not harmful to plants.

Making the cold frame lid

1 Cut the components to size. The two side pieces overlap the cut ends of the front and back pieces. Drill and counterbore holes for fixing screws; glue and screw the frame together.

2 Lay the assembled frame over the glazing material – this is twin wall polycarbonate, a tough and rigid translucent plastic sheet. Use a felt pen to mark the size required.

3 Glue and screw strips of 2.5x5cm (1x2in) softwood to the sides of the lid to protect the edges of the glazing sheet when it is in place and cover the corner fixing screws.

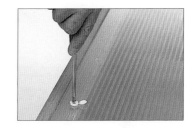

4 Position the hinges about 23cm (9in) in from the corners, and attach using 20mm (³⁄₄in) screws.

5 When the stain is dry, place the glazing sheet on the lid and drill and screw. Use plastic screw cups with snap-on covers.

8 Complete the screw fixings all round and check that all the screw caps are snapped in place. Prop the lid open for ventilation.

WATER FEATURES

BELOW: *Wall-mounted water features are ideal for small gardens. Here a section of the wall has been built to incorporate a lion head mask which spouts into a raised pool below, while the surround to the pool creates space for a themed display of white-flowering annuals and perennials.*

EVEN THE SMALLEST of gardens is large enough for a water feature. With its light-reflecting properties, water will appear to enlarge the space rather than reduce it, and you can choose from a whole range of sizes and shapes, from a small sink sunk into the soil to a water feature that takes up most of the available space in the garden. Even in the tiniest, shadiest back yard, you can incorporate an attractive water feature, for example by mounting a mask on a wall (like the one shown above) which drips or pours water into a small pool below – either a simple cistern or tank, or a small raised pool, or even a shallow pebble splash pool, if you prefer.

As with any garden feature, a pool must be in sympathy with the rest of the design. If you have opted for a formal garden, stick to a formal shape for the water feature – a smart formal channel or rectangular pool, for example. If your garden has a more cottage feel to it, you can make a naturally shaped pebble pool or shallow irregularly shaped water feature.

Water gardens, surprisingly, are low maintenance, so if you are not too keen on gardening, and enjoy the sight and sound of water, why not think about creating a large water feature, even if you have only a very small site. The surrounding ground can be decked to create a seating area, with bridges over a water feature that could, perhaps, fill the whole width of the plot. Many Dutch gardens, where water is an inescapable part of the natural landscape, are constructed around this kind of theme.

If your garden has more than one level to it, you could use these changes in level to create a cascade leading down to your pool, and install water pumps to circulate the water back up to the top again.

A fountain is a great delight in a small garden; not only is it attractive to look at, but also the sound of splashing water is extremely soothing.

LEFT: *A pretty little water feature in soft ochre, its fish sculpture spouting water into the raised pool below, makes an ideal feature for a small courtyard garden.*

BELOW: *Water can take the form of canals or streams, rather than ponds, running down one side of the garden, as here. A raised walkway, here of brick and decking, makes the ideal viewing platform.*

pool surrounds

The surroundings to the water feature are an important part of its whole appeal. However you choose to construct your pool, make sure that it is edged with suitable material and planted up appropriately. Certain plants flourish in the wild in naturally damp and waterlogged conditions, and a pond will only occur in nature where the ground retains moisture. You are not so limited in your own garden, but nothing looks more garish than an artificially constructed pool surrounded by plants that naturally love dry sun – generally silver-leaved plants with bright flowers. The larger, more leafy foliage plants that tend to seed themselves in damp situations will definitely create a more natural, appealing surround to your pool.

If you do not want to edge your pool with a formal hard surface, and you have opted for a shallow pool, then a pebble beach effect at one end of the feature can look very effective. Plants such as *Caltha palustris, Trollius europaeus* and *Astilboides tabularis* make excellent poolside plants for this kind of situation, as do the candelabra primulas, various ferns, and a tough geranium with pink or white flowers, *Geranium macrorrhizum*. Japanese ornaments – including small buddhas nestling in ferns or ivy, or the typical Japanese deer-scarer, in

which a reed pipe trickles water into a container – go well with this kind of look.

If you want to opt for the more formal canal-style water feature, then consider including some other interesting features – perhaps a small Gothic bridge over the water, a little Chinese pavilion, or just a couple of log stepping stones or a simple stone bridge, depending on the size and scale of the garden.

stepping stones and bridges

There are many ways to create crossings over water. For a shallow pool, you might include some stepping stones, for example. These can take the form of single slabs of York stone, or sawn-off and treated rounds of timber, or even small constructed squares of teak decking. Make sure you lay them in an inviting and interesting formation rather than in a regular straight line.

LEFT: *For a more naturally planted garden, decking is the ideal companion for a large water feature, in particular because you can bridge the water easily and successfully using it. The overlap of the wooden decking masks the edges of the pond, so that the water seems to flow beneath it.*

BELOW: *Water is a key feature in Oriental garden design, and it has been used very successfully in this small town garden to give an illusion of space, with its pebble shores, stone bridges and stepping stones.*

Very simple bridges can be constructed from just a couple of thick planks bridging two hard surfaces, or they can be supported on simple thick timber joists. Fancier bridges, with handrails and steps to provide an arch, can also be used if space and style permit.

ponds for fish and wildlife

If you want to keep fish, you should allow approximately 0.18sq m (24sq in) of water surface area to every 15cm (6in) of fish body length, and koi carp will need a large pond and a water depth of at least 1.2-1.5m (4-5ft). The deeper the pond, at least at one end, the better the survival chances of the fish. You will need to ensure any pond for fish has plenty of oxygenating plants to keep the water fresh, and you will have to feed them yourself in the summer months. In colder weather, their metabolism slows down and they live largely off their own body fat.

If part of your aim in having a pool is to have, or encourage, wildlife into the garden, then you will need to consider their requirements. Birds and small animals need to be able to reach the water easily, so the pool should incorporate a shallow area at one end. Any pond for wildlife should have some natural cover around the edges of the water, and at least a few plants growing in the water: reeds, irises, *Pontederia*, and marsh marigolds are ideal. Deeper water will provide a home for water lilies.

bog gardens

If you do not want a full-scale water feature, you can always opt for a bog garden, giving yourself the chance to grow some unusual and attractive plants through manipulating the soil conditions. If you sink a black plastic liner about a metre beneath the surface, puncturing the base in places to allow drainage holes, you will create an area where the soil retains more moisture than normal, thus allowing you to grow some handsome moisture-loving plants – rodgersias, ligularias, hostas, the big ornamental rhubarb (*Rheum palmatum*) and even a *Gunnera manicata* – the huge-leaved perennial from Brazil. The latter is slightly tender and will need to have its crowns wrapped in winter in colder climates, but it will make a wonderful architectural feature in the garden during the spring and summer months, growing to a good 1.8–3m (6-10ft) or more.

INSTALLING A POOL

BEFORE YOU INSTALL A POOL, consider the options for a pond liner, as this is likely to be your greatest expense. The easiest type of liner to buy is the preformed pool, which is available in a choice of sizes, a choice of colours and in both formal and informal styles, including rectangular, square, round and irregular curved shapes. Most rigid preformed liners incorporate a marginal shelf for plants. Rigid pools are available in thin or very thick plastic, the cost depending on the thickness and therefore the quality. Even stronger than the rigid plastic pools, but more expensive, are the preformed GRP (glass reinforced plastic) shapes. You can also buy flexible liners that stretch to fit every contour of the excavation. These range from inexpensive forms of PVC (polyvinyl chloride) and polyethylene (polythene) to butyl rubber liner, a highly durable material available in various thicknesses at different prices.

Mark out the shape of your proposed pool on the ground and when you are satisfied, dig out the subsoil to your required depth – a minimum of 60cm (24in) and usually no more than about 1.2m (4ft). Incorporate a shelf for marginal plants about 25cm (10in) below the final water level. Check the level of the excavations by knocking a 1.2m (4ft) post into the centre of your pool area. Use this to balance one end of a straightedge extended from a series of small 30cm (12in) pegs or posts sited around the edge of the bank. Place a spirit level along the top to show where any adjustments need to be made. Make sure there are no major bumps or hollows, and remove any sharp stones.

1 To protect the liner against damage from sharp stones, use a custom-made pond cushioning material or use a layer of sand, old carpet, sacking or loft insulation material as shown here.

2 Lay the pool liner over the excavated hole, taking care that there is an equal amount of excess around the outside. For large pools, you will need help moving the liner.

How much liner?

POOLS VARY IN SIZE; to calculate the amount of liner you will need, add twice the maximum depth of the pool to both the overall length and width. Thus, a 3x1.8x0.6m (10x6x2ft) pool needs a liner 4.2x3m (14x10ft). Liner is flexible and stretches to fit with the weight of the water, so there is no need to allow for the gentle contouring of an informal pool, or the extra few inches of a marginal shelf.

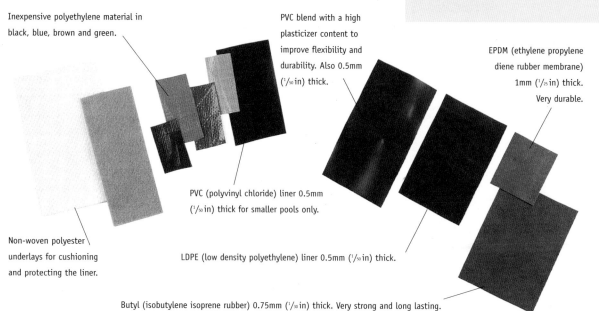

Inexpensive polyethylene material in black, blue, brown and green.

PVC blend with a high plasticizer content to improve flexibility and durability. Also 0.5mm ($\frac{1}{50}$in) thick.

EPDM (ethylene propylene diene rubber membrane) 1mm ($\frac{1}{25}$in) thick. Very durable.

Non-woven polyester underlays for cushioning and protecting the liner.

PVC (polyvinyl chloride) liner 0.5mm ($\frac{1}{50}$in) thick for smaller pools only.

LDPE (low density polyethylene) liner 0.5mm ($\frac{1}{50}$in) thick.

Butyl (isobutylene isoprene rubber) 0.75mm ($\frac{1}{30}$in) thick. Very strong and long lasting.

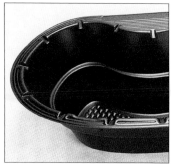

BELOW: This rigid plastic liner is typical of a wide range of preformed shapes that enable you to create an instant pond.

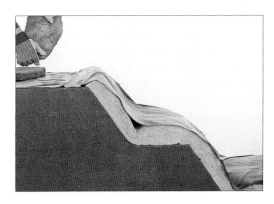

3 *Anchor the edges of the liner with smooth slabs, boulders or bricks. You can move these around as the pool fills with water to help the liner settle into place.*

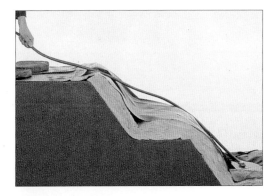

4 *Now fill the pool slowly using a hosepipe to produce a steady trickle of water. The weight of the water will gradually pull the liner into place.*

5 *When the pool has filled to its level, cut away any excess liner, leaving about 30cm (12in) to be anchored and hidden by your choice of edging.*

6 *This profile shows a small pool filled for the first time. It is used (right) to show the edging options.*

Pool edging ideas

There are several ways of edging a garden pool. The aim is to provide access to the water and to soften and disguise the junction of the pool liner and the surrounding garden. Here are a few options.

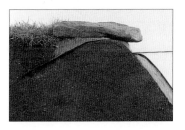

ABOVE: Turf edging produces a natural look and is easy to lay. The pool liner can be anchored beneath the soil.

LEFT: Grass, with stone slabs set at intervals around the edge and slightly overlapping the water, hide and anchor the liner.

RIGHT: Brick edging that slightly overlaps the pool needs good foundations: a 15cm (6in) layer of hardcore, 2.5cm (1in) of sand and 2.5cm (1in) of cement will be sufficient.

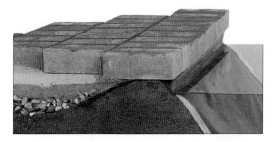

RIGHT: Paving slabs have a larger surface area to spread the weight of people walking on them. Lay a 7.5cm (3in) layer of hardcore to give substance to a damp or crumbly soil base.

RIGHT: Unless you want to create a natural sloping beach running into the pool, contain an edging of pebbles with wooden battens to prevent them spilling into the water.

INSTALLING
A WATER PUMP

IF YOU HAVE SUFFICIENT DEPTH of water, a submersible pump is a neat way to run a water feature, such as a fountain or waterfall. Submersibles are easier to maintain and more economical to run than surface-mounted pumps. Be sure to calculate accurately the size of pump you need or the results may be disappointing, especially if you hope to run more than one feature from the same pump. As the head of water increases, so the output will decrease; the length of pipe, its bore and the number of bends also affect performance. It is better not to run a pump at full capacity all the time, so buy a model slightly larger than your needs. Installing the pump is simple enough if it is close to an outdoor electrical point. This should be installed by a qualified electrician.

Setting up a pump for a fountain

1 *If you want to use the built-in filter, which contains a block of plastic filter foam, simply push it over the inlet pipe of the pump until it clicks into place. It is easy to remove for cleaning.*

2 *If you plan to run a fountain and perhaps a waterfall as well, push the T-piece adapter on to the outlet pipe of the pump. Make sure the two pieces fit firmly together so that they do not come apart once the pump is below water.*

3 *Set up like this, the pump is ready to have a fountain head fitted on top of the outlet pipe. The built-in foam pad will filter the water as it is sucked through the vents in the casing.*

Setting up a pump for fountain and waterfall

1 *Remove the blanking cap. Push on plastic tubing to supply the waterfall. This tube has a 2.5cm (1in) bore. Use an adapter for different diameters.*

2 *Use the adjuster to control the flow of water. Fully screwed in, all the water will go to the waterfall; when fully out, the flow will be split both ways.*

The water will flow up this pipe. ——————

With this outlet blanked off, all the water will flow upwards. ——————

Fit this adjusting screw to whatever outlets you plan to supply. As you screw it further in, the projection obstructs the upward flow of water.

Here, the tubing has been left exposed to show where it runs. You can hide the tubing so that the water appears to spring from the stones.

The maximum size of the fountain depends on the height of the waterfall and the length of tubing involved.

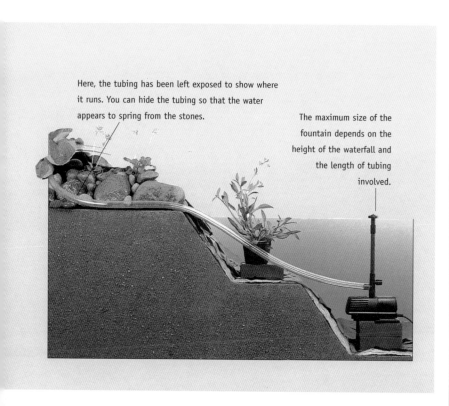

Setting up a water filter

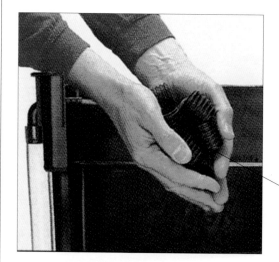

1 *Fill the base of the tank with a biological filter medium, here plastic corrugated pipe sections. There are inert and do not affect the water chemistry.*

These provide a large surface area for beneficial bacteria to colonize.

The top layer of foam is a coarser grade than the lower one.

Different types of fountain

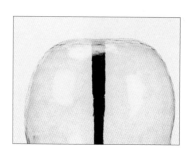

ABOVE: Correctly adjusted, a bell fountain head produces a smooth and symmetrical dome of water.

RIGHT: Change the bell shape by pushing in the plastic cone at the top of the head. Start with a reduced water flow and slowly increase it.

ABOVE: A fountain head with two circles of holes produces a tall, two-tier pattern of water droplets.

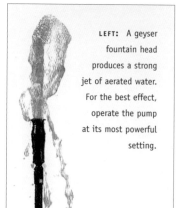

LEFT: A geyser fountain head produces a strong jet of aerated water. For the best effect, operate the pump at its most powerful setting.

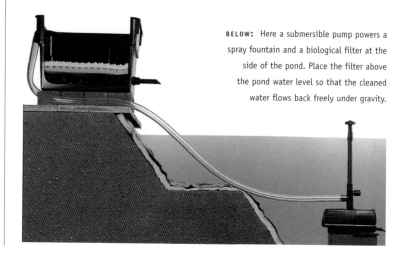

BELOW: Here a submersible pump powers a spray fountain and a biological filter at the side of the pond. Place the filter above the pond water level so that the cleaned water flows back freely under gravity.

GARDEN ORNAMENTS

THE SMALL GARDEN is the ideal place to display garden ornaments. In a limited space, any ornament will immediately have a far greater effect, and you can use statues, containers, mirrors, sundials or whatever takes your fancy, and suits the style of the garden, to add interest to the garden design.

BELOW: Ceramics and terracotta make an attractive addition to this sunny garden, creating a splash of colour. Yuccas, cordylines and agaves make an excellent planting choice.

RIGHT: This painted metal cockerel weather vane has cheered up a small pot of clipped box. Ornaments can be chosen both for their ability to enhance the garden and to create an element of surprise.

containers

Containers are, without doubt, among the most versatile of garden ornaments, and do not necessarily have to be planted up, although you will probably wish to do so in particular situations.

A very wide range of handsome large containers, in terracotta, lead or stone, is available, and they can be used as focal points in any design if chosen carefully. The main point to bear in mind is to keep the concept fairly simple, and not to mix materials too freely. If you like terracotta, it is best to stick to this as a unifying theme. There are some

RIGHT: *Siting a statue at the end of a walkway or alley will help to create a focal point, and acts as a frame for the ornament. Planting the pergola with wisteria, roses and clematis softens the structure while providing colour throughout the summer months. The space under it makes an ideal eating or relaxing area on hot days.*

wonderful imported large terracotta containers, handsome enough to stand as sculptural objects in their own right, if they are positioned carefully.

sculpture

Sculptures in a range of styles and forms can enhance the garden too. You can choose special pieces at garden sculpture galleries or visit artists direct to commission your own. A sculptor will usually specialize in a particular material, be it clay, ceramics, stone, bronze or wood, and your choice will be determined by your own taste. Texture plays an important part in any sculptural piece, and you may be more attracted to the natural warmth of wood than to the cool surface of granite, for example. Again, you need to choose a material that works well with the others in your garden; colours and textures should combine harmoniously.

If you have just a little money and are wondering what you can afford, it pays to buy one good, notable piece than to dissipate your cash on several small ones. The garden setting demands a reasonably dramatic, theatrical concept, and a large piece will return your investment with dividends by being noticed and appreciated by garden visitors. Lots of small sculptures may simply jostle for attention.

It is important when siting a good piece of sculpture to find a situation that shows it off to advantage, and possibly one where it can be lit in the evening for maximum effect. Small busts can be sited on plinths or set against a wall for example, surrounded by appropriate planting – ideally attractive foliage plants that form a soft frame; ivy, for example, is ideal.

other ornaments

Architectural relics of various types, including broken pieces of pilaster or coping stones, make good garden ornaments. Try to treat them sympathetically and incorporate them into a design that bears some echo of their original style – be it classical, Gothic or post modern.

Cisterns, water tanks, and even old sinks can all be converted to garden use. If handsome enough, they can stand alone, or they can be planted sympathetically or converted into useful water features.

Mirrors can be used to great effect in small gardens to increase the apparent space by reflecting views. This approach works very well in small basements, where a mirror will not only increase the available space but will also help to reflect light. You need to be a little careful where and how you site mirrors, since the angle is important. One way it is often done is to surround the mirror with a trellis arch, thereby creating a trompe l'oeil effect of a doorway into another part of the garden.

DECORATIVE DETAILS

MAKING THE MOST OF A SMALL GARDEN is all about detail. In a large garden the main concern is to fill the big picture: creating a landscape with giant shapes, big blocks of colour and broad sweeps of grass; fine detail would never be noticed. In a small garden, it is the little things that count. Borders should be as varied as possible. Because you only use one or two plants of each kind, it is vital to make good plant associations so that each individual looks its best. Dwarf edgings of lavender or box will visually unite even the widest mixture of plants while taking up very little of the limited space available. Raised beds provide another level and offer opportunities to grow compact and miniature plants in scaled-down surroundings where it is easy to enjoy them. Containers in small gardens are always on show so they must look immaculate all year round; attention to detail here is essential. Evergreens can be clipped, and shrubs trained as standards to save space and add interest. Every plant needs to look well groomed for the whole garden to shine.

As already discussed, a few suitable garden ornaments will do much to bring out the character of a small group of plants, or a particular area within the garden. Avoid anything too enormous or fussy for the situation, and make sure it follows the general theme of the plants and garden around it. Ideally, choose the ornament and plants at the same time, but if this is not possible try to take a photograph of the garden with you when shopping. In some small gardens, simple, natural props made from everyday objects picked up from the ground can create a better effect than expensive ornaments.

RIGHT: These simple decorations made from bits and pieces collected from around the garden break up a plain white wall very effectively. It is easy to alter or replace them whenever you feel like a change.

BELOW: Old items of garden equipment are good for themed decorations. They should look as if they have been casually abandoned and overgrown by plants, not deliberately placed in the border.

LEFT: A small group of flagons and interestingly shaped bits of wood bring this corner to life. The secret is to apply the same rules as for plant associations. Here, the three main objects are all similar but differ slightly in shape and size.

RIGHT: Terracotta pots can be used in all sorts of creative ways around the garden, both with and without plants. This flowerpot man is held together by a metal plant support, and makes a striking centrepiece among the low leafy plants.

RIGHT: You need not pay a lot for garden ornaments; these stones have holes through the middle and have been threaded on to a cane pushed into the ground.

BELOW: Wind chimes are a good way of drawing attention to a taller plant in a low background. This bamboo version makes a low, hollow sound in a light breeze.

BELOW: A layer of pebbles over the potting mix in a container adds decorative detail and helps to keep the mix cool and moist. Pick a colour that matches the pot.

Decorative plant supports

A little light support props up tall plants and those that fall forward or lean over the edge of the lawn and get in the way of the mower. Rustic supports made from woven or bent twigs not only do their job, but also make more of the plants. They are easy to make yourself from prunings.

RIGHT: Bent hazel stems, wired or tacked together, make decorative low plant supports. They usually last two or three years if taken under cover in winter, but are cheap to buy and easily replaced when past their best.

LEFT: An even simpler support like this can be pushed into a border temporarily at any time of year. You cannot hide the support, but this does not matter as it becomes part of the display, adding a touch of rustic style.

BELOW: Low sections of willow or hazel hurdle keep the lawn edge clear without looking unduly fussy – ideal for a country or cottage garden. Taller sections will discourage pets from taking short cuts through borders.

AWNINGS & UMBRELLAS

BELOW: *A canvas awning extends the shelter from the sun in this small corner patio. Awnings are ideal if you already have a supporting vertical structure in place from which to stretch them.*

IN A SMALL GARDEN, you can use the space much as you would a room in the house, with soft furnishings adding colour and interest, as well as providing protection from the elements. Awnings and canopies can be used to create much-needed privacy and seclusion, particularly if you have a ground-floor flat and garden, and the garden is overlooked by other tenants occupying the floors above you.

There are various possibilities for covering the ceiling of the garden, including the partial shade afforded by pergolas (see pages 86–9). Large canvas umbrellas, imported from the Far East, have become very popular recently and are fortunately still relatively cheap. For something larger, you could support sailcloth strips on posts with stout string ties. You will, however, need some rapid means of removing these or lowering them to a vertical position in the event of rain, otherwise they will fill up with rain water and tear loose from their moorings under the weight. You could also use very lightweight muslin, rather like mosquito netting, to create a summer awning, or a range of hand-dyed cottons in earthy colours – saffrons, terracottas and burnt oranges.

Reed screens are another possibility for overhead shade. They are relatively light and

LEFT: *A large canvas umbrella in white or cream looks particularly smart and is also effective. With its sturdy supporting pole and spokes, it offers a much better solution, in both design and functional terms, than the ubiquitous floral parasols so often used for this purpose.*

very easy to fix in position to timber supporting struts and posts. You can, if you wish, grow flowering or foliage climbers and creepers over them. In normal climatic conditions, they will last for around five years, but as they are relatively inexpensive, it is not a great problem to replace them when they wear.

Fabric can be a wonderful source of colour in the garden and there are a myriad ways to employ it to jazz up the appearance of a dull city garden in particular. The most obvious application is for colourful cushions – for seats and as floor cushions, if you have decked your patio area with timber – and tablecloths. These kinds of colourful additions work particularly well in shady gardens, which have very little natural colour of their own and benefit enormously from the addition of some imported brightness.

Many people have transformed their living space by stealing a portion of the garden to create a conservatory. If you do not want the full cost of a conservatory, you can make yourself a lean-to shelter with open sides and a roof of clear PVC. Beware that in a city this is inclined to get dirty, and if it is not to look gimcrack, you do need to give it a good annual scrubbing down. If the posts are painted a deep green, and you grow some interesting climbing plants up them, you can turn this into a surprisingly effective loggia for the spring and summer months.

LIGHTING

RIGHT: *Subtly positioned,
uplighters can create rich shadows,
outlining features and creating a
sense of drama in the garden –
only a few such lights are needed.
Organize the electrical plan
carefully to provide the best position
for the lights on one circuit.*

IF YOU ARE GOING to spend time and energy creating a lovely garden, it is well worthwhile expending a little more time and money lighting it. Lighting the garden has many benefits, not all immediately obvious. In any garden it is a boon for security. Very few burglars will walk through a lit garden to

start fiddling with windows or locks, and it also gives you and your neighbours a good view from indoors.

Lighting the garden will also mean that you can enjoy the grandeur of your garden at night as well as in the daytime. Just a couple of judiciously placed lights can give your

garden some of the dramatic appeal of a stage set. Trees and shrubs take on wonderful new outlines, the contrasts in light and shade enhancing their qualities and character enormously. If you want to use the garden for entertaining, then lights are a must, allowing you to extend your opportunities to do so into the evenings. Make sure the seating area is well, but subtly lit, the lights facing away from the area, not glaring on to it.

choosing lighting

Lighting schemes do not have to be elaborate or expensive. At their simplest, they can take the form of a few flares on supports. Flares – rather like candles on stilts – are available from most garden centres and will burn for about six to eight hours, depending on size. They cast a beautifully soft warm glow and look extremely romantic in any setting.

A simple lighting system might incorporate two or three all-weather lights, fixed to spikes

LEFT: *Lighting does not need to be a major outlay.
A few candles in holders, judiciously positioned, can
transform the atmopshere of the garden at night. Flares
are also good and will burn for six to eight hours. They
provide an effective deterrent to flying insects as well.*

secured in the ground and angled to create a spot of light wherever it seems most suitable or convenient. One light, for example, could be a downlighter on to the seating area, and two more could be fixed at further points in the garden to focus on specific features – a water feature, perhaps, or a particularly attractive shrub or tree.

If you are using the patio for entertaining, then make sure that you also install any necessary lights for safety of access as well – for example, lighting the way along a path or down steps. The aim is to sit bathed in a subtle light, not the full glare of a floodlit football pitch, so direct the light upwards or downwards as required, away from any seating.

If you have an attractive water feature, you can light it using waterproof underwater lights, which can enhance its appeal greatly. If you can afford to, make sure some of the lights are on separate circuits so that you can switch different lights on or off, as required.

Lights suitable for outdoor use are generally available in the three following types: tungsten lights which create a warm, golden glow; discharge sodium or mercury lights which give a diffused slightly greenish tinged glow; and low-voltage halogen lights which give a very white light.

BELOW: *More ambitious lighting schemes can turn your garden into an outdoor room – a true extension of the house. This courtyard blends seamlessly with the living space.*

CONTAINERS

CONTAINERS ARE PROBABLY among the most important ingredients in a small garden. The type you choose makes it easy to identify the general style of the garden instantly; clay pots equal cottage garden, patterned terracotta says Mediterranean, while hand-painted pots state fashionable designer garden, and expensive lead or stone planters suggest formal gardens. Containers make natural focal points, drawing attention to key places such as porches and entrances. In groups they form the main decoration for patios, while a single large container makes a striking centrepiece for a courtyard or garden room. Because they are so important to the garden, they must look good all year round. For most gardeners, this means filling them with colour. Several changes of annuals, planted for short-term seasonal effects, is the very best way to make the most of containers. True, this creates extra work, but planting and replanting containers involves much less effort than using bedding plants in a garden bed. There is virtually no soil preparation or weeding to do in containers and very little pest control. Deter slugs and snails by applying anti-pest 'glue' around pot rims, and take advantage of special potting composts with added pesticide. However, feeding, watering and deadheading are regular vital chores that you must make time for, but even these do not really take long compared to the spectacular displays that containers create in a garden. And by choosing suitable plants and products such as automatic watering systems, you can enjoy the benefits of glorious containers without most of the work.

Self-watering containers

Self-watering containers, such as the trough shown here, have a reservoir in the base. These containers can keep plants watered for up to a week before the reservoir needs refilling, even in summer.

ABOVE: Now that dwarf sunflowers are available, you can grow these delightful plants in terracotta pots on the patio. Raise your own from seed or buy ready-grown plants in spring.

ABOVE: Choose several good-sized plants for a large container. They should be one-and-a-half to two-and-a-half times the height of the container to look in perfect proportion. These are abutilon, *Lobelia cardinalis* and helichrysum.

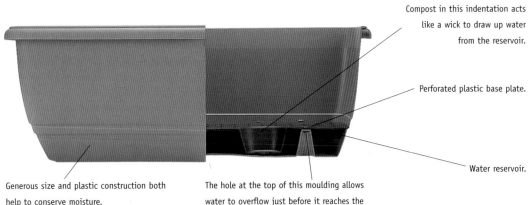

Compost in this indentation acts like a wick to draw up water from the reservoir.

Perforated plastic base plate.

Water reservoir.

Generous size and plastic construction both help to conserve moisture.

The hole at the top of this moulding allows water to overflow just before it reaches the main potting compost.

LEFT: Hanging baskets are the most popular containers. For stunning results, fill them with fuchsias, pelargoniums and brachycome, as here. Kept well-fed, regularly watered and deadheaded, they flower prolifically all through summer.

ABOVE: A striking container often looks more spectacular when planted all with the same species. Use as many plants as it takes to create a well-filled display straightaway. This is *Lotus berthelotti*.

RIGHT: Windowboxes are the containers most likely to miss out on frequent watering, so plant drought-tolerant sunlovers such as pelargoniums. But try not to forget them.

Ideas for using pot shards

1 Part-fill a shallow terracotta pan with compost. Lay curved pieces of clay pot in a circular pattern on the compost. Plant a lewisia in the centre, with shards around it.

2 Add more small alpines with similar growing requirements – full sun and good drainage. Leave space to see the pattern made by the shards. Finish with a layer of fine gravel to prevent neck rot in wet weather. Stand the container in a sunny spot.

Recycling a broken pot

1 Lay a broken pot on its side and bank up compost to form a slope from back to front. Plant a large sempervivum in the deeper end at the back of the pot.

2 Plant a low spreading sedum on its side in the shallow end, so that the stems and flowers spill out forwards. Add more compost between the rootballs.

3 To prevent it rolling, bed the finished container into loose soil or, better still, gravel (which is more decorative). Set the back of the pot slightly deeper so that water does not run straight out of the compost.

Stencilling with masonry paint

Masonry paint is ideal for decorating terracotta containers. Since it is designed to protect brickwork and house walls, it forms a weatherproof finish. The only drawback is that the colours are usually in the pastel range, but you can create new, brighter shades by adding colourizers. Add a few drops of pigment to a little paint and apply to the pot with a stencil brush.

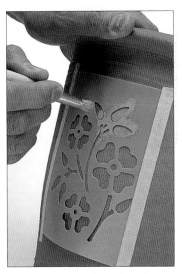

1 *Attach the stencil securely to the pot with tape and apply the first colour by dabbing carefully with a stubby bristled stencil brush.*

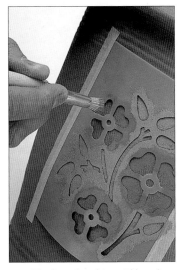

2 *The first colour dries quickly and then you can add the second one. Make this by adding blue colourizer to basic white paint.*

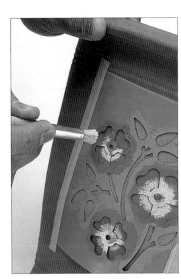

3 *To create a contrasting central ring in each flower, simply dab in some white paint. Ensure that the stencil does not move while you work.*

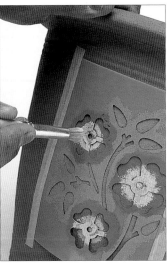

4 *The final touch in this floral decoration is to add a yellow blob that reflects the pollen-bearing stamens of a real flower.*

DECORATING CONTAINERS

Decorative paint effects, such as stencils, have been fashionable indoors for some time. Now they are moving outdoors; painted flowerpots are the latest patio accessories. But there is no need to spend a fortune because you can paint your own. Use stencils, handpainted patterns or colour washes to make new pots look much more expensive than they really are, or to give old pots a new look. You can also make new terracotta pots look weathered by dabbing shades of green, grey and yellow on to a colour-washed pot with a sponge, to simulate moss and lichen growth. After painting, add a coat of varnish to make the colours weatherproof. But since repainting is so simple, why not just repaint them every year or two? Clean the pots well and remove loose or flaky paint, then cover them with a light colour wash (use two coats if needed to cover the old pattern) and redecorate when completely dry.

Painting is also an effective way of overcoming the grey drabness of cement and concrete containers. You can buy paints formulated for concrete surfaces or use those sold for masonry and house exteriors. The latter are also available with added grit to produce a textured finish, which may suit some containers. The range of colours available is very wide, although generally speaking the more natural earth shades will suit containers better than some of the sweeter hues destined to adorn a country cottage or a seaside home. Follow the manufacturer's instructions when using these paints – some require protective gloves, for example.

You need not limit yourself to conventional pots. Wicker baskets, cane picnic hampers and woven log baskets all make good containers, first lined with plastic and treated to protect them from the elements.

This terracotta pot has a rough-textured finish that is ideal for masonry paints.

5 *When all the colours have dried, peel off the stencil to reveal the finished pattern. You can reuse the stencil, but wash it before applying it again.*

Gilding a container

1 Painting and gilding can transform a humble cast cement planter. Start by applying a coat of exterior wall paint all over – here lovat green. Choose from a huge range of pastel tones on offer.

Make sure that your paint reaches into all the crevices.

2 Lightly brushing with gold paint emphasizes the intricate detail of this wall planter. Filled with suitable plants, it would grace the walls of a stylish conservatory.

3 Fill the painted wall planter with compact plants such as primula, pansies and trailing ivy. Attach it securely to the wall.

The patterns on the cement casting are ideal for picking out in gilding.

Painting wicker baskets

New or secondhand wicker baskets need treating to protect them from rotting when left outdoors in all weathers. Since their natural colour soon fades in the sun, stain or paint them in natural or bright colours, depending on your planting scheme. Line them before planting.

LEFT: Wicker baskets with loop handles are available in many styles and sizes. Treated with water-based wood stain, they make charming planters, ideal in a country garden.

RIGHT: An informal mixture of pink flowers in various shapes give this well-filled basket its air of country charm. They include drooping fuchsias, flaring petunia trumpets and snapdragons.

Using colour washes on pots

Terracotta can look raw and orange when new. You can 'age' the surface quickly, using a dilute colour wash of artist's acrylic. As the water is absorbed into the terracotta, an uneven and natural-looking covering of white pigment remains. This is how to create a pink finish.

LEFT: Using diluted white artist's paint, roughly apply a wash to a dry container. Mix your colours together, here ultramarine and crimson, with some more white paint. Apply in downward strokes to create darker and lighter 'weathered' streaks. Apply the darker colours cautiously.

MAKING A WINDOW BOX

Wooden planters and windowboxes are versatile and easy to build yourself in virtually any shape or size. The aim of this project is to make a wooden surround that will enclose a standard-sized plastic trough; these are widely available in a range of colours and sizes. Tongued-and-grooved cladding is an ideal material to make the sides of the windowbox; simply use as many planks as necessary to give the height of container you want. You can choose from several cladding profiles, but be sure to use the heavier weight structural cladding rather than the thinner type supplied for facing surfaces. The one used here has a detailed profile that gives the finished box more style. There are two good reasons for using a plastic trough inside a wooden windowbox. One is that the interior of the box is not in direct contact with the compost and is therefore less liable to rot. The other is that it is very easy to change the display simply by replacing the trough with another one planted up in a different way. The plastic trough featured here is 60cm (24in) long and a convenient size for a small windowbox that will not be too heavy or unwieldy to fix up. The box is particularly sturdy around the end panels and these are the ideal points for support when attaching it to a wall or balcony railing. Treat the windowbox with preservative stain or paint. You can also add stencilled motifs and decorative mouldings. The possibilities are endless and it is easy to match existing house or garden colour schemes.

1 Measure and mark the pieces of cladding that will form the end panels of the box. For a snug fit, make these 17cm (6¹/₄in) wide.

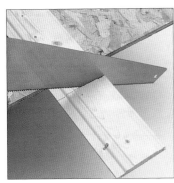

2 Saw the end panels to length and sand the cut edges for a smooth finish. Each end panel will consist of two pieces of cladding.

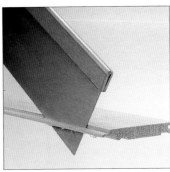

3 Using a tenon saw, cut off the thinnest part of the tongue on the piece of cladding chosen to form the top of each end panel.

4 Squeeze some woodworking adhesive in the groove of the top piece of cladding and carefully push the two pieces together.

5 Using panel pins or fine nails, attach the bottom edge of the end panel to a batten cut to the same width. Use adhesive to create a firmer bond.

6 Nail and glue battens along each side edge of the end panels. Punch the nail heads below the surface. Wipe off any excess adhesive with a damp cloth.

7 Cut long pieces of cladding and assemble them in pairs to make up the side panels. These should measure 63cm (25in).

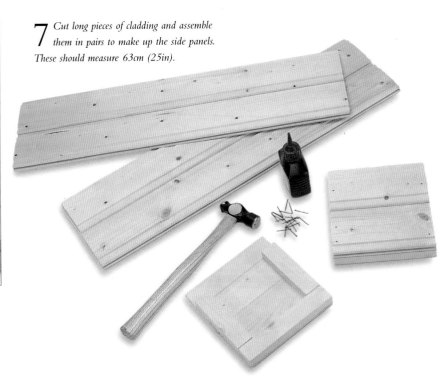

8 *Add adhesive and attach the side panels to the end panels with nails, creating a bottomless box that will fit around the trough.*

9 *Cut two pieces of roofing lathe to fit inside the box, sawing notches at each end so that they rest on the battens.*

10 *Push the support rails down on to the end battens. Screw them in place or leave them loose for removal when cleaning the box.*

11 *Drop the trough inside the windowbox so that it rests on the two rails. Drill holes in the plastic base of the trough to let water drain out. Plant up the trough like any other container and place inside the wooden box.*

Staining a wooden windowbox

Some years ago, the only options for staining wood were varying shades of brown. Today the range of stains and preservative paints is quite staggering. And what is more important, many are water-based, making them more pleasant to apply and safer to use with plants. Coordinate your plant displays with the colour of the container.

ABOVE: Translucent, water-based wood stains such as these are available in a range of bright colours. They allow the grain of the wood to show through.

BELOW: Here, the yellow daffodils echo the cheerful colour of the windowbox. The centres of the primroses pick up on it, too.

Narcissus 'Tête-à-Tête'

CHAPTER 4

PLANT FEATURES

CHOOSING THE APPROPRIATE

plants for the setting and situation taxes even

experienced gardeners. In this chapter, the

different kinds of setting that determine the

range of plants you can successfully grow are

examined, from sunny dry patios to damp shady

parts of the garden. In additional, special

plants are needed for particular purposes – for

screening, for creating a focal point, or for providing a few delicious fruits or vegetables – and

this section offers a range of choices, plus useful planting lists and details of how to go about

creating plant features. It is important, when space is limited, to choose the plants that offer the

most value – ideally with more than one season of interest.

LEFT: Pelargoniums are deservedly popular for small gardens. They flower for a long season, require almost no maintenance and look terrific, particularly in a single colour theme.

RIGHT: Foliage has its part to play as well as flowers, as this shady patio with its topiary, beautiful ancient fig tree, trained standards and tree fern demonstrates.

PLANTING THE SMALL GARDEN

CHOOSING APPROPRIATE plants for a small garden is an amalgam of common sense and imagination. It is important to make some practical choices, because of the constraints of small spaces, often difficult planting conditions and the need to choose plants that offer the best value. The element

LEFT: *A study in green, white and silver, this small urn, filled with* Helichrysum petiolare *and surrounded by ribbed hosta leaves and clipped box, makes a perfect scheme for a small shady corner.*

of imagination is equally important, as it is the planting that will bring the garden to life.

To get the most from a small space, it pays to have a clear planting theme in your mind's eye, to appreciate the limitations of the conditions – shade, sun, damp ground and so on – and then to try to unify the planting. But, to the uninitiated, what does this mean? For a start, it probably means having a balance of vertical interest – climbers, larger shrubs and even the odd tree – and horizontal interest in the form of smaller shrubs, perennials, bulbs and annuals. You do not need a wide variety of different plants to make a garden look well planted, but their position in the garden is crucial.

Not everyone grasps that big plants can in fact do very well in small spaces. As a consequence, they tend to choose lots of smaller plants, which will not only give the garden a bitty, restless look, but which are much more labour intensive. Among the big bold plants that would do well in a small

garden are evergreen shrubs, such as the broad-leaved *Fatsia japonica* and the yellow-splashed *Aucuba japonica* 'Crotonifolia', spiky cordylines and yuccas and the attractive *Choisya ternata*, with its whorl-like leaves and clouds of scented white flowers that appear in early summer.

It is important to ensure that the garden has some kind of structural frame of planting, around which smaller groups of plants, including perennials and annuals, can be composed. Even if you have no more than a balcony or terrace, it is still worth including a couple of evergreen shrubs – maybe in the form of twinned containers of topiary shapes of box or myrtle – to provide a peg on which to hang the remainder of the planting.

If you cannot afford in the first year of the garden to plant it up extensively, then concentrate your planting efforts and, if you can, buy the bigger elements first, perhaps filling in the empty spaces with big annuals that you grow yourself from seed – tobacco plants are excellent space fillers and do well in partial shade as well as sun, unlike many of the annuals. In the first summer, take any cuttings you can and make sure you do this each year to increase your stock of shrubs. Quite a few perennials can be layered or divided to augment supplies.

Pairs of containers, whether of architectural plants, such as these topiary box spirals, or of flowering plants, such as standard marguerites or fuchsias, are ideal for creating emphasis in the garden, for instance to mark a doorway, as here. Try to ensure that the scale of the planted containers suits the setting.

It is often best to pick several species from one genus that you know will work well in the environment than to go for a range of different plants. Planting gains its impact from making a bold statement, and grouping plants by type certainly increases the effect. Pelargoniums are a must for any small garden, not least because of the many different forms, which include trailing types for hanging baskets, richly scented ivy-leaved ones that can be used in cooking, and brilliant-coloured flowering regal and zonal pelargoniums, some of which can even be trained into architectural standards. Fuchsias are another good candidate, again with a wide range of flower types and colours. Like pelargoniums, they can be trained into standards, if you wish.

It is well worth considering the seasonal element of the planting, and doing your best to ensure that the garden offers year-round interest. This is obviously harder to do in very small spaces, but even on a windowsill you can change the planting as the seasons progress, so that you always have something interesting to observe. A windowbox could house spring bulbs, followed by a selection of summer flowers and herbs, with late-summer annuals and chrysanthemums for autumn, and heathers, cyclamens and ivies in winter, for example.

PLANTED SCREENS

RIGHT: *If you have a pergola, roses are the ideal companion for it, possibly with other climbing plants, such as clematis or honeysuckle, climbing over and among them to provide a longer flowering season.*

BELOW LEFT: *Trellis, over which you can grow climbers such as this handsome ivy (Hedera canariensis 'Gloire de Marengo'), makes an excellent screen for a small garden and an attractive backdrop for this pair of architetural plants trained as standards.*

ONE OF THE MOST essential requirements of a small garden is to provide privacy from neighbouring flats and houses and screening from cold winds and pollution, or, for that matter, from marauding cats. You may also want to obscure an unattractive view. In classic garden designs, screening is usually provided by formal clipped evergreens, which are dense and impenetrable – yews and hollies, for example, make excellent dark solid screens. However, both are fairly slow growing, and you may well need plants that will do their work faster, unless you plan to stay in the same apartment or house for some time to come.

Climbers

Abutilon megapotamicum

Akebia quinata

Aristolochia macrophylla

Campsis x tagliabuana

Clematis armandii

C. macropetala

C. montana

C. tangutica

Eccremocarpus scaber

Hedera

Humulus lupulus 'Aureus'

Hydrangea anomala petiolaris

Ipomoea tricolor

Jasminum officinale

Lathyrus latifolius

Lonicera periclymenum

L. x tellmanniana

Passiflora caerulea

Rosa

Solanum crispum 'Glasnevin'

Trachelospermum jasminoides

Tropaeolum speciosum

Vitis vinifera 'Purpurea'

Wisteria sinensis

climbing plants

For faster cover, climbing plants trained over tall trellis are a better option. There is a wide choice of suitable plants, some offering much more dense cover than others. Ivies are great value as they are fairly quick growing – you will get a couple of meters in two or three years out of some of the swifter varieties – and so are the creepers, some of which you might find a little too enthusiastic, however. Parthenocissus can put on many feet in one season, but it is a deciduous plant, unlike ivy, so it will provide a screen only during the summer months.

Tall bamboos are an excellent choice for cover up to about 3m (10ft) in height, but you may be best advised to plant them in containers. Bamboos spread by underground rhizomes and your whole garden may well turn into a bamboo thicket unless you control their spread in some way. If you do grow them in containers, you will need to root prune them every couple of years. One solution is to grow them in a plastic container within a larger terracotta one. Every couple of years, you can dismantle the plastic container, trim out the roots (up to one-third) and then replant the bamboo into a similar-sized pot.

One of the nicest screening plants is a grape vine – either a fruiting sort or a strictly ornamental one. The leaves are large and attractive, and turn a pretty russet color in autumn before they fall. Another good screening plant is Dutchman's pipe

---

Shrubs to grow against walls

Acca sellowiana (z8–10)

Ceanothus 'Burkwoodii' (z9–10)

Chaenomeles speciosa (z5–8)

Choisya ternata (z8–10)

Cotoneaster horizontalis (z5–9)

Crinodendron hookerianum (z9–10)

Escallonia 'Apple Blossom' (z8–9)

Euonymus fortunei (z5–9)

Forsythia suspensa (z6–8)

Garrya elliptica (z8–10)

Magnolia grandiflora (z7–10)

Myrtus communis (z8–9)

Pittosporum tenuifolium (z9–10)

RIGHT: *This singularly beautiful formal foliage garden demonstrates just how successful a garden can be without the benefit of flowers; here the varying shapes and forms provide an almost sculptural feel to the garden. Compartmentalizing the garden, by screening the view with evergreens, as here, helps to enlarge the apparent space as the eye cannot take in all the areas of the garden in one go.*

Plants for a Quick Screen

Chamaecyparis lawsoniana
Cotoneaster x *watereri*
Eucalyptus gunnii
Fallopia baldschuanica
Hedera helix
Ligustrum japonicum
L. lucidum
Pleioblastus
Pyracantha
Sorbus aria
S. aucuparia
Thuja plicata

Flowering Small Trees

Cercis siliquastrum
Cornus controversa
Crataegus laevigata
Hamamelis mollis
Laburnum
Magnolia salicifolia
M. x *soulangeana*
Malus
Prunus serrulata
P. subhirtella
Robinia kelseyi
Syringa vulgaris

Evergreen Trees

Arbutus x *andrachnoides*
A. menziesii
Ceanothus arboreus
Chamaecyparis lawsoniana
Elaeagnus x *ebbingei*
Eucalyptus gunnii
Ilex aquifolium
Laurus nobilis
Magnolia grandiflora
Nothofagus menziesii
Quercus coccifera
Taxus baccata
Umbellularia californica

(Aristolochia macrophylla), which has vine-like leaves and can be trained along poles or wires to form an attractive ribbon shape at the top of a fence, for example. Equally good is the golden hop *(Humulus lupulus* 'Aureus').

There is nothing to stop you using flowering climbers for screening purposes, and roses can make the best screens against cats, their thorny branches forming an impenetrable thicket, while offering the bonus of a once- (or twice- if you pick a remontant rose) a-year glorious display of flowers, most with delicious scent as well. 'New Dawn' seems universally popular and does well in most situations, its pale pink flowers blending well with most colour schemes. Another tough and vigorous rose is the richly scented, bright pink 'Albertine', or you could try one of the really big varieties, such as *Rosa filipes* 'Kiftsgate' if you have enough space for it to stretch itself – it will climb to 9m (30ft) or more, covering itself in clouds of white flowers in summer.

trees as screens

If you have an unsightly view to screen, a tall columnar tree – *Chamaecyparis lawsoniana,* for example – does the trick most effectively.

Plant it as close to the house as you dare without doing damage to the foundations. How close you can go will depend on the type of tree. Another good screening tree is *Eucalyptus gunnii,* which will survive furious pruning to twist and turn towards the light. The leaves on the adult tree are long, light and feathery, and although few would recommend it for a very small garden, it should do very well in a garden of, say, 12m (40ft) or more in length. Silver birches are also good for screening with dappled light and shade, as is the delicate winter-flowering cherry, *Prunus subhirtella* 'Autumnalis'.

FEATURE PLANTS

RIGHT: *This brilliantly coloured planting scheme for a hot, sunny corner of the garden makes a strong statement with a variegated phormium, deep red lupins and bright orange calendulas in the foreground.*

WHEN PLANNING A SMALL garden you need to ensure that the eye is drawn to specific elements in it, rather than allowed to meander over it in an apparently random way. In larger gardens, designers normally create a series of compartments which help to focus attention on individual elements within the larger whole. In a small garden, this luxury is not really applicable, as the space will not normally allow it, although you can copy the concept by giving different parts of the garden a specific theme, or by creating points of interest with garden ornaments or particular plants.

The plants that serve this kind of purpose best are those with strong eye-catching interest, simply because you need something reasonably large to notice it. Ideally, such a plant should look good most of the year, becoming a more or less permanent feature of the garden. You can, of course, use perennials or deciduous shrubs for the same purpose, but you will want to make sure that the garden landscape still looks good without them in the winter months.

eye-catching shrubs

Among the best shrubs to act as a focal point are those with distinctive foliage and a handsome form. A good subject is *Fatsia japonica,* an evergreen with large glossy divided leaves and attractive berries in winter. It forms a pretty large bush eventually, and can make a good end-of-border plant to screen the end of the garden from the house. Another good candidate is the Mexican orange blossom, *Choisya ternata,* or the winter-flowering *Mahonia* x *media* 'Charity'; both have the benefit of being scented, too, although not everyone likes the rather foxy perfume of the Mexican orange blossom. Equally good for this purpose would be large spiky cordylines or yuccas, perhaps in a container, or the Abyssinian banana plant, *Ensete ventricosum,* again in a container, as you will need to overwinter it indoors. A large palm, such as *Trachycarpus fortunei* or the tree fern, *Dicksonia antarctica,* makes a good focal point for a paved or gravel surface.

using arches

If you do not want the plant in a solo spot, then consider creating an arch, over which you can grow a few climbers or twining plants. This, again, will draw the eye, particularly in summer when plants are in flower, though of course you could, if you prefer, turn it into a permanent feature by planting evergreen climbers, such as ivies, over it. Alternatively, use it as a support for some exotic-looking foliage climbers, such as big-leaved vines, the evergreen clematis *Clematis armandii* which is also scented, or the climbing hydrangea, *Hydrangea anomala petiolaris,* with its large flat corymbs of creamy flowers. In warmer areas, you could try *Campsis* x *tagliabuana* 'Madame Galen' with its wonderful burnt orange trumpet-shaped flowers.

**Eyecatching
Shrubs and Trees**

Brugmansia

Buxus sempervirens

Camellia

Catalpa speciosa

Dicksonia antarctica

Ensete ventricosum

x *Fatshedera lizei*

Fuchsia

Hydrangea

Lonicera

Magnolia x *soulangeana*

Rhododendron yakushimanum

Taxus baccata

Trachycarpus fortunei

Large Flowering Perennials and Bulbs

Allium christophii (z5–8)

Camassia leichtlinii (z4–10)

Campanula latifolia (z4–8)

Canna (z8–11)

Cardiocrinum giganteum (z7–9)

Cosmos bipinnatus (annual)

Crambe cordifolia (z6–9)

Crocosmia 'Lucifer' (z6–9)

Delphinium (z3–7)

Digitalis purpurea (z4–10)

Hemerocallis (z3–10)

Heracleum mantegazzianum (poisonous) (z3–9)

Ligularia dentata 'Desdemona' (z4–8)

Lilium hybrids (z3–8)

Lobelia cardinalis (z3–9)

Nicotiana sylvestris (z10–11)

Verbascum olympicum (z5–9)

Foliage Perennials

Angelica archangelica (z4–9)

Arundo donax (z6–10)

Astilboides tabularis (z5–7)

Bergenia cordifolia (z3–8)

Cordyline australis (z10–11)

Cynara cardunculus (z7–9)

Darmera peltata (z5–9)

Gunnera manicata (z7–10)

Hosta sieboldiana elegans (z3–8)

Macleaya cordata (z4–9)

Miscanthus sinensis 'Zebrinus' (z4–9)

Petasites japonicus giganteus (z5–9)

Rheum palmatum (z5–9)

Yucca gloriosa (z7–10)

Zantedeschia aethiopica (z8–10)

perennials

A small bed of large perennials can also provide a focal point. Try creating a bed with some show-stopping perennials that grow to 1.2m (4ft) or more – *Euphorbia characias wulfenii,* ligularias, rodgersias and the big hellebore, *Helleborus argutifolias,* are all good candidates for this kind of treatment, with perhaps smaller perennials edging the bed and sprawling over the paving – try the small campanulas, epimediums and geraniums for this purpose.

To create interest at the furthest point of the garden, use some really big perennials. Clouds of *Crambe cordifolia,* with its big blue-green leaves and starry white flowers, and some silver-leaved giants, such as *Eryngium giganteum,* would be good for a fairly sunny spot, while *Macleaya cordata* would combine well with *Crocosmia* 'Lucifer' in a slightly less sunny situation.

plants in containers

A big container with a handsome plant such as *Hosta sieboldiana elegans* or a hydrangea could provide a punctuation point where two different kinds of surface meet. In a formal, Oriental-style design, you could use single specimens of mound-forming shrubs to create a similar full-stop. Yakushimanum rhododendrons, a neat *Skimmia japonica* or *Viburnum davidii* will all make handsome, fairly low mounds, or you can clip plants, such as box or privet, into ball shapes.

ARCHITECTURAL PLANTS

A BORDER CONSISTING ENTIRELY of short fuzzy plants would look very dull; even a small garden needs some height and structure to contrast with low, ground-hugging shapes. A few architectural specimen shrubs or perennials are the answer. *Hamamelis* (witch hazel) or *Mahonia* x *media* 'Charity' team well with more compact shrubs to form a group, or to add height at the back of a border. Plants with particularly good architectural shapes, such as *Yucca filamentosa* or *Aralia elata* 'Variegata', make stunning specimen features used on their own in a paved courtyard or patio, perhaps surrounded by a circle of cobblestones, or in minimalistic gardens of gravel and stones. *Cornus controversa* 'Variegata' makes a spectacular specimen, with its tiered layers of branches. You can cut off the lower branches to make an unusual flat-topped small tree. Specimen shrubs with a more conventional shape but a striking appearance include *Magnolia stellata*. In

BELOW: Cordyline palms (*Cordyline australis*) are fairly hardy, but in cold or wet areas grow them in containers and move them under cover in winter to protect them from the worst weather.

a sheltered, slightly shaded spot or in a more traditional small garden it can be grown in the lawn. Surround it with a circle of bare soil to avoid grass competing for nutrients and water and to prevent the base of the magnolia stems being damaged by the lawnmower or rotary cord trimmer when you cut the grass.

Spiky shapes
Cordyline australis
Phormium
Yucca gloriosa

Prickly/spiky foliage
Acanthus spinosus
Colletia armata or *cruciana*
Mahonia
Paliurus spina-christi
Poncirus trifoliata

Finely cut foliage
Acer palmatum dissectum
Caragana arborescens 'Lorbergii'
Rhamnus frangula 'Aspleniifolia'
Rhus glabra 'Laciniata'
Salix babylonica 'Crispa'
Sambucus nigra 'Linearis'
Sambucus racemosa 'Plumosa Aurea'
Sambucus racemosa 'Tenuifolia'
Sorbus 'Chinese Lace'
Syringa x *laciniata*

Reed-shaped stems
Arundo donax
Bamboos (any)
Miscanthus

Contorted stems
Chaenomeles speciosa 'Tortuosa'
Corylus avellana 'Contorta'
Robinia pseudoacacia 'Lace Lady'
Tilia platyphyllos 'Tortuosa'

Eye-catching bark
Acer capillipes
Acer griseum
Arbutus menziesii
Betula albosinensis
Betula utilis jacquemontii
Broussonetia papyrifera

Large striking leaves
Coppiced *ailanthus, catalpa, eucalyptus* and *paulownia*
Fatsia japonica
Ficus carica
Trachycarpus fortunei

Dramatic flowers and foliage
Carpenteria californica
Dendromecon rigida
Fremontodendron californicum
Romneya coulteri
Sophora microphylla
Tree peony
Trochodendron aralioides

Narrow upright shapes
Ballerina apple trees and 'Maypole' crab apple
Ginko biloba 'Fastigiata'
Malus 'Golden Hornet'

Weeping shapes
Betula pendula 'Youngii'
Caragana arborescens 'Pendula'
Malus 'Red Jade'
Prunus subhirtella 'Pendula Rosea'
Pyrus salicifolia 'Pendula'
Salix caprea 'Kilmarnock'
Salix integra 'Hakuro-nishiki'

Striking shapes
Aralia elata 'Variegata'
Corokia cotoneaster
Genista aetnensis
Melianthus major
Musa basjoo
Pseudopanax crassifolia

ABOVE: The hardy banana *(Musa basjoo)* is a real stunner if you want lush, exotic, tropical-looking foliage. It is only truly hardy in milder areas and even here may die down to ground level in winter. If grown in a pot, it can be moved under cover.

RIGHT: *Aralia elata* 'Variegata' makes a wonderful shape with layers of tiered foliage, but loses its leaves in winter. It is perfect for a small garden, reaching 3m (10ft) in time. Trim off the lower branches if you want to turn it into a tree.

BELOW: *Mahonia* 'Charity' has neat rows of prickly evergreen foliage that looks good all year round. Even the flowers are architectural, appearing in cartwheel shapes all over the top of the plant in winter. They are beautifully scented, rather like lily-of-the-valley.

Making the most of a specimen plant

UNLESS YOU ARE in a hurry to see the final effect, there is no need to pay extra for a large plant; small specimens establish themselves better than large ones and quickly catch up in good conditions.

Plant them a suitable distance from other plants in the garden to avoid overcrowding, shading or the risk of smothering smaller species.

Select a site where the full beauty of the plant can be appreciated from various parts of the garden. Place it so that it becomes part of several different views when seen from different directions.

Since a small garden only has room to house a very few of the larger shrubs, be sure to choose only the most striking examples. Plants that provide the right effect for the style of garden and that suit the site and growing conditions are always the best value for money.

Choose only top quality plants, well-furnished with evenly spaced stems and healthy foliage. Species that provide interest in more than one season are especially valuable; witch hazel for example has autumn foliage tints and flowers in winter and spring.

GRASSES

GRASSES ARE THE MOST FASHIONABLE of perennial plants. Huge lists of hitherto never seen varieties are now appearing in nursery catalogues and on plant stands at gardening shows. The description 'grasses' covers a huge range of plant species, many of which may seem difficult to get to know at first as they do not have common names. To complicate things further, 'grass' is also loosely applied to any grassy-looking plants, such as sedges and bamboos. But bear with them. What they all have in common is linear leaves, and in the garden, long narrow leaves make wonderful contrasts with other, more rounded shapes of foliage and flowers. This makes grasses indispensable go-anywhere plants. You can sprinkle a selection of medium-sized flowering and foliage grasses through-out a perennial border to improve it in an instant. Use taller grasses, such as miscanthus and bamboos, among shrubs to add a variety of plant shapes and forms. Grasses are particularly valuable in a heather and conifer garden or one composed mainly of evergreens, where they add movement, seasonal variation and sounds; rustling foliage is a great feature of grasses. And shorter, more drought-tolerant species, such as festuca and many of the sedges, are outstanding for rockeries and containers. You can even get grassy plants that grow in bog gardens and pond margins. So despite the difficulty with their names, grasses are well worth using all round the garden. If you like the look of it, try growing it.

Colour and shape

Grasses make wonderful tall, vertical shapes, splayed fountain shapes, short tussocks or even hairy mats with serrated edges. They can be very colourful, too; there are grasses in various shades of blue, green, bronze, purple and red, or greens with cream, white or gold variegations.

BELOW: This group of compact, slow-growing grassy plants features a bamboo, a sedge, a grass and a member of the lily family *(Ophiopogon)*, which is often regarded as an honorary grass because of its linear leaves.

Grasses for wet soil and bog gardens
Carex elata 'Aurea' (Bowles' golden sedge)
Carex grayi (mace sedge)
Carex pendula
Juncus effusus 'Spiralis' (corkscrew rush)
Schoenoplectus 'Zebrinus' (zebra rush)

Larger grasses to go with shrubs, heathers and conifers
Miscanthus sinensis 'Morning Light'
Miscanthus sinensis 'Zebrinus'
Pleioblastus auricomus
Pleiobastus variegatus

LEFT: *Carex elata* 'Aurea' is actually a sedge, but is usually included along with grasses as it looks like one. This species thrives in sun or light shade and needs damp soil.

Briza media

Pleioblastus variegatus

Acorus gramineus 'Ogon'

Ophiopogon planiscapus 'Nigrescens'

**Decorative grasses
for borders**

Bouteloua gracilis (mosquito grass)

Hakonechloa macra 'Alboaurea'

Imperata cylindrica (Japanese
blood grass)

Milium effusum 'Aureum' (Bowles'
golden grass)

Stipa gigantea (ornamental oats)

Stipa tenuifolia

**Good grasses for rock
features and containers**

Acorus gramineus 'Ogon'

Carex comans

Carex 'Evergold'

Carex hachijoensis

Festuca glauca cultivars, such as
'Blue Fox' and 'Golden Toupee'

**Grasses for a hot,
dry, sunny border or
gravel area**

Festuca glauca cultivars

Elymus arenarius

Helictotrichon sempervirens

Pennisetum alopecuroides

Stipa gigantea

BELOW: These compact grasses and sedges
are particularly showy and make superb
contrasts with plants with rounded leaves
such as hostas, bergenia and *Alchemilla
mollis*. The molinia is suitable for dry shade,
but the others all need a reasonably
sunny situation.

Grasses for small gardens

Medium-sized grasses, such as pennisetum and decorative miscanthus, look attractive
in borders with other perennials. Or make a bed entirely from a mixture of tall and
medium-sized decorative grasses. Although grassy plants are grown mainly for their
foliage, many kinds also have superb flowers and seedheads. You can find feathery plumes,
arching tassels, 'foxtails' and millet-like sprays, as well as ornamental oats, quaking grasses
and fluffy caterpillar-like heads. Leave the dead heads on the plants throughout winter;
they look brilliant rimmed with frost, and birds will feed on the seeds.

Festuca
*These dwarf evergreen grasses need
sun and well-drained soil.*

Pennisetum
*These have spectacular plume-like
seedheads. Provide winter protection
in cold regions.*

Bamboo
*Bamboos look good grown in a row
as a screen, but since many popular*

*species can become invasive, grow
them in large tubs or pots in a small
garden, which keeps them naturally
compact. Choose compact, slow-
growing varieties for planting in
borders in small gardens.*

Miscanthus
*These are mostly tall cane-stemmed
plants that tolerate wet and clay soils.
Some very decorative new compact
varieties are now also available.*

Alopecurus pratensis
'Aureovariegatus'

Carex ornithopoda
'Variegata'

Molinia caerulea
'Variegata'

Carex 'Evergold'

Deschampsia flexuosa
'Tatra Gold'

Koeleria glauca

Above: *Festuca glauca* is a slow-growing,
drought-proof dwarf grass, ideal for a gravel
garden, rockery or scree area. Plants form a
neat hummock shape, with blue feathery
flowerheads in summer.

ANNUALS &
BEDDING PLANTS

DESPITE ALL THE WORK needed to grow, plant and look after bedding plants, they are more popular than ever, especially for growing in containers and hanging baskets on the patio. Bedding plants are ideal for instant colour, as they are generally planted out just as they are starting to bloom. They also have a long flowering season and prolific blooming potential, so they can be relied on to keep a small area ablaze with colour for months on end, unlike other kinds of plants that come and go during the summer, leaving large expanses of green. Nowadays, the trend in bedding plants is away from traditional delicate pastels and old formal favourites, such as *Begonia semperflorens* and ageratum, towards stronger, bolder colours, such as reds and orange. Subtropical-looking tender perennial plants, such as datura, canna and hedychium (ginger lily), are particularly popular. Named varieties of gazania and compact 'patio' dahlias are very much in demand, while species fuchsias and shrubby salvias (which look nothing like the bedding varieties) in bright reds and blues are also becoming very sought-after. Exotic-looking annual climbers, such as mutisia, *Mina lobata* and *Lablab purpureus* (hyacinth bean) are perfect for covering arches or trellis quickly and a decorative way of screening sheds or walls.

Plants for a continuous display of flowers in containers and baskets
Argyranthemum
Brachycome
Fuchsia (bush and trailing)
Lobelia
Petunia
Swiss balcon pelargoniums (a specially free-flowering ivy-leaf type with small flowers)
Zonal pelargoniums

Scented annuals and bedding plants
Lathyrus odoratus (sweet pea; knee-high varieties are suitable for containers)
Malcomia maritima (Virginian stock)
Matthiola bicornis (night-scented stock)
Matthiola incana (stock)
Nicotiana 'Fragrant Cloud'
Zaluzianskya capensis (night stock)

LEFT: Annual flowers create an instant riot of colour, perfect for filling a new garden or bed for the summer while you decide on a more permanent planting scheme.

ABOVE: Create an impression of rapid maturity by using a mixture of tall climbing and trailing bedding plants so they run into each other. The effect looks very natural.

Trendsetting plants

IF YOU WANT to stay ahead of trends, look out for unusual half-hardy perennials with striking flowers, such as *Leonotis leonurus,* which has tiers of pompon-like orange flowers, and *Sutherlandia frutescens,* which has silvery foliage and scarlet pea flowers followed by big inflated green pods. Many of these plants can be spotted in the 'new varieties' pages of the mail order seed catalogues, making it relatively inexpensive to raise your own plants from seed or plantlets.

If you want to be first with the latest in new plants, it is worth cultivating the specialist nurseries known for their new introductions. Find them at plant shows and put your name on their mailing lists, then sit back and wait.

RIGHT: Pelargoniums are fairly drought-tolerant and keep flowering throughout the summer as long as they are regularly deadheaded. Do not overfeed; they will grow leafy instead of flowering well.

BELOW: *Sutherlandia frutescens* is easily raised from seed, although plants are sometimes available from nurseries specializing in tender perennials. It has curious inflated seed pods after the flowers are over.

ABOVE: Gazanias love a hot sunny spot and are fairly drought-tolerant. Raise plants from seed every year or take cuttings of your favourites and keep them over winter.

BELOW: A mass of informally planted calendula, impatiens, begonia and bedding dahlias make a colourful, summer-long, cottage-style display.

Keeping tender perennials

While seed-raised bedding plants can be replaced every season, it becomes expensive to treat choice tender (half-hardy) perennials in this way. If you want to maintain a sizeable collection of these plants, a frost-free greenhouse is a very useful facility. Take cuttings of half-hardy perennials in late summer, root them in small pots and keep them in a light frost-free place for the winter.

PLANTING FOR SUN

BELOW LEFT: *Succulents, such as the agaves and echeveria shown here, do well in hot sunny gravel gardens, along with smaller succulents, such as sedums and saxifrages and some of the Mediterranean herbs, including thyme and marjoram. The soil must be free-draining, however.*

RIGHT: *The gravel around this small patio provides a home for a rich display of dry-loving plants, including catmint, lady's mantle, ornamental thistles and anchusa. Gravel gardens present a good opportunity to plant Mediterranean plants, which enjoy drought conditions, in a loose, cottage-style design.*

THERE IS A rich and varied selection of plants, many of them from the Mediterranean regions of Europe, that do best in dry sunny situations. These are ideal plants for a hot, sunny patio or roof garden, or even a south- or west-facing balcony. Because they are so well adapted to drought conditions in their natural habitat, such plants are relatively low maintenance, requiring little attention and doing surprisingly well in fairly poor soil. Many of them have attractive silvered leaves, and you can make this a theme of the planting if you wish, perhaps marrying them with some plants with variegated leaves.

Among the best plants for dry sunny conditions are the wormwoods *(Artemisia)*, of which there are many different forms and sizes. *Convoluvus cneorum* is a pretty slightly tender plant with very attractive blue-green foliage and white flowers with a prominent yellow eye. Pinks do particularly well in hot sun, and those with the strongest scent, such as 'Mrs Sinkins', are always popular. Potentillas also do well in sunny places, and there are many different forms to choose from, from quite large shrubs to little mat-forming ground-covering ones.

Rue *(Ruta graveolens)* is another good foliage plant – a herb in fact – with strongly

Medium Plants for Dry Sun

Achillea

Agapanthus africanus

Anthemis punctata cupaniana

Alstroemeria hybrids

Centaurea

Crambe cordifolia

Crocosmia

Cynara cardunculus

Euphorbia

Gladiolus

Kniphofia

Lavandula

Linum

Papaver

Penstemon

Perovskia

Phlomis

Phygelius

Salvia sclarea turkestanica

Sisyrinchium striatum

Verbascum

Small Plants for Cracks in Paving

Acaena

Achillea (dwarf forms)

Anemone fulgens

Armeria

Aubrieta

Aurinia

Dianthus

Diascia

Erigeron karvinskianus

Geranium (dwarf forms)

Helianthemum

Lewisia

Origanum

Oxalis

Potentilla (dwarf forms)

Raoulia

Sedum

Sempervivum

Silene

Thymus

aromatic divided blue-green foliage; 'Jackman's Blue' is one of the most popular forms. *Santolina chamaecyparis* is another aromatic herb with silvery foliage that makes a good border edging. You can clip it back each autumn to make a mini hedge. *Brachyglottis laxifolia* is another good silvery leaved shrub, but a bit bigger (about 1.2m/4ft) and will make a good edging to a patio, sprawling attractively over the paving. Lavender, too, makes an excellent edging for a path or border, and can be clipped back to keep it to a more formal shape.

Of the bigger shrubs, buddlejas thrive in light soil and dry conditions, and the pretty *Buddleja alternifolia* 'Argentea' has attractive silvery leaves and lavender, scented flowers in early summer.

plants for cracks and crevices

If your garden has a sunny patio area, you can use the cracks and crevices to plant a range of sun-loving small perennials, which will help to soften the look of the paving. The same principle can be applied to the tops of walls, or crevices in a dry stone wall. Stone troughs and shallow containers also make ideal homes for these kinds of small sun-loving plants.

Among the best plants for this kind of situation are small saxifrages and sedums, which thrive in very dry poor soil. They have large fleshy leaves that retain moisture well, and make an attractive carpet of foliage, studded, when the time comes, with flowers on taller stems. For

planting in the cracks of paving stones, try the little and aptly named daisy-gone-crazy, or *Erigeron karvinskianus*, with its array of pink fading to white daisy flowers. Also good for crevices and cracks are the little campanulas, which will seed themselves happily almost anywhere, as indeed does the larger *Alchemilla mollis*, with its velvety green-grey leaves and lime-green flowers. Another good candidate is baby's tears (*Soleirolia soleirolii*).

SHRUBS FOR SUN

MOST SHRUBS DO BEST in situations that provide direct sun for half the day or more, but a site with strong direct sun all day which also has hot, dry, impoverished soil is difficult to colonize. Few shrubs are happy in such conditions. But by choosing carefully from among the more drought-resistant shrubs, and taking some trouble to get new plants established, it is possible to garden in even the most difficult spot. If the soil is not too impoverished, buddleja, *Lavatera olbia* 'Rosea' and hardy hibiscus will fare well, adding extra colour later in the season. And in poor dry soil in front of a wall, ceanothus or *Fremontodendron californicum* make good drought-resistant shrubs suitable for wall-training. Low spreading shrubs, such as cistus, senecio, santolina, *Genista lydia* and hebe, are ideal for covering dry banks or for the front of a border. Larger shrubs, including olearia, tamarix, *Romneya coulteri* with its huge white poppy flowers, Japanese bitter orange *(Poncirus trifoliata)* and brooms, including the Spanish broom *Spartium junceum*, make a taller back row for a border. It is always worth improving problem soil as much as possible, since this makes it possible to grow a much wider range of plants. By adding plenty of well-rotted organic matter and nutrients, plants such as hardy hibiscus, buddleja, clerodendron, helianthemum and others will all thrive in previously difficult places.

ABOVE: All the Californian lilacs *(Ceanothus)* thrive in a hot, sunny, sheltered spot. Most make large bushy plants, but 'Blue Cushion', shown here, makes a low mound.

ABOVE: The green, rush-like stems of *Spartium junceum* (Spanish broom) do the job of foliage in this virtually leafless plant, so the large yellow pea-flowers show up well against it.

Shrubs for hot sun

Salvia officinalis 'Tricolor'

Perovskia atriplicifolia 'Blue Spire'

Cistus

ABOVE: *Fremontodendron califomicum* is a large evergreen shrub for a mild region on dry neutral to chalky soil; it does well trained against a sunny wall. The bristly leaves may cause irritation.

ABOVE: *Hibiscus syriacus* 'Woodbridge'. Hardy hibiscus thrives in a warm, sunny, sheltered spot with well-drained soil. Wind can damage buds and blooms.

RIGHT: *Helianthemum* (rock rose), such as this 'Rosa Königin', makes good summer-flowering ground cover for a hot sunny spot. It pays to improve the soil before planting.

BELOW: Tamarix is an exceptionally wind-tolerant large shrub, suitable for seaside situations and exposed hot dry beds. *Tamarix tetrandra* (seen here) flowers in mid spring.

Coping with poor soil

First improve the soil by digging in as much well-rotted organic matter (such as garden compost or animal manure) as possible. On sandy or gravely soils this quickly breaks down and disappears, but it will last long enough to help hold water while new plants get established. You can assist poor dry soils further by digging in water-retaining gel crystals, which last virtually forever. A 2.5–5cm (1–2in) layer of gravel, granite chippings or even cobblestones works as a good mulch on these soils (water condenses underneath the stones overnight, thus helping plants survive), and only needs topping up every few years. The secret of planting in these conditions is to plant in autumn, when the soil is moist and winter rains will help new plants to become established. Water plants in dry spells the following summer. If planting in spring is inevitable, you must water new plants regularly throughout their first season. Avoid planting in summer entirely.

RIGHT: *Genista lydia*, a small ground-hugging broom, flowers in mid to late spring. Its slightly cascading habit makes it ideal for a raised bed or bank.

Vesatile hebes

Hebes are small, bushy summer-flowering evergreen shrubs with characteristic bottlebrush-like flowers. They thrive in a sunny, sheltered spot in light, free-draining soil, flowering from early to late summer. Some are beautifully scented.

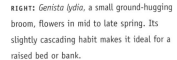

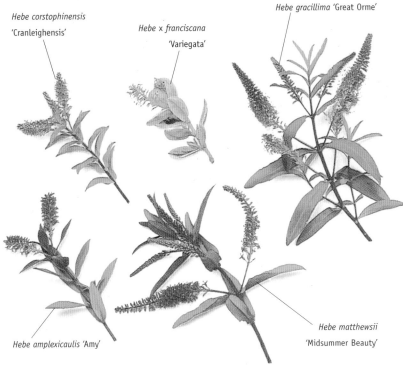

Hebe corstophinensis 'Cranleighensis'

Hebe x *franciscana* 'Variegata'

Hebe gracillima 'Great Orme'

Hebe amplexicaulis 'Amy'

Hebe matthewsii 'Midsummer Beauty'

PLANTING FOR SHADE

BELOW: *Among other good shade-loving plants, grouped here around the bole of a tree in the corner of a garden, are ligularias. Two forms, L. dentata 'Desdemona' and L. tangutica 'The Rocket', both have handsome large leaves and striking golden or orange flowers in summer.*

ALTHOUGH THERE are only a very few plants that will cope with deep shade – most notably ivies – most gardens have at least some light, and there is a much wider variety that will cope with these partially shaded conditions. Some prefer the shade to be dry and others cope better in damp soil, but provided you take the time and trouble to find out which plants will thrive, you can create wonderful gardens in relatively inauspicious conditions.

If you want privacy in your garden, and plant trees or large shrubs to provide it, the areas beneath their canopy are already ear-marked for shade-loving small shrubs and

Small Plants for Shade

Alchemilla mollis

Corydalis lutea

Epimedium grandiflorum

Geranium macrorrhizum

G. phaeum

Hedera helix (climber)

Hepatica

Impatiens New Guinea hybrids

Pulmonaria longiifolia

Symphytum ibericum

perennials. Indeed, it is well worth your while, even in a tiny garden, having at least one large shrub or small tree, just so that you can vary the habitat provided, and increase the range of plants you can grow.

In a small garden, you are unlikely to get too much damp shade, unless you live in a part of the country with very high rainfall. The shade cast by buildings in cities, let alone any trees, is more than likely to create

RIGHT: *Hostas, ferns, bamboos and ornamental maples are all good subjects for partially shaded patio gardens, seen here attractively interplanted among large York stone slabs and gravel in an Oriental-style garden setting.*

dry soil conditions as well, so it is these drier shady conditions that you will, in the main, have to contend with. Bear in mind that the area under the canopy of a tree receives relatively little rain, so this shade will be drier than most.

Fortunately, there are some very attractive plants at your disposal, although you may need to rethink some of your gardening concepts. Brightly coloured displays of hot coloured annuals will not be for you. In their place, you can grow some singularly beautiful foliage plants and a few flowering ones that cope with these conditions,

Medium Plants for Shade

Acanthus mollis

Aconitum (poisonous)

Asplenium scolopendrium

Digitalis purpurea

Dryopteris filix-mas

Euphorbia

Helleborus argutifolius

Hemerocallis

Polypodium vulgare

Polystichum setiferum

Rodgersia

Trachystemon orientalis

although their flowers tend to be in paler shades – whites and pale blues predominating. A green and white garden – the result of this kind of planting – looks extremely good in most gardens, and is very restful and relaxing to the eye. Once you have got used to the concept, you will find your eye is more attuned to noticing shape, form and texture – all virtues of shade-loving plants.

Some of the plants that do well in this kind of situation have already cropped up in other parts of this book, most notably as architectural focal point contenders, since many of them have handsome form and attractive foliage. The ubiquitous hosta is

probably the king of all shade-loving plants and should definitely be a major player in any shade planting scheme. Other larger shade-loving plants you could try include *Acanthus mollis*, big-leaved bergenias, foxgloves (*Digitalis*), hellebores, and Solomon's seal (*Polygonatum*).

Low-growing plants for shade include the bugles (*Ajuga*), little anemones and cyclamens, the deadnettles (*Lamium maculatum*), and the rather invasive evergreen *Vinca minor*, which has pretty blue flowers. Other good candidates are epimediums, with little heart-shaped leaves, and *Tiarella cordifolia*, with its spires of white flowers.

BELOW: *Ligularia in its summer guise flanks the steps in a shady corner. It looks best planted in containers, or in large drifts, as here. It needs damp soil if it is to do well, but looks equally good in a container, provided you keep it well watered.*

Shrubs for Shade

Aucuba japonica

Choisya ternata

Elaeagnus pungens

Fatshedera x lizei

Fatsia japonica

Hydrangea quercifolia

Ligustrum japonicum

Mahonia x media 'Charity'

Rhododendron

Skimmia japonica

Taxus baccata

plants for shady walls

To clothe shady walls, ivies are the obvious choice, although the yellow-splashed or silver-variegated types will revert to all-green leaf colouring if deprived of sunlight. Other good candidates are creepers and vines; *Clematis montana* and *C. alpina* will both cope with a north-facing, shady wall. *Euonymus fortunei* can be grown as a wall shrub against a shady wall, as can *Garrya elliptica*. *Cotoneaster horizontalis*, *Crinodendron hookerianum*, *Humulus lupulus* 'Aureus' and *Lathyrus latifolius*, the everlasting pea, will all cope with partial shade, and *Passiflora*

RIGHT: *Some of the more exotic plants, among them tree ferns and daturas, will cope well in semi-shaded conditions in mild climates, as this little group demonstrates. When grouping together plants in containers, try to get a good mixture of foliage types and sizes, to give variety to the planting when the flowers are no longer in season.*

caerulea, normally supposed to like sun, can also do quite well in an alleyway, although it will not grow as large or flower as freely here as in full sun.

At the foot of the wall, the shadiest part, ferns are ideal candidates, and look particularly good when planted in a ribbon formation alongside the wall. *Helleborus argutifolius,* the big evergreen hellebore with green flowers, copes well with partial shade, as do several of the euphorbias. Another good bet for this kind of situation is the big *Geranium phaeum,* a large evergreen with handsomely divided leaves.

woodland plants

For a more woodland-style shade garden, consider growing some of the plants that do well in these conditions. Pulmonarias are among the most appealing shade-loving plants, and their attractively mottled leaves and pinkish-purple bell-like flowers look particularly good when they are planted in large drifts. The hardy cyclamens, again with pretty white-splashed leaves, are another good candidate for shade under trees, as are the sweet-scented lily-of-the-valley. In the right conditions, both will rapidly spread to provide excellent ground cover.

There are a number of clump-forming plants that do well in shade, including the attractive bronze-leaved hepatica with spires of blue flowers, and Japanese anemones, with white or pink flowers. The feathery-leaved corydalis is another good plant for dry shade.

It is always worth growing a few bulbs in a semi-woodland area; snowdrops and winter aconites in particular, thrive in partially shaded conditions. Both will do well in grass around the bole of a tree. Some species of narcissus, which are more delicate than the big blowsy daffodils, will also do well in light shade, and, of course, bluebells thrive in peaty soil and partial shade. A good combination would be a couple of big evergreen *Helleborus argutifolius* underplanted with bluebells

Ground Cover for Shade

Ajuga reptans (z3–9)

Bergenia cordifolia (z3–8)

Epimedium (z5–9)

Ferns (zones vary)

Euonymus (zones vary)

Hedera helix (z5–10)

Lamium maculatum (z4–8)

Pachysandra terminalis (z4–8)

Soleirolia (z10–11)

Tellima grandiflora (z4–8)

Tiarella cordifolia (z5–9)

Tolmeia menziesii (z6–9)

Vinca minor (z4–9)

PLANTS FOR CONTAINERS

CONTAINERS ARE A MUST for most small gardens. Not only do they allow you to grow plants in inhospitable places, including high-rise roof gardens and balconies, but they also give you a great deal of flexibility, as you can move them about. This is imperative in a small space, where you need to get the most from your plants – moving a container into pride of place as the plants within it come into flower is an essential aspect of small gardening.

The choice of plants for containers is vast, and you need to get away from the traditional container plants concept, which tends to focus too much on hanging baskets and floral displays and too little on handsome architectural foliage plants, which have a very strong role to play in the smaller garden.

foliage plants

One of the greatest contenders for a container is the hosta (or plantain lily as it used to be commonly known). There are many different forms, but one of the large varieties, with huge, thickly ribbed bluish-green waxy leaves, makes a

Foliage Plants

Acer palmatum dissectum

Brassica oleracea 'Sekito'

Buxus sempervirens

Chamaecyparis nootkatensis 'Pendula'

Clivia miniata

Corydalis lutea

Dicksonia antarctica

Ensete ventricosum

Euphorbia characias wulfenii

Hedera helix

Heuchera 'Palace Purple'

Hosta fortunei

H. sieboldiana

Juniperus scopulorum

Milium effusum

Myrtus communis

Zantedeschia aethiopica

LEFT: *Foliage plants can create as much impact in containers as flowering plants. Here the contrasting forms of hostas with their broadly ribbed leaves, and ground elder, in a pretty variegated form, make an attractive display by a doorway. Make sure that any foliage plants are in attractive terracotta or ceramic pots.*

RIGHT: *A little stepped area provides a home for a number of herbs, among them a bay (*Laurus nobilis*) trained as a standard, lavender, viola and roses. Containers are invaluable for adding interest at different heights, and can be moved around as the plants come in and out of flower.*

wonderful rosette shape in a container – a very handsome sight even when out of flower. In flower it produces a tall, white spire of lily-like blooms. Hostas planted in beds are prey to slug damage, but planting them in containers helps to reduce this problem, particularly if you set the container on a bed of sharp grit. Several forms planted together make an excellent display from May until the leaves turn in autumn.

There are plenty of other foliage plants to choose from for containers. One worthwhile

---

Flowering Trees and Shrubs

Abutilon megapotamicum (wall shrub)

Actinidia kolomikta (climber)

Brugmansia x *candida*

Camellia japonica

Cobaea scandens (climber)

Fuchsia 'Leonora'

F. 'Thalia'

Hibiscus rosa-sinensis

Hydrangea macrophylla

Magnolia stellata

M. x *soulangeana*

Nerium oleander

Passiflora caerulea (climber)

Rhododendron yakushimanum

Rosa (climbers and shrubs)

---

solution is to pick a fairly small or slow-growing evergreen, plant it in the centre of the container, and change the planting around it from season to season. A clipped box ball in the centre of a medium-sized pot can play host to snowdrops or small white tulips in spring and glistening white osteospermums ('Whirlygig' is particularly striking) in summer, followed by button chrysanthemums or cyclamens in autumn. A few ivy plants to trail over the side helps to break the formality of the pot.

Even trees can be grown in large pots, and one of the best performers in this respect is the Japanese maple (*Acer palmatum*) with its delicate, hand-shaped filigree leaves. Some of them turn brilliant colours in autumn, and although expensive, are well worth including in a small garden. Be warned, however, that some

are sensitive to wind chill and may become scorched or even not survive in an exposed position unless given additional shelter.

flowering plants

In spring you can create massed displays of bulbs, ideally with some kind of orchestrated colour theme, be it a single colour or a twinned theme, such as yellow and blue, for example. If you plant a good number of tulips or hyacinths together in a pot, they look far more impressive than scattered among other bulbs.

In summer you can create a mini border effect by putting containers of larger annuals and perennials behind the smaller ones. Big tobacco plants, lilies, or alliums, with perhaps achillea or cosmos, could form the back row, while smaller plants – daisies, helianthemums,

BELOW: *The problem of displaying a lot of small containers can be solved by using vertical as well as horizontal space, as this neatly tiered stand, with its pots of matching pansies, demonstrates very effectively.*

pelargoniums and so on – form the front rank. Again, it helps to have some kind of colour scheme, but it could be either softly toning – blues, pinks, whites and silvers, perhaps – or a strong strident contrast of hot colours such as yellows, pinks and reds, for example, depending on the style of the garden and the situation, as well as your preference.

Flowering Bulbs, Annuals and Perennials

Agapanthus africanus

Allium christophii

Anemone x *hybrida*

Begonia

Brachycome iberidifolia

Canna indica

Chrysanthemum

Clivia miniata

Dahlia

Dicentra spectabilis

Helleborus

Impatiens

Lantana camara

Lewisia

Lilium 'Regale'

Lobelia

Muscari armeniacum

Narcissus

Osteospermum

Pelargonium (many forms)

Penstemon 'Andenken an Friedrich Hahn'

Petunia

Primula

Salvia sclarea turkestanica

Silene

Tulipa

Viola

If you want to grow larger climbers, you will need to ensure that they have a large enough pot in which to spread their roots, but most climbers can be successfully grown in a pot about 45cm (18in) in diameter. The plants will, of course, need to be watered regularly and fed during the growing season, as the container will limit their ability to take up food and water through the normal processes, and it will be up to you to supply it for them.

The ubiquitous pelargonium often forms the centrepiece of a flowering display in summer. There are many different forms to choose from, with attractively marked leaves as well as different shapes and colours of flower, and it is worth while going to a specialist pelargonium nursery to pick out some of the more interesting forms. Those such as the scented *P. graveolens*, with its deliciously fragrant pale green leaves and bushy habit, make excellent container plants and a good foil for some of the more brightly coloured flowering ones. They grow so easily, in the main, from cuttings that you can quickly increase your stock of them.

The new breeds of busy lizzie, the New Guinea hybrids, are also worth looking out for. Although more expensive than the usual types, their form, their leaf colour and shape, and their flowers are infinitely more striking. They do,

LEFT: *Here, too, vertical space has been well used for a mixed display of pink flowering plants in containers – asters, salvia, busy lizzies and ornamental cabbages among them. Keeping to a single or toning colour scheme will help increase the feeling of space.*

however, need copious and frequent watering, and, unlike pelargoniums, will wilt and die rapidly if neglected. However, they are an excellent choice for a shady alley, as they thrive happily even in partially shaded conditions.

wall pots and hanging baskets

If attractively planted, wall pots and hanging baskets can transform a high-walled patio or basement garden, and there is nothing to stop you using shade-loving plants, if the situation demands it. Ferns and ferny leaved plants, such as corydalis, work well in these kinds of settings. So do the delicate trailing plants like verbenas and diascia, wandering sailor (*Tradescantia*) and nasturtiums, although these all benefit from a sunnier situation. Pansies are good candidates for hanging baskets, as are begonias and lobelia, and of course trailing helichrysum and nepeta. You will get a more attractive effect if you limit the planting to three or four different plants in one container, and opt for a limited colour palette – a couple of toning colours – rather than the archetypal blaze of colour usually associated with hanging baskets.

1 *Stand the basket on a*
bucket for stability.
Place a layer of moist
sphagnum moss in the bottom
of the basket. Cut a circle
from an old potting compost
bag and place it black side
down in the base of the
basket. Fill the plastic circle
with potting compost. Even
when the top of the basket is
dry, the plant roots should
find moisture here.

2 *Using more thick*
clumps of moss, line
the basket sides. Tuck moss
under the edges of the
plastic as camouflage. Push
bedding violas horizontally
through the bars. Pack in as
many as will fit to create a
full display.

3 *Use more sphagnum*
moss to fill the gaps
between the plants, so that
the rootballs are protected
from drying out and to
prevent any soil escaping
when you water the basket.

4 *Add a group of*
cineraria, tilting one
down over the basket sides
to soften the edge. Pinch out
the tips to keep them
compact and bushy. Plant the
large sedum to one side, so
that the long trailing shoots
hang over the edge.

HANGING BASKETS

HANGING BASKETS can make an impact without being a blaze of colour. This basket contains an unusual mixture of plants in subtle shades of purple and silver-grey. The deep velvet-purple bedding viola 'Prince Henry' makes a superb contrast with the other flowers and foliage, while *Nemesia fruticans* produces airy flowers all summer long. In the top are the daisy-like flowers of *Osteospermum* 'Sunny Lady'. Like all osteospermums, the flowers close in shade, so hang the basket where it will receive sun for most of the day. The foliage ranges from the feathery leaves of *Lotus berthelotii* to the cut leaves of cineraria and the rounded, leathery, purple foliage of *Sedum* 'Bertram Anderson'.

To create a feeling of tranquillity in your garden, consider a combination of white flowers with grey, silver and green foliage. For any monochromatic scheme to be truly successful, it is vital to have plenty of textural contrast between different elements. Bear in mind that there is a noticeable variation in the colour of white flowers. Those in the basket are pure white, but the results would not have been so successful if it combined creamy whites and pure whites. Here, the large, solid flower heads of petunia are planted alongside the smaller-flowered busy lizzie, which is in turn set against white alyssum. Adding tiny amounts of an entirely different colour will often lift an all-white scheme and make the flowers stand out all the more.

5 *Plant nemesias to give height at the back. If the trailing lotus at the front produces*
orange-red flowers later on, remove them.

6 *Fill in the remaining space at the back of the basket with the osteospermum, and cover all the exposed rootballs with compost. Water the whole display thoroughly and add more soil if gaps appear.*

Allow plants to settle in well for several days by standing the basket in a shady, sheltered spot.

A classic white arrangement

1 *Having lined the basket as before, cover the sides with alyssum, feeding the rootballs horizontally through the wires.*

2 *Pack moss around the necks of the plants. Angle the busy lizzie so that it covers the rim of the basket.*

3 *Plant a pot of Lotus berthelotii to trail over the edge. Plant some petunias into the top and sides of the basket and add a trailing ivy. Squeeze a white-flowered pelargonium into the centre of the basket.*

7 *To aid moisture retention, add a thick layer of moist sphagnum moss over the compost in the top of the basket.*

Nemesia fruticans

Osteospermum 'Sunny lady'

Lotus berthelotii (coral gem)

Sedum 'Bertram Anderson'

Viola 'Prince Henry'

Senecio cinerarium

4 *Fill any gaps with compost and water well. Hang the basket where you can appreciate the scent of the sweet alyssum.*

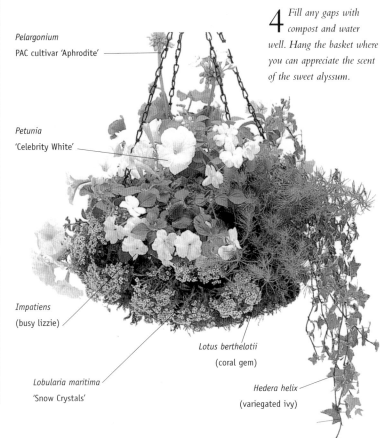

Pelargonium PAC cultivar 'Aphrodite'

Petunia 'Celebrity White'

Impatiens (busy lizzie)

Lobularia maritima 'Snow Crystals'

Lotus berthelotii (coral gem)

Hedera helix (variegated ivy)

BULBS IN CONTAINERS

WITH DAFFODILS, TULIPS AND HYACINTHS in containers, a patio can be a riot of colour from early spring onwards. Dry bulbs are on sale in garden centres in autumn; choose compact varieties. Buy daffodils as soon as they are available and plant them straight away, as they start rooting earlier than many spring bulbs. The bulbs should be plump and healthy, without cuts, bruises or mouldy bits; the biggest bulbs will bear the most flowers. You can plant containers entirely with one kind of bulb, but if you want to mix them, choose bulbs that flower at roughly the same time. When it comes to planting, normal peat- or soil-based potting compost is fine. After planting, stand the containers outdoors in a cool, shady spot protected from heavy rain. When the first shoots appear, move the containers to the patio. While the bulbs are flowering, feed them weekly with general-purpose liquid feed. When the flowers have faded, remove the bulbs from the pots and plant them in the garden. Buy new bulbs for the following year's container displays, as they will flower better than the old ones.

Potting hyacinths

1 Hall-fill 9cm (3½in) pots with potting compost. Gently press a single bulb into the centre of each pot.

2 Fill the pot to the rim, covering the bulb, then tap it down on a hard surface to consolidate the compost.

BELOW: As hyacinths come into flower, bring them inside or plunge them into containers.

3 Moisten the compost well, allowing the surplus water to drain away. Put the pot in a cool, dry and protected place.

1 If your container does not already have drainage holes, you should drill some. It is vital that containers that will be standing outdoors in winter can drain freely.

2 Place 2.5–5cm (1–2in) of coarse gravel over the base of the container to aid drainage. Bulbs can easily rot if the compost is too wet.

3 Add 2.5–5cm (1–2in) of potting compost. It may not be possible to plant bulbs in pots with twice their own depth of compost above them.

4 Press each daffodil bulb into the compost, giving it a half turn so the base makes good contact with the compost. Bulbs should not touch each other or the tub.

5 *Cover the bulbs with enough compost to leave the tips on show so you can see where they are when you plant the next layer of bulbs on top.*

6 *Gently press in Anemone blanda corms between the tips of the lower layer of bulbs. Cover these corms with more potting compost.*

Planting tulips in a container

Tulips need well-drained soil and a warm sheltered spot. If these do not prevail in your garden, try growing them in containers so you can provide these conditions.

1 *Remove the dead, brown, outer skins from the bulbs. This helps them to root well and removes any disease spores.*

2 *Put a layer of coarse gravel and then compost in the trough. Press the tulip bulbs lightly down into the compost in groups of five.*

7 *Dot another layer of Anemone blanda over the surface, about 2.5cm (1in) above the last. Fill the tub to the rim with compost.*

8 *Leave the compost roughly level on top. Take care not to knock over the bulbs as you fill the tub, as they are still quite unstable.*

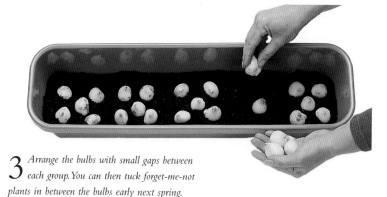

3 *Arrange the bulbs with small gaps between each group. You can then tuck forget-me-not plants in between the bulbs early next spring.*

RIGHT: Daffodils will do best in the sun, but they tolerate light shade. *Anemone blanda* grows to 15cm (6in). Blue is popular, but mixed colours are usually available.

BELOW: This cross-section shows the layers of bulbs, with 'Golden Harvest' daffodils below and *A. blanda* 'Blue Shade' above.

4 *Cover the bulbs with compost. Fill the container with more mixture to within 1cm (½in) of the rim.*

BELOW: These bulbs have been cleaned of their dead, outer skins. The planting depth shown is fine for this trough. They are bulbs of 'Spryng' (shown right).

1 *Gather the stems loosely and fit the frame over the top. With all the stems inside, press the cone gently into the compost until it is stable.*

2 *Tuck any stray shoots behind the wires. This thickens up the shape and ensures that protruding stems will not be snipped off.*

SPEEDY TOPIARY

CLASSIC TOPIARY SHAPES include domes, pillars and spirals, right through to more fanciful shapes, such as peacocks and teapots. On a smaller scale, any of the free-standing forms and many other currently fashionable shapes such as teddy bears, are suitable for growing in pots. Topiary specimens are traditionally created from box, yew and bay, which are ideal due to their evergreen foliage, dense bushy nature, slow growth and ability to withstand tight clipping. For quicker results, try euonymus and lonicera. The foundation of most shapes is a frame to which the plant's main stems are secured. Frames can be made of wire, wire netting or timber and can be bought preformed or you can make your own, which allows you to create more individual designs. Where a chunky pillar is topped by a crown or peacock, only the decorative device on top needs a frame-work. This is held up by a post driven into the pot through the foliage, which hides it from view.

3 *Working all round the plant, secure strong upright stems to the frame with ties. This makes the shape more solid right away.*

4 *Snip off any protruding straggly shoots. Remove the very tips of thin straight shoots to encourage them to branch out and become bushy.*

Tuck long new shoots up inside the frame to fill out the shape.

5 *As the shape of the cone emerges, work your way round the plant, lightly 'tipping'. Cut close to the framework at this stage.*

6 *When the horizontal side shoots start to make the outline look rather shaggy, the plant is ready for its final shaping.*

7 *Tie a string to the base of the frame. Sweeping the stems up with one hand, bind them in place with the other to fill out the shape.*

8 *At the top, tie the string firmly to the frame. Snip off any protruding stems, leaving the cone with a neatly pointed tip.*

9 *Sheep shears are used with one hand. They are ideal for trimming off any stems that stick out from the sides of the cone, leaving the sides tidy.*

10 *The finished cone has taken less than three months to complete. The same feature made in box or bay would take over a year.*

11 *Lonicera nitida is very fast growing. Trim as necessary during the growing season to keep the shape neat and to encourage it to thicken out.*

12 *Using sheep shears, clip to about 2.5cm (1in) beyond the frame. Start at the base of the topiary, using the top of the pot as a guide, and work your way up.*

Topiary in context

TOPIARY TREES suit a huge range of situations. They originated in formal gardens, and on a small scale, geometric spheres or spirals are a good way to end a row of dwarf box edging to a herb garden or formal flower bed. Potted topiary peacocks look good standing next to a doorway, and a row of different potted topiary shapes looks very decorative along the top of a wall or up a flight of steps in a country garden.

RIGHT: A pyramid is one of the easiest topiary shapes to create and maintain. If wide enough at the base, you may not need a frame for a small pyramid.

13 *Use the frame as a guide when clipping the sides, but keep standing back to check that they slope by the same amount and that the outline is symmetrical. Leave the top until last; trim it to a sharp point.*

SHAPING IVY AND BOX

TRADITIONAL TOPIARY takes years to perfect, but for quicker results try instant topiary, made by training ivy round a light framework of wire or willow. Preformed wire topiary frames – usually two-dimensional animal shapes – are sold in garden centres or you can create your own hoops and spirals by bending stiff fencing wire into shape. Make more complicated shapes, such as teddy bears, from wire netting. Plant several climbers in a large tub all round the shape and peg out the stems to ensure complete coverage. Ivy is the usual subject for instant topiary; small-leaved forms are best for modest-sized topiaries; experiment with the many variegated or gold forms, and also the arrow-head shaped *Hedera helix* 'Saggitifolia'.

For even greater variety, try other evergreen climbers: *Euonymous fortunei* varieties such as 'Blondy' or 'Emerald 'n' Gold' can be trained in this way although they are not normally regarded as climbers. For a bigger topiary, use large climbers, such as *Jasminium nudiflorum*. Grow it on the same frame as a strong-growing ivy for an interesting effect, or choose the variegated evergreen honeysuckle, *Lonicera japonica* 'Aureoreticulata'. For a scented topiary, grow *Trachelospermum jasminoides* or *T.j.* 'Variegatum', both of which have fragrant white flowers in summer, as well as evergreen foliage. Do not overlook plants that need greenhouse protection in winter, such as passion flower, plumbago and bougainvillea, all of which make good flowering topiary for summer patios.

1 Push a spiral training frame into a large pot, plant two climbing ivies and twist the stems up round the frame. You can sometimes buy ivy 'topiary' at this stage.

2 By the time the ivies reach the top, side shoots lower down start to make the shape 'fuzzy'. The topiary will need trimming three to four times a year to keep it neat.

3 Twist in all the overhanging stems around the base. Avoid cutting them off while the topiary is young, as they help to thicken the shape. Tie in place if necessary.

4 Working up, twist wayward stems firmly round the frame to keep the shape well defined. Use long new shoots to 'bind' the existing stems close to the framework.

5 Hold stems in place with plant ties – as many as you need to achieve a tight shape. Do not worry about the appearance; plant ties soon disappear under the foliage.

6 At the apex, twist the top stems together before winding them round the tip of the spiral. This creates a neater finish with more leaves and fewer visible stems.

7 *Secure the top of the ivy firmly in place. This is very important, because if it comes adrift, the rest of the plant will slacken on the frame and the topiary will 'relax' out of shape.*

8 *About 20 minutes of work restores the shape to mint condition. Repeat the process at the start of the growing season (late spring) and thereafter at regular intervals two or three times every summer.*

Planting a narrow-necked jar

LEFT: To avoid having to fill the whole jar with compost, wedge a hanging basket into the neck. Plant it with ivies and simply lodge it in place.

RIGHT: Some containers have a strong character of their own. Here, evergreen trailers, such as ivy, accentuate the shape of the jar without competing with it for attention.

Growing a box ball

BOX IS A very popular and easily managed topiary subject. Use *Buxus sempervirens*, not the miniature cultivar 'Suffruticosa'. Take cuttings from established plants in the late spring and summer.

1 *Start with a strong, rooted box cutting. Nip off the growing tips of the shoots using forefinger and thumbnail. Repeat when the side shoots are about 2.5cm (1in) long.*

2 *Use secateurs to nip back the tips of the next crop of side shoots. Each time new growth reaches 5cm (2in) long, shorten it. Pruning encourages bushiness.*

3 *As the first pot fills with roots, move the plant into a larger pot with fresh potting mixture. Clip the plant regularly using small shears instead of secateurs.*

4 *When it reaches the required size, clip back to the previous outline each time. By then, clipping three or four times each year should be enough.*

5 *It is possible to create a good box ball about 23cm (9in) across by this method in three years. Clip it two or three times a year to retain the shape and size.*

MOISTURE-LOVING PLANTS

SOME PLANTS THRIVE in deep water, some in shallow water and some simply in moist soil. If you have a small garden, you can, without too much difficulty, make a small pond or water feature, which will have the double bonus not only of creating additional visual interest, but also of increasing your choice of plants to grow. If you make the pond using a butyl liner, you could also create a bog garden alongside it. This will add an even greater variety to your plant list, and will make the pond look infinitely more natural, as in the wild, ponds are sited in marshy soil and their surrounds are populated with moisture-loving plants. (The single greatest but most commonly made mistake in water gardening is to site the pond in a desert-like area of the garden – the two simply do not work together and will never look right.)

bog and marginal plants

If you want to dispense with a pond and just opt for a bog garden, there is still a wide range of plants that like wet conditions that you can grow. The big handsome ornamental rhubarb, *Rheum palmatum,* is happy with its feet in damp soil, provided it is fed well. Ligularias and rodgersias will thrive, as will some of the hostas and the big semi-evergreen geranium, *Geranium palmatum.* Also happy in these conditions are feathery looking astilbes, the sinister (and poisonous) monkshood, *Aconitum,* and striking drumstick primulas, with their raised heads of brightly coloured flowers. These latter look best planted in quite large drifts, rather than scattered among other plants.

Grasses look particularly good and some favour damp conditions and so are ideally suited to the bog garden. Among the best are *Miscanthus sinensis* 'Zebrinus', with gold-striped leaves, and *Carex alata* 'Aurea', which also has golden foliage.

LEFT: *Among the most beautiful water-loving plants is* Iris laevigata *which comes in both purple and yellow forms. This one is I. l. 'Atropurpurea'. Moisture-loving plants tend to grow generously, in large clumps, and it is important that poolside planting echoes this feature.*

ABOVE: *For poolside plantings, in damp ground, the arum lily* (Zantedeschia aethiopica) *with its handsome white flower spathes and large green leaves, and hostas (with their thickly ribbed leaves, in the foreground) are ideal companions. For colour in this situation, candlestick primulas, in big drifts, are ideal.*

Reeds, Rushes and Grasses

Acorus calamus 'Variegatus'

Arundo donax

Carex alata 'Aurea'

Cyperus alternifolius

Miscanthus sinensis 'Zebrinus'

Phalaris arundinacea

Scirpus tabernaemontani 'Zebrinus'

Moisture-lovers

Artemisia lactiflora

Astilbe x *arendsii*

Astilboides tabularis

Eupatorium purpureum

Filipendula palmata

Hosta fortunei

H. sieboldiana

Iris ensata

I. laevigata

I. sibirica

Lysimachia nummularia

Lythrum salicaria

Persicaria bistorta 'Superba'

Primula florindae

P. japonica

Rheum palmatum

Trollius europaeus

For growing in shallow water, again some irises are ideal, in particular the Japanese irises, such as *Iris ensata* or *I. laevigata*. These have not only particularly pretty flowers, in delicate shades of blue, mauve, white or yellow, but also handsome evergreen sword-shaped leaves. Equally good for shallow water are marsh marigolds *(Caltha palustris)* and the pickerel weed, with its glossy dark green leaves and spikes of bright blue flowers.

floating plants

If your pond is at least lm (3ft) deep, you can grow singularly beautiful water lilies, which come in a range of colours. The smallest is *Nymphae tetragona* (the dwarf water lily), which is suitable for most small garden ponds with a depth of up to 30cm (12in). It comes in several colours, but the common white form is one of

the most attractive. Another good deep-water pond plant is the water hawthorn *(Aponogeton distachyos)*, which will cope with a shadier site than will the water lily. Its leaves, which are elongated and rather elegant, float in the same manner as those of a water lily, and it has waxy spires of flowers that lie horizontally above the surface of the water for a long flowering season.

oxygenating plants

If you aim to keep fish in your pond, you will need to have oxygenating plants (which will also benefit any pond, as they help to keep the water fresh). There is a wide range to choose from, but some of the most commonly used are *Elodea canadensis* (Canadian pondweed) and *Potamogeton crispus* (curled pondweed). The water violet, *Hottonia palustris,* is one of the prettiest oxygenating plants, with ferny leaves and pale mauve flowers that rise above the water.

Floating and Oxygenating Plants

Aponogeton distachyos

Eichhornia crassipes

Elodea canadensis

Hottonia palustris

Hydrocharis morsus-ranae

Nuphar lutea

Nymphaea alba

N. 'Escarboule'

N. tetragona

Orontium aquaticum

Potamogeton crispus

Ranunculus aquatilis

Trapa natans

1 *Line the tub with butyl pond liner. Drape the material loosely inside and arrange the slack in folds. Put 2.5–5cm (1–2in) of well-washed gravel into the bottom of the tub to bed the marginal plants into later.*

A BARREL WATER FEATURE

MARGINAL POND PLANTS make fascinating container subjects. Any container that holds water is suitable, but a wide half barrel is best as it has a large water surface that makes the most of the plants' reflections – one of their best assets. Marginal plants are the sort that can be grown in up to 30cm (12in) of water (measured over the top of the pot). This includes all the popular water irises, marsh marigolds and rushes, as well as many of the plants commonly grown as bog garden plants, such as zantedeschia. Avoid plants that merely grow in damp soil; although they are sometimes sold mistakenly as marginal plants, subjects such as hosta and astilbe do not enjoy standing in water above their necks and do not last long under these conditions. Marginal plants are often imposing specimens that grow quickly; to keep them at a suitable size for a half barrel, lift them out and divide them every spring, just as they are starting into growth. Once planted up, keep the barrel topped up with water. Remember that in hot weather it can lose 2.5cm (1in) of water each week due to evaporation.

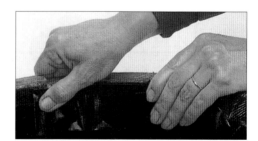

2 *Half-fill with water to weight the liner down into the bottom of the container. Rearrange the folds so that surplus material is evenly distributed around the edge.*

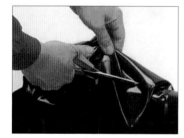

3 *Trim away the excess pond liner, leaving enough spare to allow for turning over the edge. Make small tucks to even out large folds in the material around the rim of the barrel.*

4 *Turn the liner edges under, smoothing out tucks in the material to flatten them down as you work. Use waterproof tape, ideally black, to secure the liner firmly inside the rim of the container.*

5 *Begin adding plants; choose a mixture of striking flowering and foliage marginal plants that contrast well in shape. Leave them in the net-sided pond pots that they are growing in when you buy them.*

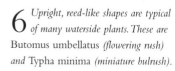

6 *Upright, reed-like shapes are typical of many waterside plants. These are Butomus umbellatus (flowering rush) and Typha minima (miniature bulrush).*

7 *Pickerel weed has striking heart-shaped leaves and blue flowers from early summer to early autumn. It works well with the tall leaves of the other plants.*

8 *Three plants are enough, as they will make quite a bit of new growth over the summer. Top up with water to the rim of the container and check that the tape holds the edge of the liner firmly.*

9 *Finally, float a handful of azolla over the surface. In full sun, this lacy-leaved plant turns bright red. Alternatively, use other floating plants, such as water lettuce or water hyacinth.*

Repotting water plants

Marginals, bog garden and water plants are sometimes sold in pots that are far too small. Often they are a good buy as they are priced according to the size of the pot, not the size of the plant. Simply move them to a bigger pot when you get them home. When your own plants outgrow their containers after a year or two, repot them in spring.

1 *If a plant is too potbound to knock out of its pot in the usual manner, cut away the pot, taking great care not to cut through the roots. Peel away the remains of the pot and discard it.*

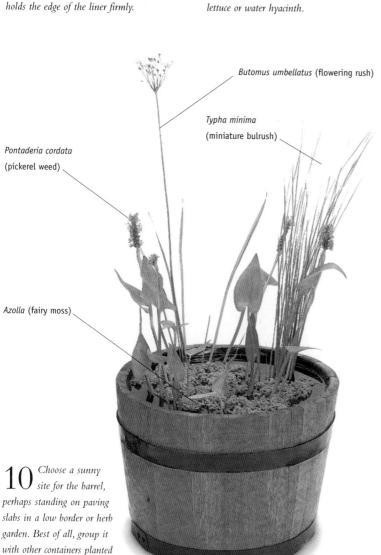

Butomus umbellatus (flowering rush)

Typha minima (miniature bulrush)

Pontaderia cordata (pickerel weed)

Azolla (fairy moss)

10 *Choose a sunny site for the barrel, perhaps standing on paving slabs in a low border or herb garden. Best of all, group it with other containers planted with a watery theme in a patio or courtyard.*

2 *Put 2.5cm (1in) of pond plant compost or garden soil with no added fertilizer into the bottom of a net-sided pot. Sit the plant in the centre of the pot.*

3 *Pot it firmly, using more of the same mix to fill round the roots. If you find the compost trickles out through the holes in the pot, line the pot with hessian.*

4 *Tap the pot to consolidate the compost and then cover the surface with 2.5cm (1in) of well-washed gravel. This weighs down the soil, preventing it from floating away when the pot is put into the water.*

A BOG GARDEN IN A TUB

BOG GARDEN PLANTS make ideal subjects for containers. This is a good way of growing them if you garden on dry soil, where they would not be happy in the open ground. It is perfect for a small garden, since many bog garden plants are large and invasive, spreading rapidly given a free root-run, so that they soon become a nuisance. Use a watertight container; if yours has drainage holes in the bottom or leaks, simply line it with butyl rubber pond liner or heavy duty black plastic before filling and planting. Since the soil will be kept permanently damp, this type of container suits all sorts of bog garden plants, including houttuynia and *Lobelia cardinalis*, as well as border plants that enjoy moist to boggy conditions, such as hostas, lythrum and astilbe. Since space is limited, restrict yourself to plants with a long summer flowering season and those with good architectural foliage. Those that have both, such as zantedeschia, are doubly valuable. Bog garden plants are often sold growing in special net-sided pond pots. They are best left in their pots; the roots are intended to grow out through the sides so that you can lift them out later if they grow too big and you want to replace them. Otherwise, the whole container becomes over-run with roots, and you have to empty the whole tub and replant it all at once.

1 *Line a large half barrel with butyl pond liner, loosely cut to shape, and put half a bucketful of washed gravel in the bottom.*

2 *Fill the container to just below the rim with pond plant compost or garden soil with a high clay content but no added fertilizer.*

3 *Place a tall plant at the back. This striking* Lobelia cardinalis *'Queen Victoria' produces spikes of red flowers in mid to late summer.*

4 *Choose plants that contrast well with each other. Use drooping or trailing plants round the sides and shorter plants towards the front to make the best possible display in a small space.*

Zantedeschia aethiopica (arum lily) grows 45cm (18in) high and makes a bold statement in the middle of the display.

5 *Add a trailing plant at the front; this is a golden-leaved form of creeping Jenny,* Lysimachia nummularia *'Aurea'. Top up the soil level to within 2.5cm (1in) of the rim. Add at least a full watering can of water, leaving the soil boggy.*

6 *Leave the barrel for about 30 minutes and then water it again if the soil has absorbed so much moisture that the surface is no longer boggy. Level it roughly and then scatter 2.5cm (1in) of washed gravel over the surface of the soil.*

7 Decorate the surface with a small cluster of attractively coloured, smooth rounded pebbles. When watering in future, trickle water over the pebbles to avoid soil splashing up on to the gravel or plants.

8 Now that the weight of the soil and water have pulled the liner down into the barrel, neatly trim the excess butyl liner with sharp scissors. Roll the edges over and tuck them out of sight below the gravel.

9 These plants will thrive in a sunny spot on a patio or by a pond and look good all summer. They die down in winter but come up again the following year.

Lobelia cardinalis 'Queen Victoria'

Zantedeschia aethiopica

Houttuynia cordata 'Variegata'

Lobelia syphylitica

Milium effusum 'Aureum' (Bowles' golden grass)

Caltha palustris alba

Lysimachia nummularia 'Aurea'

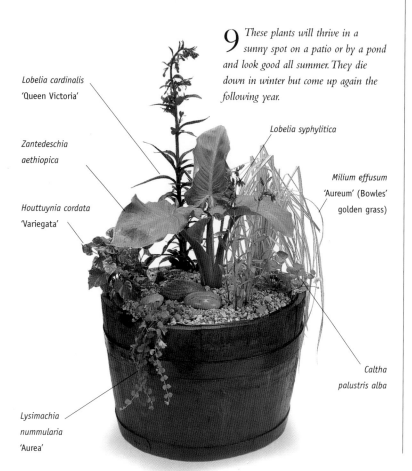

Creating a bog garden feature

Excavate an informally shaped depression, about 30cm (12in) deep, and lay a sheet of thick black plastic over the depression, holding it in place with stones. Perforate the lowest part of the liner with a garden fork to allow surplus water to drain away.

Sink a perforated hosepipe through the gravel, leaving the unperforated end exposed for watering during dry spells.

1 Place a 2.5–5cm (1–2in) layer of gravel in the base to facilitate drainage. Bog garden soil needs to be moist but not totally under water. Fill the bog garden up with a mixture of border soil and organic matter, such as old grow-bag compost or garden compost.

2 Make a hole for each plant the same size as the pot in which it is growing. Remove the plants from their pots and group them together in small 'cameos'.

3 Choose plants with a wide range of shapes and a mix of flowers and foliage. Tuck smooth, rounded pebbles between the plants for colour and texture.

BELOW: After about three years, dig up the groups of plants and divide them in early spring.

PLANTS FOR SCENT

BELOW: *Among the best scented plants are roses, here surrounding a small seating area. Scented climbing roses, mingled with honeysuckles, are ideal candidates for this kind of setting.*

WITHOUT QUESTION, if there is one attribute that no garden should be without, it has to be scent. Although so subtle as to pass unremarked occasionally, scent adds a magic ingredient to any garden, and is particularly valuable in a small city garden as an antidote to the less attractive smells of pollutants of one sort or another.

Many plants are scented, and their fragrance is by no means restricted to the flowers. In some plants the leaves are deliciously scented or aromatic – sage (*Salvia*), thyme (*Thymus*) and mint (*Mentha*) among them. Herbs are among the best plants for scent and if you have a sunny corner of the garden, it is well worth growing a small selection (see pages 176–7 for details of making a small herb garden). Herbs are not only useful, but highly decorative too – good all-purpose plants for the small garden.

roses and other scented climbers

If you ask anyone to name any scented plants that they can think of, roses are going to come high on the list. Indeed, there are so many different forms of scented rose, all exquisite, that it is hard to know which to choose. It helps, therefore, to have some idea of the different kinds of rose. Entire books have been written on rose classification, but for the

LEFT: *Wisteria does need a firm hand to keep it under control and to encourage flowering. The aim is to train the stems horizontally and reduce the flowering spurs to two or three buds. This is best done in two hits: once in late summer and again in mid-winter.*

Scented Shrubs and Climbers

*Brugmansia (*syn *Datura)*

Buddleja davidii

Chimonanthus praecox

Daphne bholua, D. odora

Elaeagnus pungens

Hamamelis mollis

Jasminum officinale

Lavandula

Magnolia grandiflora

Myrtus communis

Philadelphus 'Beauclerk'

Rosa

Salvia

Santolina rosmarinifolia

Sarcococca

Syringa

Viburnum x *bodnantense* 'Dawn'

average novice gardener, it is sufficient to group them into climbers, bush roses and little patio roses, and to say that there are old roses, which have been grown for centuries, and more modern versions (of which the patio rose is one). The aim of modern breeding has been to get the best of all possible worlds – great scent, good looks, good habits – but despite all the efforts, some of the very old roses are still hard to beat. Everyone has particular favourites, but in a small garden, you cannot go too far wrong if you concentrate on climbing roses, as they will give you the maximum amount of flower power and take up the minimum amount of space – at a premium anyway in a small garden.

There are many different types of climber, including huge rambling roses, such as 'Rambling Rector', 'Kiftsgate' and 'Bobbie James', which will happily scale any tree or building, reaching up to about 10m (33ft) or more. There are also more ladylike climbers, which will adorn the front or back of your house. Do be aware, however, that roses need plenty of sunshine, and they also like deep clay soil with plenty of good organic matter added to it. Among the most popular climbers for walls are 'New Dawn' – a relatively new delicate pale pink rose, and 'Marigold' – a loose-petalled semi-double yellow rose which is very pretty – both of which are well scented. The white, pink-tinged 'Madame Alfred Carrière', with double flowers that are also richly fragrant, is also a good bet. In addition to the roses with scented flowers, there is also the incense rose, *Rosa primula*, which has wonderfully aromatic leaves, an unusual quality in a rose.

There are many other good scented climbing plants, not least among them the honeysuckles (although beware – not all species and varieties are scented). *Lonicera fragrantissima* is partially evergreen and has richly fragrant creamy white flowers in winter and early spring. *L. periclymenum* 'Serotina' is deciduous but is also highly scented. Jasmine has a very powerful scent; the summer-flowering, white-flowered *Jasminum officinale*, in particular, can literally fill the garden with heady scent.

BELOW: *Some magnolias are exquisitely perfumed as well as eye-catching, at a time of year when scent in the garden is in short supply. There is a wide range, of which the smaller forms, like* M. stellata *and* M. soulangeana, *are excellent for small gardens.*

scented shrubs and trees

It can be a great delight to have a winter-scented shrub in the garden. *Chimonanthus praecox,* or wintersweet as it is commonly known, has spicy scented flowers in pale yellow that appear on the bare branches in winter. *Hamamelis mollis,* the Chinese witch hazel, also has sweetly scented little yellow flowers on bare branches. *H. m.* 'Pallida' has dense clusters of paler yellow flowers flushed with red. Other good shrubs for winter scent are the pretty pinkish-mauve flowered daphnes, such as *Daphne bholua,* and Christmas box (*Sarcococca*), with its small shiny green leaves and little white highly scented flowers.

Other good scented shrubs, for other seasons of the year, are mock orange blossom (*Philadelphus*), which has clouds of highly fragrant white flowers; lilac (with white or mauve flowers, which are wonderful for cutting for the house); and the scented flowers of some of the viburnums, in particular *Viburnum* x *burkwoodii*. As a star performer in a small space, grow the little magnolia, *M. stellata*. It has singularly beautiful starry white flowers in spring that are also highly fragrant. 'Royal Star' has bigger white flowers, and 'Rosea', pink-flushed ones. If you have acid soil, you can grow some of the scented azaleas, among them the strongly fragrant *Rhododendron luteum*, which

LEFT: *The heady scent of lilies, in particular that of Regale lilies and these handsome pink-striped Stargazer forms, as well as that of tobacco plants (*Nicotiana*) can be almost overpowering on a warm summer's evening.*

Scented Annuals, Perennials and Bulbs

Convallaria majalis (spring)

Dianthus 'Mrs Sinkins' (summer)

Erysimum cheirii (spring)

Freesia (spring)

Hyacinthus (spring)

Iris unguicularis (autumn)

Lathyrus odoratus (summer)

Lilium 'Regale' (summer)

Malcolmia (summer)

Matthiola (summer)

Narcissus (spring)

Nicotiana (summer)

Pelargonium (some with scented leaves) (summer)

Primula (spring)

Thymus (scented leaves)

has rich yellow flowers in late spring and the added attraction of autumn-tinted leaves as well.

For trees, some forms of ornamental cherry are scented, among them the Japanese cherry, *Prunus* 'Amanogawa', which is ideal for small gardens, and has semi-double scented pink flowers. The bird cherry, *P. padua*, has almond-scented white flowers in spring, as do *P.* 'Shirotae' and *P. x yedoensis*.

other scented plants

There is also a wide range of scented perennials, bulbs and annuals to choose from. Among the most strongly scented are those in the carnation family, including pinks such as the old-fashioned 'Mrs Sinkins', stocks (*Matthiola*), tobacco plants (*Nicotiana*) and bulbs, such as narcissus and freesias. No small garden should be without a short row of wallflowers, as there

is nothing to beat their perfume on a sunny day in late spring before other bedding plants have come into flower. Sweet peas are also deliciously scented, and ideal for cutting for the house. Grow them up a wigwam to save space, choosing a mixture of old-fashioned shades. Make sure the ones you choose have been bred for scent. Lilies are also among the most scented flowers, with a particularly rich, heady fragrance.

EDIBLE PLANTS

BELOW: *Tomatoes are among the most practical edible plants to grow as they need relatively little space, but they must have a sunny corner and very generous supplies of water to thrive.*

ONE OF THE GREATEST joys for any gardener is the thrill of picking home-grown produce, and nothing tastes more delicious than even the most gnarled carrot, if you have lovingly grown it from seed yourself! There is, of course, nothing to stop you from turning your whole small plot into a kitchen garden, provided that it gets enough sun and, if you want to grow vegetables, that you are prepared to put a lot of effort into ensuring that the soil is sufficiently rich in nutrients to support a good crop. Alternatively, you could grow just a small amount of produce in a sunny corner of the garden or, if the fancy takes you, cottage-style among the ornamental flowering plants.

vegetables

The most important requirement for vegetables, apart from sunlight and water, is that the soil is rich in organic matter. One of the best ways of providing this is to make your own compost heap – an art in itself – from kitchen waste, plant clippings and so on (see page 188–9). Another point to remember if you are growing vegetables is that you need to rotate them according to type, ie root vegetables, brassicas and other crops, because if you grow the same crop in the same place year after year, diseases build up in the soil.

For a small garden, it is best to concentrate on plants that produce rewarding vegetables from a relatively small area of soil. Among the best are tomatoes, which can even be grown in special growing bags on a roof top or balcony; so too can lettuces and other small salad crops, such as radishes or spring onions. If you do not have much space, then look out for vegetables that offer particularly good flavour. Some of the more unusual tomatoes, or the little salad tomatoes, such as 'Gardener's Delight', are unfailingly good, taste delicious, crop heavily and are easy to grow. Other good salad vegetables are beetroots, corn salad (also called

LEFT: *Salad bowl lettuces, in red and green forms, can be used ornamentally as well as for their edible crop. They also make a pretty edging to a flower bed in summer. Curly parsley can also double as an attractive edging.*

BELOW: *This brightly coloured little herb garden has been formally designed, with lemon balm and calendula making the central feature, surrounded by thyme and chives.*

lambs' lettuce), rocket (with a delicious spicy flavour), different kinds of lettuce – such as the Italian coloured curly lettuces like Lollo Rosso, and dwarf cos lettuces – Welsh onions and peppery radishes.

To make an attractive feature, you could grow any of the above in a neat square, with a brick surround, and perhaps even border the vegetable plot with a small brick path. If you wish, you could put a gooseberry bush, trained as standard, or a wigwam of runner beans, as a central point and make the beds as the four quarters of the square.

You can also plant globe artichokes (*Cynara scolymus*) in the back of a flower border – their silvery leaves and handsome purple-tinged heads (which you can eat) make an architectural statement of their own. The variety 'Gros Vert de Lyon' is a good eating form. Courgettes can be grown up a fence or trellis if you wish, but they need a rich soil and plenty of sunshine, as well as regular watering.

culinary herbs

Whether or not you want to grow salad vegetables, it is well worth your while cultivating a few culinary herbs. Even if all the space you possess is a windowsill in front of the kitchen window, you can manage to raise a few herbs, provided it gets some sun.

Herbs are relatively easy to grow, and demand very little attention. Apart from in containers, the best position for them is by the kitchen door in a narrow border. Two or three plants of each kind will probably be more than enough. The following are among the best types to grow for culinary purposes:

BELOW: *A narrow section of the garden has been devoted to an attractively organized vegetable and herb garden, with soldierly rows of parsley and spring onions, backed by beans and artichokes.*

basil There are two different kinds, bush basil and sweet basil. Sow seed out of doors after the last frosts.

coriander Best grown in a border in drills about 30cm (12in) apart from seed sown in April, but the seed can be slow to germinate. You can use both the leaves of the plant, and the seeds, which will be ready in August.

dill This is pretty enough to be grown in the flower border. The seed should be sown in April in drills about 30cm (12in) apart and the plants thinned out to a distance of about 23cm (9in). You can use both leaves and seeds.

garlic If you enjoy garlic, it is not difficult to grow. Plant the cloves in autumn in a sheltered spot, at twice their own depth. They will be ready when the leaves start to fade. Store the bulbs hanging in bunches in cool, dry conditions.

marjoram There are several forms and it is most easily grown from rooted shoots from an existing plant. It is best to harvest the leaves before the plant flowers in July.

mint This can be grown easily from root cuttings. Mint prefers richer soil to most herbs, and will also grow better in partial shade. It is inclined to spread, so either plant in containers or insert slates around the mint bed to prevent the roots running.

LEFT: *Containers can provide a home for herbs, which are decorative as well as useful, as these terracotta pots of chives and purple-leaved sage (Salvia purpurascens 'Atropurpurea') demonstrate well.*

BELOW: *Walls and fences can be used as a support for fruit, such as the cultivated blackberry ('Loch Ness') here, or cordons of fruit, such as apples and pears. Remember that the latter will need careful pruning if they are to bear good crops of fruit.*

parsley You can grow parsley from seed, twice a year in spring and late summer, but it is notoriously slow to germinate. It makes a pretty edging to a border and can also be used in containers as an edging plant (it looks good planted with blue pansies). It does best in light sandy soil. You can overwinter parsley in a cold frame to ensure you have some all year round.

rosemary This is a pretty shrub, with bright blue flowers and small spiky aromatic leaves. It grows best in light soil in full sun. It grows easily and very well from cuttings.

sage There are many forms, some of which are simply flowering perennials, but the sage used for culinary purposes is the shrub *Salvia officinalis*. A purple-leaved form of this, 'Purpurascens', is particularly attractive. Grow it from cuttings in a sunny spot in light soil. You can harvest it for drying in midsummer, but even if you don't, prune it back in late summer to prevent the bush becoming straggly.

thyme This little bushy shrub comes in many forms, some of which are more pungently scented than others. They like a light, limey soil and are best grown from cuttings. Harvest the leaves for drying from early to late summer.

fruit

There is plenty of room, even in quite a small garden, for some of the modern varieties of fruit, such as the cordon-trained apples or one of the family trees, with several delicious varieties grafted on to one stem. Peaches and nectarines can be grown in fan formation on a sunny wall, raspberry and blackberry bushes can be grown against a fence, and gooseberries can be trained as standards to add ornament to the vegetable plot. Currant bushes are very prolific, and even just a couple will yield enough to make generous quantities of jam, for example. A fig tree, with its beautiful glossy grey-green hand-shaped leaves, can be grown in a large tub to make a handsome ornamental tree, which may just reward you with edible fruit if the climate is warm enough. Last, but by no means least, are grapes, which are well worth growing in any small garden. Provided you have a sunny aspect to the garden, a vine will reward you with beautiful foliage for a large part of the year, and the bonus of grapes (edible or for wine) in the autumn of most years.

1 Herbs need good drainage; on heavy soil spread 2.5–5cm (1–2in) of grit or gravel over the planting area and dig it in thoroughly. Remove weeds and debris and rake the soil level.

2 Shovel gravel on to the areas where the paving slabs are to go. Compact the soil down first by treading it well with your feet. Avoid walking on the areas that are to be planted.

3 Sit the paving slabs in place so that alternate slabs and soil make a pattern like the black and white squares on a chessboard. Wriggle the slabs down into their gravel bases as you lay them, so they are firmly bedded down and will not move later once you start walking on them.

A FORMAL HERB GARDEN

THIS CONTEMPORARY VERSION of a traditional geometric herb garden is more in keeping with the style of a modern home, and can be adapted for a space of any shape or size. It is based on the alternate black and white squares of a chessboard and could easily be created in a quiet corner of a patio by removing some of the slabs and improving the soil underneath. It also makes a good form of flooring for a small fragrant courtyard garden, but could also become an attractive herb feature in a family garden, especially if linked with a seat and taller potted herbs. The combination of herbs and paving is a particularly effective one, since the paving reflects heat and light, which provide ideal growing conditions for the plants. In this situation, herbs produce more concentrated essential oils, which in turn perfume the air when the plants are crushed if you step on odd sprigs overhanging the paving. The most suitable species to use are the more decorative but naturally compact bushy herbs that will not get overgrown quickly, such as purple sage, double-flowered Roman chamomile, purple basil, orange thyme, and pineapple mint. Choose a mixture of evergreen, flowering and coloured foliage plants for a herb garden that looks varied and interesting all the year round. To accentuate the chessboard idea, why not trim potted box plants into the shape of chessmen to stand on some of the paving slabs; if you are feeling ambitious you could even have a game!

6 Plant up the soil squares. This formal bed resembles a historic geometric herb garden, but on a scale in keeping with today's modern gardens.

4 Surround the feature with a line of contrasting bricks laid on their narrowest edge and sunk to about half their depth into the soil. This is enough to hold them firmly.

5 Tap down each brick as it is laid, using the handle of the trowel on a wooden batten. For the rest of the time the trowel is only used to take out the flat-bottomed 'bed' for each brick.

7 *Choose low spreading herbs for this style of bed, as they will billow out over the slabs, releasing their scents when they are crushed. Take the pots off before planting and avoid breaking up the rootballs.*

Maintaining a herb garden

A feature like this is very quick and easy to maintain as the gravel mulch helps to retain moisture. After the plants have been watered in they should not need much more water except in dry spells. If it is deep enough (at least 2.5cm (1in) and ideally 5cm (2in) thick) the mulch will also prevent weeds growing from any seeds that may be present in the soil. However, in time, new weed seeds will blow on to the surface of the mulch from other gardens, so to stop them spoiling the appearance of the bed, rake the gravel over briefly every week. This way, germinating weed seeds are disturbed before they can really take a hold, and any footprints or dead leaves and so on are removed so that the bed always looks neat and well cared for.

suitable plants

Most non-invasive Mediterranean-style herbs that like well-drained soil and sun will thrive in a bed like this. Choose the most decorative of the low-growing bushy kinds or creeping varieties. Good ones include purple sage, variegated sage, golden marjoram, or prostrate rosemary. Choose well-scented kinds and those with good flowers for the container in the middle; French lavender, a purple frilly-leaved variety of basil such as 'Fluffy Ruffles', pink lavender, gilded rosemary (silver- and gold-variegated varieties are both available), pineapple sage or a trimmed bay tree are ideal.

8 *A small sphere-trained box tree in each corner suits the formal style. This golden-variegated box is slower-growing than the green forms, but looks more distinctive.*

9 *Snip off the tips of any long shoots that spoil the outline. Side shoots will soon grow and thicken out the shape. Box balls may take a year or two to fill out.*

10 *Spread a 2.5–5cm (1–2in) layer of gravel over the surface as a mulch. These pink granite chippings set off the plants and tone in with the red brick surround.*

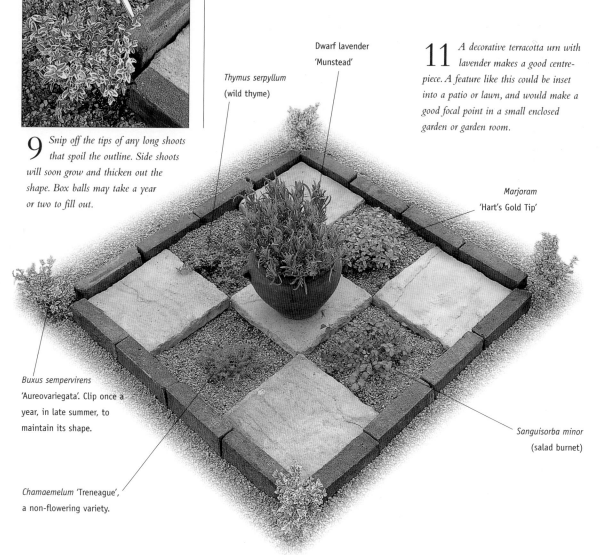

Thymus serpyllum (wild thyme)

Dwarf lavender 'Munstead'

11 *A decorative terracotta urn with lavender makes a good centre-piece. A feature like this could be inset into a patio or lawn, and would make a good focal point in a small enclosed garden or garden room.*

Marjoram 'Hart's Gold Tip'

Buxus sempervirens 'Aureovariegata'. Clip once a year, in late summer, to maintain its shape.

Chamaemelum 'Treneague', a non-flowering variety.

Sanguisorba minor (salad burnet)

SALAD CROPS ON A SMALL SCALE

1 Loosely fill a wooden planter (with drainage holes) with rich potting mixture. There is no need to add fertilizer. Choose plants with a floppy or low, semi-trailing habit for the edges and corners.

2 Place the plants as close to the edge as possible to make full use of the space. Turn plants so that their best sides face forward.

EVEN IF YOU DO NOT have space for a vegetable plot in your garden, you can fill a large container with salad plants and keep it by the back door where the crop will be convenient for picking. Nowadays, many kinds of edible leaves are popular as garnishes and ingredients for green salads; planted together, they make a decorative and useful container display. The best 'ingredients' for a container salad garden are those that can be picked little and often: sorrel, purslane, rocket, land cress, salad burnet and cut-and-come-again lettuce, such as 'Salad Bowl'. Planted in spring, the same plants can be picked over lightly for most of the summer. If the container is large enough, add a few hearting salads, such as Chinese cabbage, Cos and normal lettuce and radicchio-type chicory. Where available, choose miniature varieties, as they take up less room and are faster-maturing than full-sized varieties. As soon as a plant forms a heart big enough to use, cut it, remove any remaining foliage, pull the root out carefully and put in a new plant. This way you can obtain a regular succession of salads from a small space.

3 The low plants allow light to reach all parts of the container. Add an edible-flowered plant, such as nasturtium, in the centre, where it will make a focal point for the display.

4 French sorrel is a leaf salad, with large, lemon-flavoured leaves. This perennial plant can be cut little and often over several years, but it will die down in winter to reappear the following spring.

5 Chinese cabbages grow quickly and are safer from slugs and snails in a raised container, but make sure that the potting mixture does not dry out, otherwise they are likely to run to seed. Plants form chunky hearts.

6 *Put in all the remaining plants 15cm (6in) apart. Water well after planting, and check daily, as the compost will start drying out fast when the tub fills with roots, and in hot weather. Begin liquid feeding after four weeks.*

Radicchio 'Pallo Rossa Bello' – firm red hearts with white veins

Lettuce 'Blush' – a baby iceberg type

Chinese cabbage

Buckler-leaved sorrel (*Rumex scutatus*)

Purslane (*Portulaca oleracea*)

French sorrel (*Rumex acetosa*)

Rocket (*Eruca sativa*)

Salad burnet (*Sanguisorba minor*)

Nasturtium 'Alaska' has variegated foliage

7 *Although the tub will soon look crowded, plants around the edge will spread out over the sides, while plants such as sorrel and purslane will be picked regularly.*

Sowing lettuce seeds

Sow lettuce little and often in summer and early autumn. Raise young plants under glass and transplant for early crops. In summer, sow in situ and thin out. Lettuce seedlings do not transplant well in summer.

1 *Fill a suitable size pot with a good-quality seed-sowing or multi-purpose compost. Gently level out and firm the surface.*

2 *To aid seed germination, dampen the soil with a fine rose before sowing until water runs out of the holes in the base.*

3 *Sprinkle the seeds evenly and thinly over the surface of the soil. If you sow too thickly, the seedlings will be lanky and weak.*

4 *Cover the seeds with sifted potting mix. Firm the surface lightly to ensure that the seeds are in contact with the soil.*

5 *If you prefer to water after sowing, stand the pot in a bowl of water until moisture soaks up to the surface.*

6 *Cover with glass or plastic to keep moist. Label it and stand it in a warm, but not too sunny, spot.*

1 *A good way of preventing an opened grow-bag from spilling its compost is to cut off the end beyond the heat seal to form a plastic ring.*

2 *Slip the ring over one end of the unopened bag and move it into the centre. Do not be rough with the strap if it is not very wide.*

3 *Make a V-shaped cut at each end of the bag, with the point of the V towards the centre. Join the points of the two Vs with another straight cut running under the strap.*

4 *Fold under the edges of the single planting compartment and work the compost down the sides and into the corners of the bag.*

5 *Plant three tomato plants in each grow-bag if it is to stand in a greenhouse. If growing them outdoors, plant four single-stem or three bush plants in each bag.*

GROWING TOMATOES

ONE OF THE BEST WAYS of growing tomatoes, in a greenhouse and outdoors, is in a grow-bag – a long plastic bag filled with a specially formulated planting medium. Grow-bags are free of pests and diseases and the plastic isolates plant roots from any diseased soil. Tomatoes are susceptible to root diseases at the best of times and greenhouse plants are especially vulnerable. Both cordon (single-stem) and bush varieties grow well in bags. Generally speaking, grow one less plant of a bush variety than a cordon, because a bush type takes up more room. Follow the general rules for watering grow-bags; wait until the surface of the soil has dried out and then give at least 4.5 litres (1 gallon) of water at a time. Feeding is not necessary for the first few weeks, but once the first fruits are pea-sized, feed according to the instructions on the bag or the feed packaging. To allow sun and air to reach the bottom fruits, remove the leaves from the base of the plant up to the lowest truss that has fruit showing red. A container arrangement is another good way of growing a few tomatoes in a small garden. Compact, bushy varieties are ideal for hanging baskets, as they have a prostrate growth habit and you do need not remove their side shoots. For best results, use a large container (which holds more compost than a small one and takes longer to heat up or dry out) and insulate it with a thick liner. To keep moisture levels even, add water-retaining gel crystals to the compost mix and water up to twice daily in hot weather. A sunny spot and frequent feeding with a high-potash liquid tomato feed are essential for tomatoes. Leave the ripening tomatoes on the plants until they are completely ripe to develop their full flavour, but do not leave them until they become soft.

6 *Apply up to 6 litres (1½ gallons) of water at the first watering to rehydrate the compost. Delay the next few waterings until the compost dries out slightly, to avoid lush growth.*

When to plant out tomatoes

DO NOT PLANT OUT tomatoes until you see yellow petals in the bottom truss of flower buds. This takes about ten weeks from sowing seed.

BELOW: This tomato is ready to plant out. Turn it upside-down, tap the pot rim and drop the plant into one hand.

ABOVE: Extra growth induced by overwatering young plants will lead to an unfruitful bottom truss.

The rootball should be full of healthy roots at this stage.

LEFT: As the fruits mature on this bush variety, they provide an array of attractive colours, ranging from pale green to bright red. The fruits on each truss usually ripen at different times, which avoids having a glut to eat up and means the fresh crop is spread over a longer period.

7 The same grow-bag some weeks later. Being a bush variety, the side shoots have not been removed from the plant. After a few weeks, there are plenty of flowers and the promise of a good crop.

Growing tomatoes in a hanging basket

Several kinds of edible plant make attractive hanging baskets, especially when teamed with complementary ornamental flowers. Tomatoes are a good example and are here teamed up with French marigolds. The marigolds attract beneficial insects that help prevent pests attacking tomatoes, so you should not need to spray, which is ideal for organic gardeners.

1 Line a large hanging basket with a thick coco-fibre liner for insulation and an inner lining made from black plastic to hold moisture.

2 Loosely fill the basket with potting compost and firm the mix down gently. The weight will settle the liner into all the curves.

3 Trim the edges of the liner. Space three trailing tomato plants evenly around the basket, angled outwards. Fill the spaces between them with a few French marigolds.

4 Water the basket well. Use diluted liquid tomato feed to encourage heavy fruiting and avoid excess leafy growth.

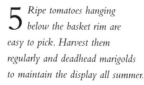

5 Ripe tomatoes hanging below the basket rim are easy to pick. Harvest them regularly and deadhead marigolds to maintain the display all summer.

1 Make a support to stabilize the tower of pots by screwing a length of wooden pole to a flat base and sit the biggest pot over it.

2 Part-fill the pot with any good-quality potting compost. Leave a deep depression in the middle where the second pot will rest.

3 Put six strawberry plants around the edge of the pot, spreading the roots out as much as possible and then firming lightly.

GROWING STRAWBERRIES

STRAWBERRIES MAKE EXCELLENT subjects for hanging baskets, windowboxes, grow-bags, tubs and troughs. High-rise containers, such as strawberry pots with planting pockets in the sides, are a particularly good space-saving way of growing them in small gardens. Unlike many edible crops, strawberry plants are neat and compact, and also highly decorative with their apple blossom-like flowers in spring followed by cascading green unripe berries. They associate well with tubs of flowers, or can be added to a herb garden or potager-style vegetable garden to give height to a ground-level display. When grown in pots, ripening strawberries are far more easily protected from birds. Drape containers with netting or crop protection fleece from the time the first green fruits appear. Prevent slugs and snails spoiling the fruit by smearing crop protection jelly around the base of containers to prevent them climbing up. A strawberry container can be started any time in autumn or spring. Strawberry runners are available in autumn and should be planted straight away so that the roots do not dry out. If you have access to a strawberry bed, you could also dig up spare runners from established plants in autumn to replant in containers. Small pot-grown plants are also sold in spring; the earlier in spring you plant them the better.

4 Set the second pot in place. This should be sufficiently smaller to allow room for the first tier of plants to develop freely.

5 Firm and level the pot and part-fill with compost, mostly around the edges, leaving a depression in the center for the smallest pot.

6 Plant four strawberry plants around the edge, but not directly above those in the lower pot, so the fruits hang down evenly around the edges.

7 Fit the smallest pot in place, taking care to keep the tower upright to prevent it toppling over once the plants are heavy with fruit.

8 *Put two plants in the top and fill to the brim with compost mix. Fill any gaps between the lower plants with compost to prevent plants drying out.*

9 *Water each tier well. Moisture will drain down from the top pot, so after the initial watering, it will need more than the others.*

10 *Pour gravel into the saucer for extra stability and to hide the base plate. To move the tower, lift and steady using the 'handle'. Feed weekly with half-strength liquid tomato fertilizer.*

RIGHT: As the fruits reach full size, protect them from birds with a net supported on a frame. Tuck the netting loosely around the plant and hold it down with bricks. Pick the fruit daily. By early summer, the plants will have filled the container with fruit cascading down over the tiers.

Planting strawberries in the ground

Strawberries are probably the most popular and easily grown fruit, and you can include some plants even in the smallest garden. Strawberry varieties are either of the summer-fruiting or perpetual-fruiting type. Summer-fruiting are the most popular and you can advance them under cloches or even in an unheated greenhouse. For later crops, use one of the perpetual varieties. Reduce the risk of infection from botrytis by putting down plenty of clean straw or proprietary matting between the rows so that the fruits are not splashed with rain or mud.

1 *Buy strong, bare-rooted plants in late summer or early autumn. If you already grow strawberries in the garden, save about 12 of their best runners to transplant then. Or buy young plants in small pots available from nurseries in spring.*

2 *It is important to plant strawberry plants deeply, so that the lower leaves rest on the surface of the soil. You should not be able to see the top of the roots. If you can, dig them out and replant them in a slightly deeper hole.*

3 *Place hoops over the green fruit to support netting. If the net rests on the fruit, birds will peck at it through the holes. Secure the edges of the netting with bricks.*

CHAPTER **5**

GARDEN TECHNIQUES

IN ADDITION to planning, constructing and planting your garden, you need to know how to keep it looking good, so that you can enjoy it all year round. Not only do you need to choose appropriate plants and know how to maintain them in a healthy state – feeding, watering and pruning them as and when required – you also need to be able to increase your stocks of plants inexpensively by sowing seed or taking cuttings, for example. This chapter shows how, with the helpful addition of step-by-step photographs. Although small gardens require relatively low levels of maintenance, you will need to pay particular attention to feeding and watering, since plants in containers dry out very quickly and also have no natural replenishment of nutrients apart from what you supply.

LEFT: *Build staging against the walls of a small garden to increase the planting space, and to give you a place to propagate your own plants.*

RIGHT: *Every inch of space has been used in this garden, along with a range of containers, to get the greatest value from the garden. Herbs, perennials and annuals create a wonderful cottage-garden display.*

SOILS & MULCHES

GOOD GARDEN SOIL takes several years of regular cultivation to create, and soil improvement should be part of every gardener's regular routine. This happens in several stages. First, whenever you make a new bed or border, dig plenty of well-rotted organic matter, such as garden compost or composted manure, into the whole area, burying it to the full depth of the spade. Use about a barrow-load per square metre (yard); you will need more on light sandy or chalky soils. Then each time you add a new plant, dig a bucketful of organic matter into the bottom of the planting hole. Finally, spread a mulch over the soil surface to trap moisture in the soil and smother out weed seedlings. Reapply mulches each spring (or spring and autumn on dry sandy or chalky soils). If low maintenance is your aim, spread a decorative layer of a long-lasting surface mulch of gravel or bark chips over a weed-suppressing membrane, which totally prevents weeds.

Types of soil

These are the main types of soil found in gardens; each one can be improved with soil conditioners and by feeding and mulching to make good conditions for growing a wide range of plants.

Improving the soil

DUE TO THE special characteristics of organic matter, the same materials can be used to open up heavy soils and improve their aeration and drainage, and improve moisture retention in dry, sandy or chalky soils. Dig in organic soil improvers, such as well-rotted garden compost or horse manure, coir or moss peat, before planting, fork them in between established plants or use them as a surface mulch.

Soil improvers

Moss peat is naturally acidic. Use it to acidify neutral or slightly acid soil before planting acid-loving plants. Use peat substitute when possible as peat bogs are under threat.

Well-rotted garden compost is made up of kitchen and disease-free garden waste (no perennial weeds, weed seeds or woody material).

Sedge peat or old grow-bag composts serve to lighten clay soils and increase the moisture-holding capacity of light soils.

Gritty sand contains a mix of particle sizes. Dig it in to break up clay.

Composted horse manure. Stack it in a heap until soil-like in consistency or layer it between kitchen and garden waste to help compost heaps rot down faster.

Coir. Use it alone as a soil improver or in the form of ready-made seed and potting composts.

Clay soil forms hard clods in summer, when cracks often appear in the soil. When wet, the soil is sticky and a handful forms a ball that holds its shape.

Chalky soil is very alkaline, fast-draining and low in nutrients, which are locked up chemically. It looks pale, with a whitish cast if chalk rock is present. Particles of pure chalk may be visible. Pale soil may cover a layer of chalk rock lower down.

Water runs quickly through sandy soil; puddles vanish immediately after rain and a handful of damp soil will not hold together in a ball.

Good garden soil holds moisture, but is never boggy. Its dark colour is due to the organic matter added over several years of regular cultivation.

Woodland soils contain large amounts of leafmould. They are usually slightly acid, rich, fertile and free-draining.

Testing the soil

ONE OF THE FIRST TASKS to do in a new garden is to test the soil to discover whether it is alkaline, neutral or acid. This in turn determines the types of plants that will grow best in it, and whether any remedial treatment is necessary. Before testing the soil, ensure that you take a representative sample by gathering several specimens from all round the garden. Take the samples 10cm (4in) below the soil surface and avoid obvious abnormalities, such as areas that have been used for bonfires, compost heaps or mixing cement. This investigation can save expense and disappointment later on.

Soil-testing kits

1 With this type of kit, put a little dry soil into the tube, up to the level indicated. Add water to the next mark on the side of the tube, replace the cap and shake well.

2 When the water changes colour, compare it to the chart provided to see if your soil is acid, neutral or alkaline. Now you can tell which kinds of plants will suit your garden.

Conditioning the soil

Once you know whether your soil is acid, neutral or alkaline, you can use soil additives to condition it so you are more likely to be able to grow the types of plants you want. Don't expect miracles, however. You will only be able to change the soil a little and will need to reapply the conditioner regularly.

Calcified seaweed breaks down clay soils and neutralizes acid ones. A source of magnesium, calcium and trace elements.

Sulphur chips acidify a neutral or slightly alkaline soil.

General-purpose fertilizers restore the soil's major nutrients.

Mulches

A mulch is a layer of material spread over the soil surface to seal moisture into the soil, smother annual weeds, and give a decorative finish. Garden centres stock a wide range of suitable mulch materials.

Cocoa shell chips are slightly acid and break down quickly. Apply to damp soil in early spring.

Use gravel on dry gardens or over a weed-suppressing membrane for low-maintenance gardens.

Chipped bark, a long-lasting mulch, is ideal for shrub borders. Top it up every few years.

RIGHT: To help retain moisture, mulch heather and conifer beds in spring with 2.5–5cm (1–2in) of well-rotted organic matter such as garden compost. Alternatively, apply bark or wood chippings, or cocoa shell chips.

ABOVE: Coarse bark chippings applied while the soil is still wet retain moisture in the soil and help to suppress weed growth.

LEFT: Unlike organic mulches that slowly rot, gravel lasts forever. Push it right up close to the neck of the plant for maximum effect.

MAKING GARDEN COMPOST

GARDEN COMPOST is one of the most common and effective forms of bulky organic matter to add to the ground. It is the perfect soil conditioner, improving the texture and structure of the soil as well as increasing nutrient levels. And what's more it is free. Good garden compost is made from plant remains, including annual weeds, vegetable kitchen waste, lawn mowings, hedge clippings, leaves and soft prunings. You can also add sawdust, straw, hay and bulky animal manures, but be sure to mix them in with green waste to make the best compost. Never add anything of a meaty nature, and avoid any cooked foods as these encourage rodents into the garden. Also avoid adding perennial weed roots as these will regrow, and weed seedheads as the seeds will germinate when you add the compost to the soil. The secret of good garden compost is to use a good mixture of raw materials: plenty of soft vegetation plus a high proportion of shredded woodier things. The choice between a compost heap or composting bin rests largely on the amount of raw material available. If there is plenty, a full-size compost heap is better, but where raw material is limited, use a smaller compost bin. Small heaps never make good compost. Fill up compost bins in one operation; they quickly heat up and make the best compost. If you have the space in your garden, consider having two compost heaps. Then you can be filling one up while the other is rotting, ready for use.

1 *With a new heap or bin, try to make the first batch of material a coarse and woody layer, such as these rose prunings. It ensures that the heap will have good drainage and aeration.*

2 *Keep adding more coarse material until you build up a foundation layer of vegetation about 15cm (6in) deep in the bottom of the bin or heap, once you have firmed it down.*

3 *Now you can start to add soft materials as well, such as these grass mowings. It is vital to build up alternate layers of fine and coarse material to allow the rotting process to work properly.*

4 *When the heap is about 25cm (10in) deep, sprinkle on an activator to help micro-organisms break down the material. You can use a granular or liquid activator, or layers of fresh manure or soil.*

5 *Continue adding more raw material. These potato tops are soft and full of water so, ideally, you should follow them with rougher material to keep the heap open. Shred or chop woody prunings before you add them to the heap.*

6 *Add more shredded prunings to assist the decomposition process by aerating the heap. This, in turn, leads to heating up. Woody flower stalks, thorny prunings, cabbage and other brassica stalks are all suitable at this stage.*

7 *With this bin you add slats as the heap rises. The gaps ventilate the heap. Add more activator for every 25cm (10in) of vegetation. The activator contains an agent to reduce acidity; the micro-organisms prefer an alkaline environment.*

8 *An important part of good composting is to stop the generated heat escaping. Any covering, such as a thick layer of black plastic or old carpet, will do this and it will also stop rain from cooling the heap.*

9 *The result is humus-rich, fibrous garden compost that will improve your soil physically and chemically, either as a mulch or when dug in.*

Shredding woody and thorny waste

Some of the best raw materials are woody or thorny and cannot go directly on to the compost heap. By shredding these prunings you can make sure that none of this valuable vegetation is wasted. Alternatively, you could burn prunings and put the ashes on the heap.

Autumn flower stalks, woody prunings, cabbage and other brassica stalks are first rate, but chop or shred them first.

Thorny prunings after they have been put through an electric shredder.

Comfrey as compost

LEFT: To make a rich compost for the garden, layer comfrey leaves with other plant material. Include vegetable waste, but avoid adding perennial weeds and roots. Use compost from an existing heap as a starter.

Liquid manure

It is worth growing a few comfrey plants in a corner of the garden simply for the purpose of making a powerful and nutritious liquid manure. Infuse an armful of fresh comfrey leaves in a barrel or bin of rainwater for about four weeks and then use the liquid as a plant food. Use the decomposed leaves to enrich the compost heap or fertilize your tomatoes.

LEFT: When spraying, make sure that your applicator can reach under the foliage. This is just as important as covering the top surface. Always read the manufacturer's instructions and follow them carefully.

ROUTINE TASKS

LITTLE AND OFTEN is the key to gardening success. This explains why the gardener who spends an hour or so every evening apparently wandering about enjoying their borders usually has a much better-kept garden than the person who only appears on fine weekends, and then spends all their time in a sunlounger. For, of course, the wanderer is not merely wandering, but also observing and, where necessary, doing something. If you attend regularly and promptly to the weeding, watering, feeding, tying up, trimming and deadheading, it is much quicker and easier to take care of a garden. But if things get out of control, then instead of a few light chores, gardening becomes hard work, involving serious undergrowth clearance and resuscitating half-dead plants. There is more than one way of doing most key jobs. Plants in containers, for example, can be fed using slow-release products that last a whole season, as an alternative to weekly liquid feeding. If time is tight, simplify frequent jobs, such as watering, by using irrigation systems that ensure that plants stay well cared for when you cannot be there. A huge range of products and equipment is available to help take care of routine chores. The trick is to find out which suits you best; if a job is enjoyable, you will feel more inclined to do it. And the results of a little light gardening regularly will be a garden that looks and feels loved and responds accordingly – without creating problems.

RIGHT: Nip out the soft terminal bud on a green shoot rather than wait until it has grown and then have to shorten an overlong shoot.

LEFT: Never tie a young shoot to a wire too tightly. The shoot will expand, but not the string. Leave a little slack to allow for growth. String is available in a range of strengths and thicknesses.

Watering

In very dry weather, give newly planted plants a good soaking every few days, rather than light waterings more often. Water in the evenings, especially in hot weather, to give plants time to take up the water before the following morning's sun causes it to evaporate from the soil again.

LEFT: Irrigation systems that use porous water pipes do not waste water, as only the area under the piping gets wet. This also ensures that weeds are not watered.

RIGHT: Irrigation systems that deliver water to individual plants via drip nozzles are ideal for plants in containers. Systems like this can be connected to an outdoor tap via a preset water computer.

LEFT: Having planted a new shrub such as this rose, water it in well, concentrating the water near the stem and around the edge of the rootball. Continue watering through the first season when the soil is dry.

Feeding plants

1 *Feed flowering plants regularly from spring to midsummer. Sprinkle a good general-purpose fertilizer between the plants and fork it lightly into the soil.*

2 *Water thoroughly after feeding to dissolve the feed and make it available to plants. In prolonged dry spells, give liquid feeds instead.*

RIGHT: Keep all powdered feeds in a closed container, as they take up moisture from the air. Keep the feeding program simple – your plants will be the better for it.

BELOW: Liquid feeds are very popular. Follow the maker's directions carefully; do not be tempted to make the feed too strong. It is better to feed your plants at half-strength twice a week than to overdo it.

Deadheading

Deadheading is specially worthwhile for plants with a potentially long flowering season, such as hybrid tea roses and bedding plants. But even when the flowering season is short, deadheading keeps plants looking tidy and removes dead petals on which grey mould may form. Do not deadhead plants from which you expect fruit or hips later on.

LEFT: Deadheading roses. Cut the heads back to a bud or to a shoot that has yet to flower. Then cut back the other half to a bud. This will usually grow into another flowerhead.

BELOW: Once a heather bed is established, wait until flowering is over, then clip back the old blooms with shears and tidy up the plants. This will encourage strong growth next season.

RIGHT: As camellia flowers start to fade, gently nip off the dead heads between thumb and fingernail. This improves the shrub's appearance and lets new shoots emerge from behind the old flowers. Avoid damaging the new shoots when deadheading.

PLANTING

IT IS IMPORTANT TO MAKE SURE that you give your plants a good start when you plant them. They need, first and foremost, the right kind of soil and appropriate light conditions. There is no point in trying to get a heather or a rhododendron, for example, to grow in alkaline soil – they need the fairly acid conditions of their native habitat to do really well.

Almost any plant will suffer as a result of being moved. It will recover more quickly and therefore grow better if the shock is minimized and the conditions are optimum. Be careful not to damage the fine feeder roots of the plants in the planting process. Once the plant is in position, these roots should be able to spread out and become operational, so make sure that you don't cram them into a planting hole that is too small, and that the surrounding soil is not too hard. Fork the area over, dig out a planting hole that is large enough for the roots to spread and grow into, firm the plant in well and water thoroughly. Thoroughly is the key word, since even apparently copious amounts of water only penetrate about an inch below the soil surface (as you will quickly discover if you insert a stick into the soil in a container you have just watered).

The best times for planting out new plants are in spring and in autumn. These seasons offer the best combination of temperature and moisture: not too hot and dry to stress the plants unduly and mean lots of work watering, and not too cold tó allow the plants to establish themselves before the onset of winter.

Planting a clematis

It is important to plant clematis at least 7.5cm (3in) deeper than the soil level in the original container. This ensures that if wilt strikes, or you run a hoe too close to the stems when weeding, the plant will regenerate from the base and grow on strongly.

1 Remove the plant from its pot and lower the rootball into position. Make sure that the surface of the rootball is at least 7.5cm (3in) below soil level.

2 Fill the space around the rootball with a soil and compost mixture. Ideally, add some organic material to the soil at the base of the planting hole.

3 Once the plant is in place, firm the soil down around the base to ensure that the rootball makes close contact with the soil in the hole.

4 Give the plant a very good watering to ensure that the soil is settled and there are no air pockets. If the soil level sinks, add more soil as necessary.

Ideal planting depths for bulbs

1 *Iris reticulata*: 5cm (2in) deep

2 *Anemone blanda*: 5cm (2in) deep

3 *A. 'De Caen'*: 5cm (2in) deep

4 Crocus: 7.5cm (3in) deep

5 Pushkinia: 7.5cm (3in) deep

6 Ornithogalum: 7.5cm (3in) deep

7 Chionodoxa: 10cm (4in) deep

8 Allium: 10cm (4in) deep

9 Muscari: 10cm (4in) deep

10 Hyacinth: 10cm (4in) deep

11 Tulip: 10cm (4in) deep

12 Daffodil: 12.5cm (5in) deep

Planting bulbs

A bulb planter is useful for planting a few bulbs individually or for spacing them widely over a larger area. Still plant the bulbs at the correct depth for their type. Some bulb planters have depth markings to help – if not, use a permanent marker pen to show the required depth. You can also use bulb planters to plant individual bulbs in grass.

LEFT: The elegant blooms of *Tulipa* 'West Point' would grace any garden in late spring. It is one of the so-called 'lily-flowered' types.

1 Space the bulbs on the soil, then lift each one to make a hole under it. Press the planter into the ground and twist to remove a core of soil.

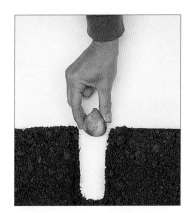

2 Place the bulb in the hole. If you can, press it slightly into the soil to ensure it remains upright. If the hole is too narrow or deep, just drop in the bulb.

3 Reinsert the planter into the hole and squeeze the handle to drop the core of soil back into place over the bulb. Gently firm the soil back down level.

Planting a tree

If you are planting trees, make sure you stake the stems securely so that the rootball does not rock about afterwards. Bare-root trees should only be moved in autumn or early spring; container-grown plants can be planted at any time, as long as you water them very well in warm weather.

1 Remove the tree from its container. Plants lift out easily from rigid plastic pots. In the case of plastic bag-type pots, first slit the sides carefully with a knife.

2 Dig a planting hole larger than the tree's rootball, hammer in a short stake to one side of it, then plant so that the top of the rootball is roughly flush with the soil surface.

3 Firm the soil down well to make sure that there are no air pockets left in it. These would leave roots hanging in space, where they tend to dry out and die.

Raising seeds in trays

1 Slightly overfill the tray with loose multi-purpose or seed compost and remove the excess by levelling the surface with a flat piece of wood.

2 Lightly firm the surface with the base of a clean flower pot, leaving it level and about 6mm (¹/₄in) below the rim of the tray.

3 Tip the seeds into a piece of folded paper and tap it gently over the tray so that the seed is sown thinly and is evenly distributed.

4 Cover the seeds to their own depth with more compost. Sieve the compost to ensure an even covering of fine material over the seeds.

5 Label the tray and water it by standing it in a dish of tepid water. When the surface of the compost turns a darker colour, you know that it is wet right through.

6 Remove the tray from the water and cover it with a clear lid or slip it into a large, clear plastic bag with short sticks inside to lift the bag into a tent. Alteratively, cover the tray with a sheet of glass or stiff plastic.

SOWING SEEDS

ALTHOUGH GARDEN CENTRES offer quite a good selection of flowers in bloom and ready to plant, it is much more satisfying to grow your own right from the start. Mail-order seed catalogues offer a far larger range of plant varieties to grow at home, including unusual ones that you may not be able to buy as plants. And, particularly if you want many plants of the same kind, raising your own can be far cheaper. Some kinds of flowers can be sown straight into the garden, but half-hardy annuals must be sown early on in reasonable warmth if they are to be in flower by the start of summer. Sow these in pots or seed trays under controlled conditions. If you intend raising a lot of plants, it is best to use an electrically heated propagator inside a frost-free greenhouse. This way you not only have the means of maintaining the right temperature for germination (60-75°F/15-24°C, depending on the type), but you will also have room to grow them on when the seedlings are pricked out. If you only need a few plants, then use warm windowsills. Choose shady sills for pots of seed that are germinating, as direct sun can harm them. Then when the seedlings are pricked out, move them to a brighter spot after a few days so that they do not become drawn and spindly. If space is short and you only need a few plants of each kind, do not prick the seedlings out into trays; just plant them into small pots as these are likely to fit better on a windowsill.

Sowing seeds in the ground

HARDY ANNUAL, biennial and perennial flower seeds, along with hardy vegetable seeds, are best sown either where they are to mature or in nursery rows in the ground. They will make much better plants if they are not cosseted.

ABOVE: Sow small seeds evenly and thinly in a shallow drill. Thin the seedlings in position or transplant when large enough.

LEFT: Sow large seeds, such as beans, singly or in twos where they are to stay. On heavy soil, use a stick to make a hole.

Raising seeds in pots

1 *Fill clean 3½in (9cm) pots with multi-purpose or seed compost. Tip the seeds into a fold of paper and scatter them thinly over the surface.*

2 *If the seeds are very fine, sprinkle a thin layer of vermiculite over the surface of the pot before sowing them.*

3 *Tip the fine seed into a fold of paper and sow it thinly and evenly. Seeds fall between the granules; don't cover them.*

4 *Cover larger seeds to their own depth with sieved compost. Use a clean pot with small holes if you do not have a sieve.*

5 *Label the pots with the plant name and date of sowing. Stand them in a dish with a few inches of tepid water and leave them until the surface of the soil turns dark, showing that it is wet right through.*

6 *Put the pots into individual clear plastic bags to create a humid atmosphere and secure them with rubber bands. Place on a warm windowsill (about 70°F/20°C) in good light but away from direct sunlight.*

Sowing larger seeds in pots and cells

If you are sowing medium to large seeds, you can avoid the job of pricking out seedlings by sowing directly into small individual containers, such as 5cm (2in) pots or cells. Since only about 50 per cent of flower seedlings germinate, sow two medium-sized or one large seed per small container. As the volume of compost is so small in these tiny cells, they dry out very quickly, so regular watering is vital.

LEFT: Fill the cells smoothly and evenly with compost and make a shallow depression in each one. Drop in two seeds. Sow only as many of one variety as you need plants, plus a few spares.

RIGHT: You can sow large seeds, such as nasturtium, singly into small pots. Fill each pot with seed compost and press one seed into the middle. Young plants are ready for planting out when the pots are full of roots.

Pricking out seedlings

1 *Prick out seedlings while they are tiny to give them more space to develop. Water the pot well the day beforehand.*

2 *Hold the seedlings by a leaf and transfer them to a clean tray of fresh compost. Use a dibber to make holes.*

3 *When the whole tray has been filled with seedlings, water them in using a fine rose on a watering can. Water again when necessary; keep the soil moist but take care not to overwater the tiny plants.*

Taking semi-ripe cuttings of buddleja

TAKING CUTTINGS

1 *Select a stocky shoot; these will grow on the sunniest side of the shrub. Cut the shoot off as close as possible to the older wood.*

2 *Pull or cut off the lowest leaves, leaving 2.5cm (1in) of clear stem at the base. This will be the part under the rooting compost mixture.*

3 *Trim off the very bottom of the cutting immediately below a leaf scar. Roots will form most readily from these leaf joints.*

4 *Dip the base of the cutting in hormone rooting powder and tap off any excess. Make a hole in the compost to accommodate the cutting.*

5 *With the cutting in place, gently firm in around the base of the shoot so that there are no large air spaces and to ensure that the cutting is held firmly in the compost mixture.*

6 *When all the cuttings are in place and have been given a good watering, put the pot in a large plastic bag and tie up the top to keep the air inside the bag moist to encourage rooting.*

CUTTINGS PROVIDE THE MOST successful and productive way of propagating many plants. Hardwood cuttings taken in the early winter are the least troublesome, but only certain plants, notably the currant family and some roses, are suitable. Softwood cuttings taken in spring are probably the most difficult to root because they are the most fussy. If they are too wet or too dry, too hot or too cold, rooting will be delayed and they may die. In the right conditions, however, they will root very quickly. Fuchsias are a good example. Semi-ripe cuttings of many trees and shrubs will root fairly easily in the late summer. A propagator in a heated greenhouse is the surest way of rooting these and softwood cuttings. Treating the base of the cuttings with hormone rooting powder is a good idea but it does not make up for poor growing conditions. Semi-ripe and hardwood cuttings rooted outdoors are best left for a year before being moved.

Semi-ripe cuttings of hydrangea and lavender

HYDRANGEA AND LAVENDER have virtually nothing in common and look totally different, but both are propagated from semi-ripe cuttings taken at more or less the same time of year and given the same conditions.

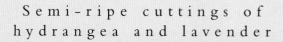

BELOW: Take lavender cuttings in late summer and prepare them as for buddleja. Use stocky growth shoots without old flower stalks at the top. The rooting medium is a 50/50 mix of peat substitute and coarse grit.

ABOVE: Take hydrangea cuttings in midsummer, when the base of the shoot is mature but not woody. Cut below a leaf joint. If leaves are large, cleanly cut off the top half.

Stem and leaf bud cuttings

1 Cotoneaster horizontalis *shoots are small, but root well. In late summer, remove pieces of the current year's growth.*

2 *Next, take off the bottom leaves and trim the base of the cutting to just below a leaf joint. It is now ready to pot up.*

3 *Although stem cuttings root perfectly well, you can raise more plants by cutting up the stem into short lengths, each with one leaf and its accompanying bud. Shown here is ivy.*

4 *Push each leaf bud cutting into the compost so that the bud is just visible but the base of the leaf is just beneath the surface. The roots will form just below the leaf.*

5 *The cotoneaster and ivy cuttings can be rooted in the same propagator. Water them thoroughly with a fine rose.*

6 *To help the single good watering last until the cuttings have rooted, cover the propagator with a transparent lid.*

Pelargonium cuttings

Although many bedding pelargoniums are now grown from seed each year, the only way to propagate a favourite old variety true to type is to take tip cuttings from the plants in early autumn. It is seldom necessary to use rooting powder for pelargoniums and, indeed, too much powder can delay rooting. Insert the cuttings in a peat-and-grit or similar rooting mixture and overwinter them, preferably in a cold but frost-free greenhouse. During that time, only give them enough water to prevent wilting.

1 *Use a sharp knife to remove the lower leaves from a strong, young stem about 7.5cm (3in) long. Take care to avoid cutting your thumb, or cut on a board.*

2 *Remove any developing buds and flowers in the same way. Now the cutting will have two or three leaves at the top and a length of clean stem.*

3 *Make a clean cut across the base of the stem just below a node, or leaf joint. This is where new roots will emerge. Any ragged tissue left here will rot.*

4 *Push individual cuttings into a 5cm (2in) pot of compost, or put a few cuttings around the edge of a 10cm (4in) pot, making sure they don't touch. Water in.*

Potting up the cuttings

Once the cuttings have rooted and are growing away, normally after about six to eight weeks, tip them out and pot them up separately. Use 9cm (3½in) pots and fresh multi-purpose compost for this first potting. A week later when they have settled in and you can see that they are growing again, remove the tip of the main stem to encourage a stocky and bushy plant to develop. At the same time, remove any flowers that may have grown to allow more strength to go into the young plant.

DIVIDING PLANTS

THE EASIEST WAY of increasing the number of herbaceous plants in your garden is likely to be by dividing them. This involves splitting up clump-forming plants into several separate pieces and replanting these. The only qualification is that you need to start with this particular kind of plant to make it possible. Herbaceous phlox and Michaelmas daisies are typical plants suitable for division. They are plants that spread each year by putting out short underground shoots around the perimeter that increase the size of the clumps. By splitting up the clump, retaining the younger portions on the outside and throwing away the older part in the middle, you rejuvenate the plant and, at the same time, create many more. If you want to divide a plant that is growing in a pot into many new plants, just knock it out of its container and tease it apart into as many pieces as you can make. Remember that each new piece must have at least one, and preferably more, growing shoots to make it viable. You might do this if you want to make the most of a plant you have just bought. You would also divide a clump of perennials such as Michaelmas daisies if they are cramped and crowded in the border, and the flower quality is deteriorating.

Dividing hostas

SOMETIMES, YOU MAY wish to divide a plant that you have just bought in order to make the most of it. Very often, you will find that a new acquisition is potbound and actually needs dividing.

1 This is the way to deal with a relatively small plant that either needs dividing or that you want to multiply. Tease the rootball apart so that it divides easily, but without damaging it.

2 Normally, you will only be able to divide a potted plant into two pieces. However, if the two bits are large enough to split up further, you can do so. These ones are probably not.

Dividing an iris

1 Propagate irises in the autumn or spring, or after flowering. Cut behind the one-year-old rhizome so that each new plant has one or, better still, two tufts of leaves and roots.

2 Pull off the piece you have just severed, making sure that there are no old and blind rhizomes left attached to it. These will not produce new shoots.

3 When splitting a plant straight after flowering, reduce the amount of transpiration from the leaves by cutting them back into a small fan. This will not harm the plant.

4 Replace the plant in the border, with the top of the rhizome above the ground, but the base of the fan in the soil. The new roots will grow from this part.

LAYERING

IF DIVISION IS THE EASIEST METHOD of propagating certain herbaceous plants vegetatively (as opposed to sowing seed), then layering must be the easiest and most successful method for shrubs and climbers. It involves bending down a shoot or small branch of the plant you want to propagate and burying a short section of it so that roots form on the buried part. A year or so later, you can sever the layered portion, complete with its roots, from the parent plant, dig it up and plant it out. It is also a very useful method for propagating plants that are difficult to root in other ways. In theory, you can layer at any time of the year but, because it is an advantage to have new roots growing on the buried portion as soon as possible, mid spring to late summer is the preferred time. This quick rooting ensures that any wound made on the stem before burying it heals quickly. Shoots of either the current or previous season's growth root the quickest. Older wood will take much longer to form roots and may never do so. It is worthwhile taking the trouble to find a suitable shoot that you can bend down to layer. Look all round the shrub until you find a good one.

Plants with runners

ALTHOUGH the strawberry is the obvious example, some other plants, including *Iris japonica* (right), also produce runners above or below the ground with plantlets on the end. Root these to produce new plants.

1 Push the plantlet at the end of a strawberry runner into a pot of used seed or potting compost. It will root quickly and you can move the pot later on.

2 Hold the plantlet in place with a small wire loop, so that it is reasonably firm. Any cutting or plantlet must be held still while it is forming roots or the process will not work.

Layering clematis

1 Select a strong, disease-free shoot and tease it away from the mass of stems. The leaf joint must have strong buds showing, as these will form the new plant.

2 Remove the leaves, making a clean cut as close as possible to the main stem. Take care not to damage the buds in the joints where the stem and leaves meet.

3 Using a trowel, make a hole about 2.5cm (1in) deep in which to place the shoot. It is worth sprinkling a little silver sand into the planting hole to aid drainage and prevent rotting.

4 Place the layer on to the surface of the soil with the buds over the hole you have made. Bend pieces of garden wire into a number of U-shaped staples and insert them in the soil on either side of the buds to prevent the layer from moving.

5 Make sure that you press the wires in firmly so that the leaf joint is directly in contact with the soil. This should prevent it from drying out during the summer months. It will be at least three or four months before any new shoots emerge.

PRUNING

PRUNING SERVES TO improve the shape of a plant or to increase the amount of flowers, coloured foliage or fruit it produces. However, it isn't compulsory. You should prune a tree, shrub or fruit plant only if pruning will improve its performance and not merely to satisfy a whim. Every cut should have a purpose. If you do not prune a tree or shrub, no actual harm is going to come to it; it will merely operate less efficiently. This could mean fewer flowers and/or fruit, poorer flowers, less and/or weaker growth, poorer foliage and general untidiness. If you prune something in the wrong way or at the wrong time or, perish the thought, both, you will do infinitely more damage than by not pruning. On these pages you will find advice on when to prune ornamental trees and shrubs, and fruiting plants, and how to do it.

Roses

When you prune roses largely depends on when they flower. Tidy bedding varieties (hybrid teas and floribundas) and climbers in the autumn and prune them in spring. Prune ramblers soon after their midsummer flowering. Treat shrub roses like other shrubs. Earlies are pruned after flowering and the lates in mid-spring. Prune roses with ornamental hips in spring so you don't cut the hips off.

Fruit

Apples and pears are usually pruned in winter, but prune trained trees in the summer to encourage the formation of fruiting spurs. It is best to prune plums and other stone fruit after fruit picking to reduce the incidence of silver leaf disease. Most cane fruits are also pruned after fruiting. Bush fruits are usually pruned in early winter but prune cordons in summer.

Early-flowering shrubs

There is no rigid line between early- and late-flowering shrubs, but early-flowering shrubs tend to produce their best and/or the most flowers on stems produced during the previous year. Prune these plants after flowering so that they have the most time in which to produce new shoots for flowering the following year.

Heathers

Clipping time is governed by when they flower. Prune spring-flowering ericas (heaths) in early summer; summer- and autumn-flowering ericas in late spring; and winter-flowering ericas and calluna (ling) in mid-spring. They are not really pruned in the classic sense, but clipped with shears or clippers to keep the beds or clumps compact and flowering well.

Trees and shrubs with fruits or berries

Most are early-flowering to allow time for the berries to develop before winter. Pruning after the plant has flowered would remove the developing fruitlets. If necessary, prune them in the winter or early spring. The emphasis must be on leaving as much flowering wood as you can; the flowers, after all, develop into the fruits.

Late-flowering shrubs

Shrubs flowering after about midsummer flower best on the current season's shoots. Prune them, if necessary, in the spring when growth is starting. This gives them several months in which to produce new shoots to flower later the same year. Do not prune them after flowering, because they would start growing again from the buds at the base of the pruned shoots. These would not mature and harden before the winter months and many would be killed by the frost and cold conditions.

Conifers

Conifers have their own individual shape and any pruning tends to interfere with this and spoil the plant. The main exception to this is conifer hedges. Clip them in spring, but fast-growing ones may need it in summer and early autumn as well. If a conifer is damaged, administer first aid immediately (such as tying up) and any serious remedial work in the spring.

Coloured stems

The beauty of these plants, such as *Cornus* (the dogwoods) and *Salix* (willows), lies in their juvenile growth, so prune them to produce as many shoots as possible. Mainly, it is the winter shoots that are the attraction, providing welcome colour on dull days, so prune them hard in early or mid-spring. This encourages plenty of new shoots for the following winter.

The pruning year

This summary reflects the main pruning and training tasks through the seasons, but bear in mind that trees and shrubs will not always need pruning; the aim is to improve the plant's performance and appearance.

Spring

Prune any fruit trees (though not plums) and bushes that were not pruned in winter, and also autumn raspberries. Prune shrubs that have flowered since about midsummer including winter and early spring-flowering ones, such as winter jasmine (*Jasminum nudiflorum*) and *Forsythia*. Prune climbing and bush roses, plus any evergreens and conifers. This will include cutting back hard into old wood for rejuvenation. Clip or prune evergreen and conifer hedges. Prune *Salix* and *Cornus* being grown for their colourful stems.

Summer

After flowering, prune almost all shrubs that flowered in the spring and early summer. Prune cordon bushes of red- and whitecurrants and gooseberries in midsummer and cordon, fan and espalier apples and pears in late summer. Prune plums after fruiting. Cut down the fruited canes of early raspberries when finished. Clip hedges. Deadhead roses, except those with hips, and other flowered shrubs. Summer prune wisteria. Prune rambler roses and tie in new shoots.

ABOVE: Once they are over, cut escallonia flowers off in summer to leave just the growth shoots.

ABOVE: To prune potentillas after their first flush of flowers, simply grab a handful of shoots and cut them back as far as you can.

Autumn

Summer-prune trained fruit trees that were not mature earlier along with later fruiting plums. Prune hybrid cane fruits and blackberries after fruiting and tie in the new canes. Cut down fruited canes of any summer raspberries not yet done. Cut off the dead heads of flowered shrubs. Lightly prune bush and climbing roses and tie in the shoots of the climbers. Tie in all trained fruit trees and climbers.

Winter

This is the big pruning season for fruit trees (except plums) and bushes. It is best to wait until leaf-fall so that you can see better what you are doing. Prune trained fruit trees that were not summer-pruned. Spur back summer-pruned wisteria shoots. Prune most kinds of ornamental trees, except those that flower during winter and spring.

PRUNING EARLY SHRUBS

FOR THE PURPOSE of pruning, early-flowering shrubs are those that flower before midsummer. The correct and only way to find out which group a shrub belongs to is to look at the shoots with the best flowers. If these are the shoots that grew in the previous year (like forsythia), then the shrub is described as early-flowering. If the best flowers are on shoots that grew earlier in the same growing season (such as buddleja), then it is late-flowering. Shrubs that flower best on the previous year's shoots (early-flowering shrubs) should be pruned straight after flowering to give the plant the longest possible time in which to produce long, vigorous shoots for flowering in the following year. Thus, a forsythia flowering in mid-spring will have the whole of the growing season until late autumn to produce the following year's best flowering shoots. Remember, though, it is only the best flowers that will be produced on the new shoots; there will still be plenty of flowers on older shoots but they will not be of the same high quality. Pruning consists of cutting back or completely removing the oldest branch systems in the shrub each spring after flowering. This opens up the shrub and encourages the formation of new shoots and, at the same time, gets rid of some of the oldest and poorest flowering shoots. Pruning this group in the winter is entirely wrong, as it simply takes away flowering wood; leave it until after flowering.

Heather

LEFT: While heathers are young and recently planted, grasp each plant by the spent flowerheads and clip them with secateurs. Trim over established plants with shears.

Forsythia

LEFT: After flowering, remove the ends of stems that carried the current year's flowers. Cut just above an unflowered side shoot.

ABOVE: Every branch of a well-grown forsythia has the potential to be covered with vivid flowers.

Spiraea

LEFT: Cut straggly growth from the base with secateurs. Then cut below each spent flowerhead to just above a young shoot lower down the stem. Trim long side shoots to restore the shape of the shrub.

RIGHT: Lovely spring-flowering *Spiraea* x *arguta* (bridal wreath) makes a medium-sized shrub with graceful arching branches. It is inclined to be untidy; if necessary, prune it after flowering to improve the shape of the bush.

Coloured stems

Some of the shrubs with the most attractive winter stems are found among the dog-woods *(Cornus)* and willows *(Salix)*. Prune hard in spring.

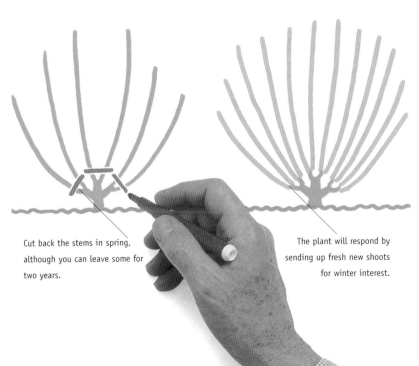

Cut back the stems in spring, although you can leave some for two years.

The plant will respond by sending up fresh new shoots for winter interest.

PRUNING ROSES

WITH THE EXCEPTION of rambler roses, which are pruned after they have finished flowering in summer, most roses, including hybrid teas and floribundas, are best lightly pruned in early winter and properly pruned in mid-spring. Lightly pruned bushes can rest in winter and will not rock about in stormy conditions. If a hole were to develop in the soil around the neck of the bush, it could fill with water and start a rot in the bark. There is one important exception to this general rule; roses that are grown as much for their ornamental hips as for their flowers, such as *Rosa rugosa* and *R. moyesii* 'Geranium', are pruned in spring to allow their hips to develop fully and stay on the bushes as long as possible. After a mild winter, growth can start in early spring and you cannot bank on the early growth surviving. That is why it is best to delay the second pruning until the worst of the winter is over. Hybrid teas and floribundas are pruned in almost exactly the same way as each other. The only real difference is the severity. The floribundas are not pruned as hard as the teas because the aim is a good display of many flowers, whereas the teas should have fewer but larger blooms. The length to which you cut back the individual shoots in spring will depend on their vigour. Cut back strong hybrid tea bushes to about 30cm (12in) high. Cutting them almost to the ground is going too far, unless they are being grown specifically for show. The extra hard pruning will make them produce later but larger flowers. For ordinary garden flowering, it is better to have the flowers earlier and for the plant to produce more of them.

Autumn pruning

It is important to prune rose bushes lightly in the autumn. Do not prune them any harder than necessary. Remove flowers, buds and hips, and cut back long shoots by about a third of their length (those taller than 60cm/24in). Remove broken and out-of-place shoots. This is not a proper pruning, just an opportunity to make the bushes smaller and tidier.

1 *A hybrid tea rose bush in early winter. Remove the long shoot to leave it about 60cm (24in) long.*

2 *Cut out branches with hips as they take energy from the plant. Remove them before winter.*

Spring pruning

In spring, first tackle any shoots that are clearly in the wrong place or causing overcrowding. Add to these any that are too weak and feeble to carry decent flowers. Cut both kinds right out or shorten them to a strong bud pointing in the appropriate direction. Cut back the strong shoots on floribundas to about 45cm (18in) long.

1 *Cut dead branches back to their point of origin. Use a saw or loppers on thick branches.*

2 *Remove any dead stems or branches left over after the plant's light pruning in the autumn.*

3 *Cut back this tall branch by about half its length to a bud pointing in the desired direction.*

4 *Hybrid tea roses need this treatment to perform well. Prune floribundas more lightly.*

Pruning hydrangeas

Unlike most late-flowering shrubs, the mid to late summer-flowering *Hydrangea macrophylla* Hortensia and Lacecap varieties produce their best flowers on strong shoots that grew the year before. Prune in spring, after winter frosts are over. Leave old flower heads of Hortensia varieties on until spring pruning to protect the terminal buds that produce the summer flowers. Deadhead Lacecap varieties after flowering.

1 When pruning the Hortensia hydrangeas, leave as many terminal buds (those on the ends of the shoots) as you can. They will produce the summer flowers. The old flowers will protect the plant in winter.

2 Cut back dead flowerheads to a strong growth bud. Cut back as far as 15cm (6in), or more, if necessary, to find a strong bud or to shorten a long, untidy shoot.

3 With nearly all the old flowers gone, reduce any congestion inside the bush. Overcrowding will lead to weak and spindly shoots that are less likely to produce flowers.

4 Shorten or remove any outer branches that are spoiling the overall shape of the bush. The final result is a well-balanced, shapely bush that should flower profusely.

PRUNING LATE SHRUBS

LATE-FLOWERING SHRUBS usually produce their best flowers on shoots that have grown during the current growing season. Prune these shrubs, if necessary, in the spring shortly before, or as, growth starts. This gives them the maximum length of time, several months, in which to produce and ripen the new shoots before flowering halts their growth. If you pruned shrubs of this sort straight after flowering, almost all the tender new shoots that grew out after the hard pruning would be killed during the winter. This is worse for the plant than if it had been left alone, because there will be far fewer strong buds left to grow out. You can carry out a secondary pruning (as with bush roses), in early winter to remove dead flowerheads and any breakages. This only applies to plants that look untidy or are liable to wind rock.

Pruning lavender

LAVENDER NEEDS REGULAR pruning after flowering to stop it becoming sparse and leggy. You can snip off dead flowerheads individually and dry them to use in lavender bags. Lavender is not a particularly long-lived plant, so replace it when it starts to deteriorate.

LEFT: Once flowers start to fade, trim the plants with secateurs or shears, removing the old heads and the tips of the young leafy shoots below them. Never cut back into old brown wood or you could kill the plant.

RIGHT: Pruning lavender every year keeps the plant tidy and rejuvenated. This is *Lavandula spicata*, the old English lavender.

Pruning a newly planted buddleja

1 *Establish a sturdy framework for a new plant by cutting back the main shoots to a suitable length in spring. This will determine the future shape of the bush.*

2 *Repeat the whole process with each stem until the plant is only a few inches tall. By autumn, several new tall flowering shoots will have developed.*

LEFT: When pruned correctly, buddleja grows about 3m (10ft) tall and 2m (6ft) across. *Buddleja davidii* produces superb tall, arching shoots of scented flowers in white and lilac shades, much loved by butterflies.

Pruning hardy fuchsias

LEFT: When new growth reaches 7.5cm (3in) remove old wood that has been killed by frost. Make clean cuts with sharp secateurs.

ABOVE: In areas without frosts, fuchsias still need partial pruning to ensure a good show. This is 'Dorothy', a fine hardy fuchsia.

Late-flowering shrubs

On the whole, late-flowering shrubs flower from midsummer onwards on shoots that have grown during the current growing season. It is fairly safe to assume that all ornamental shrubs in this category not mentioned below are pruned just before or as growth starts in spring.

ABOVE: *Cistus purpureus*, an excellent form with large pink blooms and deep green foliage.

Buddleja davidii: In mid-spring, cut the flowered shoots back hard to about 10cm (4in) to encourage strong new ones.
Ceanothus: Late-flowering ones, such as 'Gloire de Versailles', thrive on hard pruning. In early to mid spring, remove weak shoots and shorten the remaining side shoots to 15–30cm (6–12in).
Cistus: Older specimens need little pruning and, indeed, object to it most strongly. It is usually better to replace old bushes, as they seldom rejuvenate.
Deutzia: In summer, as flowers fade, remove flowered branches with no young side shoots, and the occasional old branch.
Escallonia: Lightly cut back bushes after flowering or in the spring. Cut back side shoots on trained plants after flowering.
Fuchsia: If the top growth is killed in winter, cut shoots back to ground level as soon as new growth appears in the spring.
Genista: Late-flowering brooms such as *G. hispanica* need little pruning. Remove or cut back long shoots in early spring.
Hebe: Deadhead hebes after the flowers fade. If hard pruning is required, do this in mid-spring.

Hibiscus: In spring, shorten the odd young shoot of *H. syriacus* to encourage branching.
Hydrangea: Leave the dead flowerheads of the Hortensia (mophead) kinds until the spring to protect the flower buds. Cut out weak and twiggy shoots after flowering.
Hypericum (shrubby): During early and mid-spring, shorten the previous year's strong shoots by a quarter or more. Otherwise, just aim to keep the bushes tidy and compact.
Lavandula: Cut off the old flower stalks and trim the bushes in late summer after flowering. If any hard pruning is needed to correct legginess, do it in spring.
Lonicera: To keep shrubby winter honeysuckle young and relatively compact, shorten over-vigorous flowered shoots in the spring.
Viburnum (some): No regular pruning is needed. Remove out-of-place shoots and cut back over-vigorous ones. Do this in mid-spring for autumn- and winter-flowering kinds and evergreens.

ABOVE: The handsome and compact *Viburnum tinus* 'Eve Price' has pink buds and white flowers in the autumn.

LAWN CARE

IT IS ONE THING TO CREATE what you might think of as the ideal lawn, but quite another to keep it in the best condition. This will depend on the quantity and quality of the upkeep you are prepared to lavish on it. All too often the lawn is left to its own devices after the first flush of enthusiasm. Mowing, raking, feeding, watering, spiking, weed and moss control and a host of lesser jobs will all need to be done. Here are some of the more important maintenance tasks.

LEFT: Compaction of the soil surface leads to poor drainage, waterlogging and weak grass. Spike all or part of the lawn with a garden fork, driving it 10cm (4in) deep and the same distance apart into all parts of the lawn that need aerating.

Feeding the lawn

ABOVE: Grass plants constantly compete for nutrients. You can apply fertilizer by hand, but take care to distribute it evenly.

ABOVE: Set correctly, a spreader distributes fertilizer at the ideal rate, leading to an even result and less risk of overdosing.

Raking the lawn

RIGHT: In every lawn, dead grass and other plant debris will build up among the blades of grass. You must rake out this debris regularly if the lawn is to flourish. 'Thatch', as it is called, is a contributory factor to moss and the appearance of yellow grass.

Weeds in the lawn

No matter how high the quality of the grass, weeds can ruin the whole effect of a lawn. They smother the grass and give the lawn a neglected appearance. Some, such as dandelions, have deep tap roots that are difficult to dig out; a lawn weedkiller is the only certain treatment.

ABOVE: Dandelions are difficult to dig out successfully; kill them with a lawn weedkiller. Pick off the flowers before they set seed.

ABOVE: You can rake patches of clover before mowing to weaken it, but lawn weedkiller is the only complete and lasting treatment.

ABOVE: Plantain seeds readily from brown flowerheads and dies back in winter, leaving a bald patch. Treat with lawn weedkiller.

ABOVE: Daisies are not easy to kill with a weedkiller. Apply a second dose four weeks after the first. Raking helps reduce them.

Lawn weedkillers

You can dig out a few individual weeds, but apply a selective weedkiller if there are rather a lot. Weedkillers are perfectly safe when used as directed, so always follow the manufacturer's instructions carefully.

BELOW: To treat the whole lawn, fit a dribble bar to a watering can. On a dull day, the area stays wet, so weedkiller has longer to work.

BELOW: A handsprayer is effective and economical for spot treating weeds. You can buy them filled and ready to use.

PESTS & DISEASES

Many garden pests and diseases can be avoided by good garden practices, controlling weeds and tidying away garbage. Compost lawn mowings, dead leaves and weeds so that they break down without encouraging pests or disease spores. Remove and burn plants with persistent problems. Wash empty pots, seed trays and boxes straight after use and store them out of the way in a shed. Natural predators will deal with many pests, so plant trees to encourage insect-eating birds, grow clumps of wildflowers to encourage more beneficial insects into the garden, and avoid chemical pesticides so that beneficial creatures are not harmed along with the pests. However, if a pest or disease problem is serious, use a remedy in order to save a plant. Use environmentally friendly chemical sprays where possible and spray in the evenings when bees are not about.

ABOVE: If roses suffer from fungal diseases such as rust, spray them regularly in spring and summer with a proper rose fungicide.

LEFT: Earwigs are active at night and not only damage flowers (this is a clematis) but can also reduce the leaves of a plant to a tatty network of veins.

ABOVE: Powdery mildew on roses. Spray regularly with a fungicide, evenly covering both the upper and undersides of the leaves.

BELOW: Bluetits and beneficial insects will clear minor outbreaks of aphids, a common pest, or use chemicals that only kill aphids.

Pest control

Concentrated soft soap (natural fatty acids). Dilute with water and apply with a hand-operated sprayer against common pests.

Ready-to-use sulphur spray, an organic remedy for mildew on roses. Do not use any sprays in hot sun, in windy conditions or when plants are under stress.

Slug tape impregnated with metaldehyde.

Green sulphur protects stored bulbs from rot and mould.

Hormone rooting powder with fungicide.

Liquid slug killer.

Slug pellets.

Slugs slide off this nonstick barrier tape.

Aluminium sulphate granules to kill slugs.

CHAPTER 6

SMALL GARDEN PLANTS

AN ENORMOUS NUMBER of plants are suitable for small gardens. Since so many houses nowadays have small, even tiny, plots, garden centres and nurseries cater much more for this group of gardeners than for the owners of huge gardens. Because of this it is not difficult to find a range of appropriately sized subjects. Even so, it is possible to make mistakes. This chapter features the best plants of each type to choose, offering suggestions for the best trees, shrubs, climbers, roses, perennials, bedding plants, moisture-loving plants, bulbs, and ferns, grasses and bamboos for the small garden. These are obviously not comprehensive lists of plants that can be grown in small gardens, just a small selection chosen for their all-round qualities. They will offer a useful starting point for those who don't know where to begin choosing what to grow. Most of the plants offer more than one feature of interest, really earning their valuable space in the small garden.

LEFT: *Hydrangeas make valuable plants for containers, flowering well through the summer months.*

RIGHT: *Even the smallest of gardens can accommodate a wide range of plants, from small trees and shrubs to perennials, climbers and container plants.*

Acer palmatum

Acer pseudoplatanus 'Brilliantissimum'

Cercis siliquastrum 'Rubra'

TREES

JAPANESE MAPLE

Acer palmatum

H 5m (16ft) S 5m (16ft)

Deciduous. These trees vary in height from 5m (16ft) down to 1m (3ft) making them suitable for a range of small gardens. All the Japanese maples are interestingly shaped trees, even in winter. The smaller ones of the 'Dissectum' group have very finely cut, feathery leaves and are very ornamental. They all take on wonderful autumn tints. They prefer a light shade (at least out of the hot midday sun) and a soil that does not completely dry out. No pruning is required.

VARIEGATED SYCAMORE

Acer pseudoplatanus 'Brilliantissimum'

H 5m (16ft) S 4m (13ft)

Deciduous. Unlike other sycamores, which are too large for small gardens, this variety is small enough for most, especially as it is very slow growing. The main attraction is the amazing foliage. The leaves are large like most sycamores, but they open an unusual light pink, change to darker pink and then to green before finally changing to yellow in the autumn. This makes a good tree for providing dappled shade. It is best planted in full sun but will tolerate a little shade. It grows in most soils. No pruning is required.

SNOWY MESPILUS

Amelanchier lamarkii

H 8m (26ft) S 6m (20ft)

Deciduous. A round-headed tree with attractive, butterfly-like white flowers in spring. The flowers appear before or just after the leaves open. These are light green turning to bright red-orange in the autumn. The snowy mespilus will normally grow as a shrub with multiple stems but if one of the stems is selected and the others removed it can be trained as a well-shaped tree. Once trained no pruning is required. It is best planted in full sun but will tolerate a little light shade. Any soil type is suitable for this tree.

WEEPING BIRCH

Betula pendula 'Youngii'

H 7.5m (24ft) S 5m (16ft)

Deciduous. As long as they are not allowed to get too big, many of the birches are suitable for the small garden. This birch generally stays smaller. It has a delicate weeping form and makes an excellent alternative to weeping willows which are far too large for small gardens. It is a good specimen tree for planting in or at the edge of a lawn as it sweeps the ground with its pendulous branches. However, other plants, such as shade-loving perennials, cannot be grown beneath it as the branches come down too low. It prefers sun and tolerates most soils.

JUDAS TREE

Cercis siliquastrum

H 6m (20ft) S 6m (20ft)

Deciduous. An attractive small tree or large shrub that is mainly grown for the masses of small purple flowers that clothe the naked branches in spring before or just as the leaves open. The foliage is a bluish-green with a purple tinge, especially when young. The leaves turn yellow in autumn. It can be mixed with other trees and shrubs or used as a specimen tree by itself in a lawn or border. No pruning is required. Plant in a sunny or lightly shaded position; any soil type is suitable.

CHINESE DOGWOOD

Cornus kousa var *chinensis*

H 7m (23ft) S 5m (16ft)

Deciduous. An award-winning tree that is popular because of its attractive flowers. In fact the actual flowers are insignificant but they are surrounded by creamy white bracts or modified leaves that look just like petals. They appear in late spring and being leaves they last much longer than true flowers. They eventually turn pink. The leaves also provide superb autumn colour, turning a flaming orange-red. They make good specimen trees or can be planted with other trees. No pruning required. A neutral to acid soil is needed.

HAWTHORN

Crataegus laevigata

H 6m (20ft) S 6m (20ft)

Deciduous. A neat, compact tree with a rounded shape that well suits small gardens. The clusters of flowers (May blossom) are produced in spring and vary from white through pale pink to dark pink in colour. There are forms such as 'Paul's Scarlet' which are so dark a pink as to almost be red. The flowers are single in some varieties and double in others. In autumn bright red berries are produced on the plant. No pruning is required but the tree can be clipped to keep it even more compact. Any soil conditions will do.

HONEY LOCUST

Gleditsia triacanthos 'Sunburst'

H 9m (30ft) S 8m (26ft)

Deciduous. An extremely attractive and award-winning tree. Its beauty lies in its foliage, which consists of long leaves, each made up of opposite leaflets, giving it a delicate, ferny look. The colour

is a very fresh golden-yellow which matures to lime-green before returning to yellow in the autumn. It has changing clusters of greenish-white flowers in midsummer. In many ways this is the perfect tree for the small garden, but it is relatively fast growing and should not be planted close to buildings. No pruning required. Honey locust prefers a rich soil.

HOLLY

Ilex x *altaclarensis* 'Golden King'

H 6m (20ft) S 3m (10ft)

Evergreen. This unusual variegated holly can be trained as a tree with a distinct trunk or as a bush with several main stems. The foliage is rounded with only a hint of the prickles found on most hollies. It is dark green with bright yellow margins, making it good for flower arrangements. In spite of its name this is a female plant and produces red berries in autumn, which are also good for indoor arrangements and Christmas decorations. No pruning is necessary but it can be clipped to reduce its size. Any soil is suitable.

ROCK MOUNTAIN JUNIPER

Juniperus scopulorum 'Skyrocket'

H 6m (20ft) S 60cm (24in)

Evergreen. An excellent conifer which is very useful in the garden for its vertical emphasis. It is a pencil-thin tree, forming a tall column. It takes up very little space in the garden but it adds height to any arrangement of plants. The foliage is a grey-green in colour, making it a good companion to green or lime foliage, or to flowers of many different colours. As with most conifers no pruning is necessary. It is important to knock off any heavy snow as this may bend the branches and distort the shape. It will grow in any garden soil.

Cornus kousa var *chinensis*

Crataegus laevigata 'Rosea Flore Plena'

Ilex x *altaclarensis* 'Golden King'

Laburnum x *watereri* 'Vossii'

Magnolia stellata

Prunus serrula

GOLDEN RAIN

Laburnum x *watereri* 'Vossii'

H 7m (23ft) S 5m (16ft)

Deciduous. This is one of the most suitable of the laburnums for the small garden. It has delicate foliage which offsets beautifully the long (up to 60cm/24in), hanging clusters of golden yellow flowers in late spring and early summer. The seeds of black laburnums are poisonous and the trees should not be grown if there are children around. However this form produces fewer seeds than other varieties, making it a bit safer. It needs no pruning, but it will need staking, especially if it is growing in an exposed position. Any garden soil is suitable for this tree.

BAY

Laurus nobilis

H 4m (13ft) S 3m (10ft)

Evergreen. This plant can be grown as a tree with a single stem or allowed to develop into a shrub with multiple stems. The flowers are of little significance, but it is grown for its dark green, leathery leaves. These not only make bay a good permanent structural plant in the garden, but they are useful as a herb in the kitchen. No pruning is required but it can be clipped into shape if necessary. It will grow in most soils, however it is often used in containers where a good general potting compost is required.

STAR MAGNOLIA

Magnolia stellata

H 3m (10ft) S 3m (10ft)

Deciduous. Most magnolias become too large for a small garden but this one, which is more of a shrub than a tree, is just perfect as it does not take up much space and yet is spectacular when it is in flower. The masses of flowers appear before the leaves and consist of strap-like petals which give a starry appearance. Most are glistenly white, although some varieties have pink or pink-tinged flowers. No pruning is required. Once planted star magnolias really resent being moved, so try to get their position right the first time round. Any good garden soil is suitable.

CRAB APPLE

Malus 'Profusion'

H 10m (30ft) S 10m (30ft)

Deciduous. Although in its standard form this crab apple can ultimately become a large tree it is possible to get this plant on a rootstock that restricts it to only 2–3m (6½–10ft), a perfect height for the small garden. It has wonderful purple foliage and dark purple blossom which appears in spring. In autumn small ornamental purple apples are produced. There are many other good crab apples that are perfect for the small garden. No pruning is required. It will grow in any good garden soil.

ORNAMENTAL CHERRY

Prunus serrula

H 7m (23ft) S 4m (13ft)

Deciduous. This is really an ornamental cherry tree for all seasons. The most striking thing about it is the smooth, copper-coloured bark that shines out beautifully in the winter sunshine. The bark is also prone to peeling, forming attractive copper ribbons. In the spring the tree has white flowers. The handsome green foliage creates a good dappled shade through the summer and then in the autumn small dark cherry-like fruits are produced on the tree. They are inedible but not poisonous. No pruning is required. This ornamental cherry will grow in any good garden soil. Plant it where the winter sun will strike it to best effect.

YOSHINO CHERRY
Prunus x *yedoensis* 'Shidare Yoshino'
H 5m (16ft) S 4m (13ft)

Deciduous. The perfect weeping tree for the small garden with a mass of branches cascading down from its crown. In spring it forms a waterfall of pink flowers that fade to white as they age. The flowers are slightly scented and open before the leaves. In the autumn the green leaves turn yellow before falling. A good plant for a focal point such as in the middle of a lawn. It needs no pruning and any good garden soil is suitable.

WEEPING PEAR
Pyrus salicifolia 'Pendula'
H 5m (16ft) S 4m (13ft)

Deciduous. A superb tree for the small garden especially if purchased on a rootstock that does not grow too large. It has a perfect weeping habit with branches sweeping to the ground. The foliage is an excellent silver-grey colour. In the spring it has clusters of white flowers. It makes an excellent specimen plant for the centre of a lawn or focal point elsewhere in the garden. It requires no pruning. This plant will grow in any fertile garden soil and is best planted in full sun.

ALLEGHANY MOSS
Robinia kelseyi
H 4m (13ft) S 3m (10ft)

Deciduous. An attractive tree with delicate grey-green foliage. Each long leaf is made up of up to ten leaflets, giving it a feathery look. These offset

beautifully the hanging clusters of deep pink, pea-like flowers that are produced in late spring and early summer. They are good for planting as a background to other plants, perhaps on the boundary of the garden. The trees need no pruning. They will grow in most fertile garden soils as long as they are not too wet. Avoid exposed positions.

KASHMIR MOUNTAIN ASH
Sorbus cashmiriana
H 4m (13ft) S 4m (13ft)

Deciduous. Most of the mountain ashes (*Sorbus*) make good trees for the small garden as they tend to be reasonably compact and are attractive. The outstanding feature of this one is the large clusters of white berries that are produced in the autumn which hang on well into the winter. In spring it has clusters of white flowers. The foliage is grey-green which turns to an attractive yellow in autumn. No pruning is required. It will grow in most garden soils. Plant where the autumn fruit can be clearly seen.

LILAC
Syringa vulgaris
H 4m (13ft) S 2.4m (8ft)

Deciduous. There are so many good lilacs to choose from, most being suitable for the small garden. The main attraction are the cone-like clusters of usually scented flowers that are so redolent of spring. The basic colour is lilac but there are variations available from white to dark purple. Some are more powerfully scented than others. They make good cut flowers for the house. Some standard forms have a single trunk but most have several main stems. No pruning is required. They will grow in most garden soil conditions and make excellent background plants for a border.

Pyrus salicifolia 'Pendula'

Sorbus cashmiriana

Syringa vulgaris

Abutilon megapotamicum

Aucuba japonica 'Marmorata'

Camellia japonica 'Tricolor'

SHRUBS

ABELIA

Abelia x *grandiflora*

H 1.5m (5ft) S 1.8m (6ft)

Semi-evergreen. This particular shrub is valuable as it fills the gap between late summer and autumn when there are few shrubs in flower. It has pretty small tubular flowers which are pink and white. The leaves are olive-green, often with a reddish tint. Some fall in autumn. It makes a good background shrub and can be fan-trained against a wall. About a third of the older stems should be removed in early spring each year. It will grow on any good garden soil.

TRAILING ABUTILON

Abutilon megapotamicum

H 1.8m (6ft) S 1.8m (6ft)

Semi-evergreen. A loose, open shrub that makes an excellent container subject for a small patio garden. The stems are black and stand out well against the foliage. The flowers are bell shaped with a red, balloon-shaped base and yellow petals and are well set off by the mid-green, heart-shaped leaves. This shrub is slightly tender but often hardy enough to be left outside in sheltered town gardens. Remove up to a third of the older wood every spring. Any good garden soil will be suitable.

SPOTTED LAUREL

Aucuba japonica

H 4m (13ft) S 4m (13ft)

Evergreen. This is a very solid-looking shrub with large glossy leaves. It is too massive for many small gardens, but makes a very useful, dense screen on the boundary of a garden if one is required. There are varieties with spotted leaves which lighten them and make them appear less solid, especially when grown in shade. It has clusters of pale yellow flowers in spring, followed by berries on female plants. No pruning is necessary but the plant can be cut back hard if it gets too big. Any soil will be suitable. This is one of the few shrubs that will grow in dense shade.

BARBERRY

Berberis

H 4m (13ft) S 4m (13ft)

Deciduous/evergreen. There are a large number of berberis that are suitable for the small garden. Most have small leaves, some evergreen other deciduous. Their colour varies from green to purple. Most have stiff prickly spines on their stems which make them good to plant under vulnerable windows or on the boundary of the garden to form an impenetrable hedge. The flowers vary from pale yellow to orange and are fragrant in some species. No pruning is required but it can be cut back to restrict size or keep it neat. Any soil will be suitable.

BUTTERFLY BUSH

Buddleja

H 4m (13ft) S 4m (13ft)

Deciduous. There is a wide selection of buddlejas that are suitable for the small garden although most will become too large for the smallest of gardens. The flowers, which appear in summer, are in long or round clusters and vary in colour from lilac to purple and from pale yellow to near orange. Butterflies and insects love them. They are best planted as background plants in a border. Many common varieties should be hard pruned early each spring, almost to the ground. Any soil, even dry ones, will be suitable.

BOX

Buxus sempervirens

H 5m (16ft) S 5m (16ft)

Evergreen. Box can be allowed to grow freely like any other bush but it is usually clipped tight and used to form a hedge or a topiary shape. The form 'Suffruticosa' is useful for miniature or dwarf hedges around beds and borders and along paths. As topiary, box can be clipped to virtually any shape you require. It is slow growing and has small oval, dark green leaves and insignificant flowers. Box only needs clipping over once a year and as a shrub needs no pruning at all. It will grow in any well-drained soil and tolerates situations from full sun to deep shade.

CAMELLIA

Camellia japonica

H 10m (33ft) S 6m (20ft)

Evergreen. Superb flowering shrubs that vary in height from low growing to almost tree-like proportions. The foliage is dark green and glossy and offsets the flowers beautifully. The flowers can be single, semi-double or double. They vary from light pink through to very dark pink and red. There are also white forms. Camellias need no pruning. They need a neutral to acid soil and light shade. Plant away from the early morning sun. They flower in late winter and spring and may be caught by the frost.

CALIFORNIAN LILAC

Ceanothus

H 4m (13ft) S 4m (13ft)

Evergreen/deciduous. Although these can be grown as free-standing shrubs they all make excellent wall shrubs. The evergreen ones generally have small oval leaves, dark green in colour, which set off perfectly the clusters of blue flowers that appear at varying times between spring and autumn. The shrubs are dense and tightly packed. The looser, deciduous shrubs tend to have larger leaves. Evergreen ones need no pruning but the deciduous ones need the previous year's growth cut back by at least half. Plant in a good soil in full sun.

ORNAMENTAL QUINCE

Chaenomeles

H 3m (10ft) S 3m (10ft)

Deciduous. These can be grown as free-standing shrubs or wall shrubs. In the former they usually become very loose straggly shrubs, too big and untidy for a small garden. However as wall shrubs they can be kept cut back and can be very compact and decorative. They flower in spring and often through the winter as well. The flowers can be single or double and vary in colour from orange through red to pink, and white. In autumn they have very hard, pear-shaped fruits, often with a decoratively coloured skin. Prune hard. Any soil, sun or shade.

MEXICAN ORANGE BLOSSOM

Choisya ternata

H 1.8m (6ft) S 1.8m (6ft)

Evergreen. A rounded shrub with attractive glossy foliage that sets off the clusters of white flowers that appear in late spring or early summer. There is often also a second flush of flowers, sometimes even in winter if it is a mild one. The flowers are deliciously and strongly fragrant and for this it is worth planting it near a sitting area or window that is often open. Remove up to a third of the old wood every year after flowering to help the plant rejuvenate. Plant in any good garden soil in either sun or shade.

Ceanothus 'Pin Cushion'

Chaenomeles 'Fire Dance'

Choisya ternata

Cistus 'Paladin'

Convolvulus cneorum

Cotoneaster horizontalis

ROCK ROSE

Cistus

H 1m (3ft) S 1m (3ft)

Evergreen. A large group of beautiful shrubs, most with soft hairy leaves, often grey but also bright green. The flowers are like single roses made of crumpled tissue paper and appear only for a day, but there is a continuous supply of them. The basic colour varies from white to various shades of pink. There is often purple or chocolate blotches on the petals in the centre of each flower. Some of the rock roses have resinous buds which produce a delightful aroma. Little pruning is needed except for light trimming. A well-drained soil and full sun is required by these plants.

SILVERY CONVOLVULUS

Convolvulus cneorum

H 45cm (18in) S 60cm (24in)

Evergreen. A stunning shrub with silvery foliage that appears to shine in the sun. This is complemented by white trumpet flowers throughout the summer. It is a compact plant that is perfect for the small garden. Unlike the more weedy convolvuluses this one does not spread and is not a rampant weed. It is short lived but will last several years or more if it has a well-drained soil and a warm, sunny position. It grows particularly well in walls. No pruning is required.

COTONEASTER

Cotoneaster horizontalis

H 1m (3ft) S 1.5m (5ft)

Deciduous. Low, spreading shrub that is sometimes grown as a free-standing shrub, but is more commonly grown as a wall shrub, when it will grow flat against the wall or fence. The main

branches have sub-branches arranged in a neat herringbone fashion. These are clothed with tiny oval leaves. In summer small white flowers are produced on the plant, followed by bright red berries. The berries last well into the winter and often through to the following summer. No pruning is required. This plant will grow in any garden soil in either sun or medium shade.

DAPHNE

Daphne tangutica

H 75cm (30in) S 1m (3ft)

Evergreen. Most daphnes are suitable for the small garden but this is one of the easiest to grow as well as being one of the longest lived. It forms a dense, rounded shrub, with dark green, oval foliage and pink starry flowers. These appear mainly in spring, but it often flowers intermittently for the rest of the summer and into the autumn. The flowers are very fragrant and are followed by orange-red berries which are poisonous. No pruning is required. Plant in any good garden soil that is reasonably well-drained. Light shade.

ELAEAGNUS

Elaeagnus pungens 'Maculata'

H 3.6m (12ft) S 4m (13ft)

Evergreen. A brightly coloured shrub that has bright golden leaves with dark green margins. The undersides of the leaves are duller but of a silvery-green. The young stems are a light brown dusted with gold. Altogether an attractive shrub. The flowers, however, are insignificant. It does not require pruning but its size can be contained by regular trimming. It can even be used to make a hedge. Cut out any branches that revert to green foliage. It will grow in any garden soil and can be planted in sun or shade.

HEATHER

Erica

H 30cm (12in) s 45cm (18in)

Evergreen. There is a wide variety of heathers suitable for the small garden. They are compact and easy to maintain. The foliage is small and needle-like. It is usually green but there are also golden forms. The flowers vary from white, through pink to purple and red. They mix well with conifers and other permanent subjects of a more subdued nature, rather than with annuals and colourful perennials. They need neutral to acid soil (although there are a few that can be grown on chalk) and do well on sandy soils. Full sun is best.

ESCALLONIA

Escallonia

H 3m (10ft) s 4m (13ft)

Evergreen. These are attractive shrubs with small glossy leaves that are oval in shape and light to dark green in colour. These are a perfect foil for the masses of small, bell-shaped flowers that appear in late spring and early summer and continue intermittently for the rest of the growing season. The flowers vary in colour from light to dark pink and through to red, as well as white. Prune out about a third of the old wood each year after the main flowering. It will grow on most garden soils. Sun or light shade will be suitable.

EUONYMUS

Euonymus fortunei

H 60cm (24in) s 3m (10ft)

Evergreen. Excellent shrubs for the small garden, especially for filling odd gaps or as ground cover. Although only low growing, they will scramble up through other shrubs or up walls and fences. The best forms are the variegated ones which are available with gold or silver variegations. These are bright and cheerful and are especially useful in shady areas as they lighten them considerably. No pruning is required. They will grow in any good garden soil and can be planted in situations with full sun to moderate shade.

FUCHSIA

Fuchsia

H 1.2m (4ft) s 1.5m (5ft)

Deciduous. There is a vast quantity of different fuchsia varieties to choose from and nearly all are suitable for the small garden. There is one important distinction. Some are hardy and can be left in the garden all year round, while others are tender and need to be given protection during the winter months. All fuchsias have very attractive flowers featuring pink, white, red and purple which appear over a very long season. The hardy varieties can be left unpruned, in which case they will flower earlier, or cut almost to the ground in early spring. They prefer sun or light shade.

SUN ROSE

Helianthemum

H 30cm (12in) s 75cm (30in)

Evergreen. A superb plant for the small garden. The shrubs form low hummocks and carry colourful flowers for a long period. There is a great number of varieties varying from bright brash oranges and reds, to soft, subtle pinks, whites and yellows. Some are double others single. The leaves are small, sometimes grey and sometimes green. They are perfect for the front of a border or for growing on a rock garden, raised bed, wall or cascading down a bank. Trim over after flowering. Full sun and well-drained soil are required.

Erica carnea

Fuchsia 'Thalia'

Helianthemum cupreum

Hydrangea macrophylla

Lavandula angustifolia 'Twickel Purple'

Philadelphus 'Manteau d'Hermine'

HORTENSIA HYDRANGEAS

Hydrangea macrophylla

H 3m (10ft) S 3m (10ft)

Deciduous. These are wonderful, old-fashioned shrubs with large, rounded heads of flowers over a long period from midsummer onwards. The heads of flowers can be dried for flower arrangements. The flower colour varies from pale to dark pinks and reds to blues and whites. The flowers tend to be pink on alkaline soils, reds on neutral and blues on acid soils. No pruning is required. Remove old flowerheads in spring. Any moisture-retentive soil will do but the colour of the flowers will vary. Light shade is preferred.

LAVENDER

Lavandula angustifolia

H 1m (3ft) S 1m (3ft)

Evergreen. These shrubs are grown for their foliage and flowers, especially the fragrance that is given off by both. The leaves are silvery-grey in colour. The flowers, which form on short spikes carried on stiff stems, are lavender-blue although there are some varieties with purple, pink or white flowers. This is an excellent plant for a herb garden or for lining either side of a path in a formal or cottage garden. Trim over the plants in spring to keep them compact and tidy. Remove old flowerheads in autumn. Any well-drained soil in full sun will do.

LAVATERA

Lavatera 'Rosea'

H 3m (10ft) S 3m (10ft)

Deciduous. An airy shrub that has masses of large pink, saucer-shaped flowers. The showy flowers appear over a long period from summer onwards.

If left unpruned, these shrubs start flowering much earlier but pruning helps to produce more flowers over the summer. In exposed positions this shrub can suffer from wind rock and can die in very wet winters. Frosts will cut it back but it will usually regenerate. Cut back the previous year's growth each spring, almost to the base. Any free-draining soil will be suitable. This shrub should be planted in a sunny position.

MOCK ORANGE

Philadelphus 'Manteau d'Hermine'

H 75cm (30in) S 1m (3ft)

Deciduous. This is a miniature philadelphus that is eminently suitable for a small garden. It flowers in summer with double flowers that are creamy white in colour and extremely fragrant with a typical philadelphus scent. Being small this shrub can be tucked away among other shrubs or among herbaceous plants in a mixed border. Once established, cut out up to a third of the old wood straight after flowering each year. It will grow in any good garden soil and can be planted in any situation between full sun and light shade.

SHRUBBY CINQUEFOIL

Potentilla fruticosa

H 1.2m (4ft) S 1.2m (4ft)

Deciduous. Very useful shrubs for the small garden. They make neat rounded hummocks and are covered with simple pink, yellow or white flowers over a long period in the summer. They fit in well with other shrubs or in mixed or herbaceous borders. You can get away without pruning them but the amount of flowering decreases. Once established it is best to prune out some of the old wood each year to rejuvenate the bush continually. Any soil will do and they prefer a sunny position.

RHODODENDRON

Rhododendron yakushimanum

H 1.2m (4ft) S 1.2m (4ft)

Evergreen. Many small rhododendrons and azaleas are suitable for a small garden, but this one really is one of the best. It has dark, glossy foliage that sets off the flowers beautifully. The large, handsome flowers are held in tight clusters and consist of pink bells, emerging from darker pink buds and finally ageing to white. On a healthy plant, the flowers will literally cover the shrub. No pruning is necessary. These plants need a neutral to acid soil and dislike any alkalinity. If the soil is moist enough they will grow in the sun, but otherwise they prefer a lightly shaded position.

COTTON LAVENDER

Santolina chamaecyparissus

H 50cm (20in) S 1m (3ft)

Evergreen. A very decorative shrub with finely cut silver foliage. It is a very useful colour for mixing in a border or container with very soft-coloured flowers such as pale blues and pinks. It is also useful for linking colours that might otherwise clash. This plant produces yellow flowers, but most gardeners remove these as they spoil the foliage effect. Trim the plant over lightly in spring when new growth starts. It will grow in any well-drained soil. Like all silver plants, it needs a sunny position otherwise it will languish and grow very leggy.

SKIMMIA

Skimmia japonica

H 1m (3ft) S 1m (3ft)

Evergreen. Attractive, glossy-leaved bushes that have clusters of fragrant white flowers in late spring. These flowers are followed in autumn by large shining red berries which remain on the plant all winter. Unfortunately it is necessary to have both a male and a female plant in order to produce fruit so ensure that you buy one of each. No pruning is required. These plants need to have a neutral or acid soil to thrive and dislike alkaline conditions. Skimmias can be grown in containers if the containers are large enough. They will grow in either sun or light shade.

THYME

Thymus

H 10cm (4in) S 50cm (20in)

Evergreen. A compact shrub that is ideal for the small garden. It is a valuable herb for kitchen use as well as an attractive garden plant. It can be grown in the front of a border or herb garden, or it can be grown on a rockery bed or allowed to tumble down a wall. It is perfect for growing in cracks in paving and will stand the passage of feet. It has small, fragrant leaves and clustered heads of pink flowers. It requires no pruning and will grow in most soils. It prefers sun.

VIBURNUM

Viburnum carlesii

H 1.8m (6ft) S 1.8m (6ft)

Deciduous. There are a number of viburnums that are suitable for small gardens, some of which are evergreen. This one has the advantage of being small and carrying the most deliciously scented flowers of all shrubs. The pretty domed heads of small flowers are white, opening from soft pink buds. They appear in spring. The softly hairy leaves turn orange-red in autumn. Plant this shrub with other shrubs or at the back of a border. It needs no pruning. It will grow in any reasonable garden soil and prefers a light position.

Rhododendron yushimanum

Skimmia japonica

Thymus 'Doone Valley'

Clematis 'Nellie Moser'

Clematis 'Mme Julia Correvon' (viticella)

Cobaea scandens

CLIMBERS

CLEMATIS

Clematis montana

H 12m (40ft) S 12m (40ft)

Deciduous. A strong climber that can easily fill a tree or cover a garage or shed. However, it can be controlled by pruning to fill a much smaller space. The flowers are pink or white and they have a creamy vanilla scent, stronger on warm days. Although it will scramble through trees and bushes it may need tying to other supports. No pruning required except to restrict size and remove dead wood. Any good garden soil will do. Plant with the roots in the shade but the top preferably in sun.

CLEMATIS

Clematis viticella

H 4m (13ft) S 4m (13ft)

Deciduous. A group of small-flowered clematis that are particularly valuable as they flower from mid-summer onwards and are suitable for growing through shrubs and trees that have already flow-ered. The flowers vary according to the cultivar from white through to blue, pink, red and purple. They are produced in great profusion. Prune back each spring to a pair of buds not far above the ground, removing all the old wood above them. Any good, preferably enriched, soil will do. Plant with roots in shade and top in sun or light shade.

CLEMATIS

Clematis large-flowered forms

H 4m (13ft) S 4m (13ft)

Deciduous. A very large group of some of the most decorative clematis. Some of the flowers are up to 25cm (10in) across. They vary in colour from white through pink, red, purple and blue. They vary in time of flowering from spring to autumn. They can be grown up trellis, poles, walls or through shrubs and trees. Prune each year by removing some of their growth, cutting back to a pair of strong buds, although some late-flowering cultivars need to be more heavily cut back, remov-ing most of the previous year's growth. Any good soil; roots in shade, top in sun.

CATHEDRAL BELLS

Cobaea scandens

H 10m (33ft) S 10m (33ft)

Evergreen. This is a perennial but it is usually treated as an annual in colder areas, except if grown in a conservatory. It has large, perfectly shaped bells which are creamy green turning to purple with age. Cobaea can be grown up any form of support. They are grown each year from seed and planted out after the frosts into a rich soil that does not dry out too much. They need a sunny position to flower well. No pruning is required; discard the dying plant in autumn.

CHILEAN GLORY FLOWER

Eccremocarpus scaber

H 3m (10ft) S 3m (10ft)

Evergreen. Not a vigorous climber but one that is very useful for growing through other plants, including other, early-flowering climbers. It has small tubular flowers that are a flame-red on the outside and orange on the inside. They appear over a long period from spring until autumn. They can be treated as an annual and grown from seed each year. Alternatively, in warmer areas and against walls, they can be left in the ground from one year to the next. No pruning is required. Any soil and a sunny position.

IVY

Hedera

H 5m (16ft) S 5m (16ft)

Evergreen. There are a large number of species and cultivars available. Nearly all are grown for their foliage rather than for flowers or fruit. The foliage varies in size and to a limited extent in shape. Colour also varies, sometimes with strong gold or silver variegations. Many ivies are very striking plants. They make excellent wall-covering plants and can also be used for covering the ground. They require very little attention and no pruning other than cutting the stems back from gutters and roofs where they have become a nuisance. Ivy is a self-clinging climber so no training is required. Any soil and situation from full sun to deep shade.

GOLDEN HOP

Humulus lupulus 'Aureus'

H 5m (16ft) S 5m (16ft)

Deciduous. A perennial climber that dies back to the ground every autumn. Hops are twisting climbers and readily attach themselves to poles, wires, string or trees and bushes. The stems are very rough and can cause skin burns if rubbed against. It is mainly grown for its beautiful golden foliage, but it also develops hops, which are at their best in late summer. Since it starts from ground level it does not attain any great height until midsummer. Any good soil and a sunny position.

CLIMBING HYDRANGEA

Hydrangea anomala petiolaris

H 12m (40ft) S 12m (40ft)

Deciduous. A strong-growing wall climber which can also be grown through trees. It can be rather too strong and may need cutting back regularly to prevent it invading gutters and roofs. The leaves are light green turning an attractive yellow in autumn. In summer it carries large and airy heads of pretty, lacy flowers typical of lace-cap hydrangeas. It is self clinging and needs no training or tying in. It will grow in any garden soil although preferably rich and moist. It grows in sun to medium shade.

MORNING GLORY

Ipomoea tricolor

H 3m (10ft) S 3m (10ft)

Deciduous. Although this climber is a perennial it is usually grown as an annual, especially when planted outside where it will not survive a winter. The flowers are very attractive funnels or shallow trumpets. The flared part of the trumpet is a rich and vivid blue or purple, inside which is a band of bright white with a final touch of yellow right in the base. These plants are grown from seed and should be planted outside only after the last frost of spring. They need a rich, moist soil and a warm position in the sun.

JASMINE

Jasminum officinalis

H 12m (40 ft) S 12m (40ft)

Deciduous. A climbing shrub that is grown for its deliciously scented flowers. They are white and appear from midsummer onwards. They are particularly fragrant in the evening and it is worth planting this climber near open windows or where you sit at that time of day in the garden. The plant itself is not overly attractive if it becomes restricted and over dense. To start with, tie the stems in to their supports. After the plant reaches a reasonable size, prune out dead and surplus wood to stop it forming a thick, dense mass. Plant jasmine in a rich, moisture-retentive soil and sunny position.

Eccremocarpus scaber

Ipomoea tricolor

Jasminum officinalis

Lathyrus odorata

Parthenocissus tricuspidata 'Vietchii'

Passiflora caerulea

SWEETPEA

Lathyrus odoratus

H 2.1m (7ft) S 2.1m (7ft)

Deciduous. An annual that is sown from seed every winter. It is hardy and can be planted out when large enough. It is grown entirely for its flowers, which are frequently cut for indoor use. Many cultivars are distinctly fragrant. The colours vary from white through pink and red to purple and blues. They are grown in a rich, moisture-retentive soil and allowed to climb through an arrangement of peasticks, trellis or some other support. In borders they can be grown through shrubs. They need a sunny position to grow and flower well.

HONEYSUCKLE

Lonicera periclymenum

H 10m (33ft) S 10m (33ft)

Deciduous. A twining plant that naturally grows through trees and bushes. It can be used up poles, trellis or any other form of support. It is grown for its heads of yellow tubular flowers which are highly and sweetly scented, especially around the time of dusk. Good for planting near windows and areas where you sit at that time of day. It flowers mainly in spring but is often repeat flowering. No pruning required except for removing dead wood. Any moisture-retentive soil will do. The roots can be in shade but the top should be in sun.

VIRGINIA CREEPER

Parthenocissus

H 10m (33ft) S 10m (33ft)

Deciduous. A wonderful climber for covering walls. There are several suitable species, each being reasonably vigorous and making a dense cover. The leaves are attractive throughout the summer, but it is their rich, fiery autumn colouring that makes them so appealing. The flowers are insignificant and rarely noticed, but they do attract many bees and other insects. These plants are self-clinging and need no supports. No pruning is required except to keep them back from windows, gutters and roofs. They will grow on any soil and can be grown in shade although they prefer sun.

PASSION FLOWER

Passiflora caerulea

H 6m (20ft) S 6m (20ft)

Deciduous. A slightly tender climber that is best grown on warm walls. It is grown for its curious but very attractive flowers. They are a mixture of creamy-white and bluish-purple. In autumn these are followed by egg-like orange fruits. There are other species and cultivars, but these are more suitable for indoor cultivation except in the warmest of areas. No pruning is needed but the plant can be heavily pruned every few years to restrict its size. A rich, moisture-retentive soil is required. Plant in a warm, sunny position.

POTATO VINE

Solanum crispum 'Glasnevin'

H 4m (13ft) S 4m (13ft)

Semi-evergreen. A vigorous but very attractive climber with large clusters of blue flowers through the growing season. It can be grown as a rather sprawling, free-standing shrub, but it is best trained against a wall, trellis or tall fence. It is not self-supporting and will need to be tied in to the support. The plant needs pruning; a third of the old wood should be removed to the ground each spring. It can be grown in any good garden soil and should be planted preferably in a warm, sunny position against a wall.

WHITE POTATO VINE

Solanum jasminoides 'Album'

H 5.5m (18ft) S 5.5m (18ft)

Semi-evergreen. A delightful climber that has clusters of white flowers set off against dark green leaves. The flowers are very fragrant and they appear in summer and into the autumn. This climber is on the tender side and should be grown against a warm wall although in warmer areas it can be used against a trellis or tripod. It works well in a white garden as the flowers are very bright. Up to a third of the old wood should be removed each spring to rejuvenate the plant. Plant it in a rich, moisture-retentive garden soil in full sun.

BLACK-EYED SUSAN

Thunbergia alata

H 1.8m (6ft), S 2.4m (8ft)

Deciduous. A perennial climber that is usually treated as an annual and grown from seed sown each spring. The flowers are a bright golden yellow with a distinctive black spot in the centre. It is not self-supporting and will need tying in unless it is scrambling through a bush. It can be grown up any form of support. This plant is suitable for borders or container displays. No pruning is required. Black-eyed Susan should be planted in a rich, moisture-retentive soil and should be kept watered, especially in containers which may dry out. Sun or light shade is required.

NASTURTIUM

Tropaeolum majus

H 1.5m (5ft) S 1.5m (5ft)

Deciduous. An annual climber with very distinct, trumpet-shaped flowers in bright oranges, reds and golds. These are set off beautifully by the dense,

light green, round foliage. It should be grown from seed each spring and planted out after the frosts. It can be used to climb up any sort of support or it can be allowed to spread out across the ground. Also suitable for containers. It needs no pruning. Grow in a moisture-retentive soil and preferably in light shade although it will grow in full sun.

VINE

Vitis

H 6m (20ft) S 6m (20ft)

Deciduous. There are a number of vines, some ornamental others producing grapes, that are worth cultivating. They can be used on vertical surfaces such as walls or trellis but come into their own when grown across pergolas or arbours to create shady seating areas. The leaves are large and in varying shades of usually light green. There are purple-leaved forms. The flowers are insignificant. No pruning is required except for those grown for fruit. Plant in a good free-draining, but moisture-retentive soil. Try to choose a site in sun, although they will grow in light shade.

WISTERIA

Wisteria

H 15m (50ft) S 15m (50ft)

Deciduous. A very attractive climber with long pendant clusters of mauve or white pea-like flowers. The flowers appear in late spring and occasionally later in the year as well. It is a vigorous climber and should be kept under control in smaller gardens. It can be grown up a wall as well as over pergolas and trellis. Alternatively, this plant can be trained as a free-standing standard tree. It is important to keep new growths cut back to just a few buds unless the spread is being extended. A rich soil and sunny position is preferred.

Solanum jasminoides 'Album'

Thunbergia alata

Tropaeolum majus

Rosa Abraham Darby

Rosa Cécile Brunner

Rosa Gertrude Jekyll

ROSES

ROSE

Rosa Abraham Darby

H 1.5m (5ft) S 1.5m (5ft)

Shrub rose. A delightful rose that does not get too big. It has good dark glossy leaves which set off the apricot-pink flowers beautifully. The flowers are large, double and delightfully scented. They appear over a long period from summer into the autumn. This handsome rose looks good planted with yellow roses such as *Rosa* 'Graham Thomas'. Prune side shoots back by about half in early spring and on older bushes remove up to a third of the old wood. It can be planted in any rich garden soil. It is best planted in sun.

ROSE

Rosa Aloha

H 3m (10ft) S 3m (10ft)

Shrub or climbing rose. This is an excellent rose with masses of flowers over a long period. The flowers are double, pink, getting darker towards the centre and have a wonderful scent. This pretty rose flowers from summer well into autumn and goes well with other flowers of pinks and reds. It can be pruned as a shrub rose or allowed to grow and tied in as a climber. Plant in any garden soil that has been enriched with manure or compost. This rose is best planted in sun.

ROSE

Rosa Cécile Brunner

H 1m (3ft) S 1m (3ft)

China rose. A low shrubby rose with arching stems carrying beautiful pale pink flowers that are set off by glossy dark green leaves. The flowers are double and highly scented. They appear continuously from summer into the autumn. This rose works well with deeper pink roses. Prune the side shoots back by about half in early spring and on older bushes remove up to a third of the old wood. Cécile Brunner can be planted in any garden soil that has first been enriched with compost or manure. It is best planted in full sun.

ROSE

Rosa China Doll

H 45cm (18in) S 45cm (18in)

Miniature rose. This is a dwarf Polyantha rose with clusters of small double flowers. The flowers are pink and set off against mid-green leaves. This rose is continuously in flower from summer well into the autumn. Being a small plant, it is ideal for small gardens where it can be used at the front of a border or could be grown in a container. Prune back the stems by about a third. This rose will grow in any garden soil but it will do best in soil enriched with garden compost or farmyard manure. Plant in sun.

ROSE

Rosa Dublin Bay

H 3m (10ft) S 3m (10ft)

Climbing rose. The glory of this climbing rose is its beautiful deep crimson flowers that darken towards the centre with a wonderful velvety quality. They are double blooms and have a long season, flowering from summer well into the autumn. The foliage is a good glossy dark green. This is really a marvellous rose for the small garden and can be grown against a wall or up a tripod or trellis. Once established, prune back the main shoots to maintain its shape and size and side shoots by a third. Plant in a good garden soil in sun.

ROSE

Rosa Gertrude Jekyll

H 1.5m (5ft) S 1.2m (4ft)

Shrub rose. A beautiful, award-winning (AGM) rose with double flowers of a most pleasing dark pink. They are fragrant and appear over a very long period from summer into autumn. The foliage is a mid-green. It goes well with pale pink roses. Prune side shoots back by about half in early spring and on older bushes remove up to a third of the old wood. It can be planted in any garden soil enriched with garden compost or farmyard manure. It is best planted in full sun.

ROSE

Rosa Graham Thomas

H 1.2m (4ft) S 1.5m (5ft)

Shrub rose. A very attractive rose with long arching stems carrying rich yellow flowers. These flowers are perfectly double and are carried in some quantity over a long period from summer right into the autumn. The dark glossy foliage sets the flowers off beautifully. This lovely rose mixes well with apricot and pale yellow roses. Prune side shoots back by about half in early spring and on older bushes remove up to a third of the old wood. It can be planted in any rich garden soil. It is best planted in a sunny spot.

ROSE

Rosa Iceberg

H 1m (3ft) S 75cm (30in)

Floribunda bush rose. This is one of the best white-flowered roses. It has clusters of double pure white flowers with the occasional red spot. It flowers from summer though to the autumn and also occasionally in the winter. It is an award-winning plant

(AGM). Although mainly grown as a bush rose, there is also a climbing form. It is especially good for a white garden or border. Prune back stems by about a third. It will grow in any garden soil but do best in soil enriched with garden compost or farmyard manure. Plant in sun.

ROSE

Rosa Little White Pet

H 45cm (18in) S 60cm (24in)

Miniature. A gem of a rose that should be in every small garden. It forms a low, rounded bush and is continually in flower from summer right through to late autumn. The flowers are relatively small but they are produced in abundance, making a fine showy display. The flowers are double and coloured very pale pink. As well as being suitable for borders, this rose is small enough to fit on to a rock garden. Prune back stems by about a third each year. It will grow in any garden soil but do best in soil enriched with garden compost or farmyard manure. Plant in sun.

ROSE

Rosa New Dawn

H 3m (10ft) S 3m (10ft)

Climbing rose. A wonderful climbing rose with pale pink flowers that are well set off against dark green, glossy foliage. The flowers are double and strongly perfumed. They appear continuously from summer through into autumn. One of the great benefits of this rose is that it will grow and flower in the shade of a north-facing wall. Once the rose is established, prune back the main shoots to maintain its shape and size, and side shoots by a third. Grow in any garden soil, but preferably one enriched with good garden compost. It can be planted in either sun or light shade.

Rosa Graham Thomas

Rosa Iceberg

Rosa New Dawn

Alchemilla mollis

Anemone x *hybrida* 'Honorine Jobert'

Armeria juniperifolia 'Bevan's Variety'

PERENNIALS

BUGLE

Ajuga reptans

H 15cm (6in) S 60cm (24in)

Evergreen perennial. A spreading perennial with dark green foliage and upright stems of dark blue flowers in spring. There are also variegated forms as well as ones with white or pink flowers. The foliage is pressed to the ground and so when out of flower it has virtually no height. It spreads without becoming a nuisance and makes a good ground cover. Remove the flowering spikes when they have faded. It prefers a moist soil and will grow in either sun or light shade, preferring the latter, under open shrubs or trees for example.

LADY'S MANTLE

Alchemilla mollis

H 60cm (24in) S 1m (3ft)

Herbaceous perennial. A wonderful plant that is too often dismissed as common. It has sprays of yellow-green flowers in early summer and again late in the year if the old stems are removed. The leaves are round and heavily pleated giving an attractive appearance, especially when wet with dew. Plant in the front of a border or beside water. Shear the plant over once the flowers begin to fade. Any garden soil will be sufficient. It will grow in shade but a sunny position is best.

JAPANESE ANEMONE

Anemone x *hybrida*

H 1.2m (4ft) S 1.8m (6ft)

Herbaceous perennial. Japanese anemones are an important part of any late summer border. They have single or double flowers, usually in shades of pink but there are also white versions. The flowers are carried on stiff stems that do not need staking. They spread, some forms almost invasively, but can be easily kept in check by digging round the clump. They work well with the rich blue of late agapanthus. They do not like to be too dry so a rich, moisture-retentive soil is best. They will grow in sun or light shade.

WOOD ANEMONE

Anemone nemorosa

H 15cm (6in) S 30cm (12in)

Herbaceous perennial. Delightful plants for the early spring. The flowers are pure white with a yellow central boss of stamens and are carried on nodding stems above a finely cut, filigree foliage. There are some cultivars with blue flowers. These are woodland plants and appear in early spring and have retired below ground again by the time leaves have appeared on the trees above. In the garden they can also be planted under deciduous shrubs where little else will grow. They soon spread to form a colony. These plants need a moist, leafy soil and grow best in dappled shade.

THRIFT

Armeria

H 30cm (12in) S 30cm (12in)

Evergreen perennials. Hummock-forming plants from which leafless stems rise carrying rounded clusters of pink or white flowers. These appear in late spring and early summer. The leaves are narrow and make a tight bun or hummock in many species and cultivars. These are plants of rocky cliffs and are perfect for use on the rock garden or raised bed. They can also be used at the fronts of borders, perhaps bordering a path. They like a well-drained soil and should be planted in a sunny spot.

ELEPHANT'S EARS

Bergenia cordifolia

H 45cm (18in) S 60cm (24in)

Evergreen perennial. This is a good all-year-round plant. In spring and early summer it produces thick stems carrying clusters of pink or white flowers. These appear above large rounded leathery leaves which are glossy and mid to dark green in colour. It is these leaves that give the plant its attraction for the rest of the year. In winter the leaves on many cultivars turn a rich red colour. This plant is an excellent ground cover plant and contrasts well with irises and other strap-leaved plants. It will grow in any soil and either sun or shade. Useful for a difficult spot.

BELLFLOWER

Campanula

H 1.2m (4ft) S 1m (3ft)

Herbaceous perennials. A large genus of plants with many species and cultivars varying from ground-hugging plants suitable for the rock garden to tall ones that are suitable for herbaceous or mixed borders. Although the shape of the plant varies, the flowers all have a characteristic bell shape. They are usually blue although there are white and pink cultivars and a few rarer yellow forms. Many will grow in either sun or light shade and are not too fussy about their soil as long as it is not too dry.

BLUE CUPIDONE

Catananche caerulea

H 60cm (24in) S 45cm (18in)

Herbaceous perennial. Attractive plants which have distinctive 'everlasting' flowers. The flowers are cornflower-shaped and are blue with a deeper purple-blue centre. They are carried on stiff stems above a fountain of narrow, grass-like hairy leaves that are a silvery grey-green colour. They appear in summer. The flowers can be dried for indoor arrangements. These plants are perfect for the front of a border especially when mixed with pink soft flowers, or for contrast bright yellow flowers. They will grow in any well-drained soil and need a sunny position to thrive.

LILY-OF-THE-VALLEY

Convallaria majalis

H 25cm (10in) S 30cm (12in)

Herbaceous perennials. Much-loved perennials with arching spikes of tiny white bells. These are very fragrant and wonderful for scenting a room when cut. The flowers are wrapped as in a posy within a pair of elliptical, mid-green leaves. The plant can be invasive but can easily be controlled. It grows in shade and is ideal for planting under shrubs as ground cover. It can be planted in any soil, but prefers a moist woodland-type soil. It will grow either in a sunny or shaded position.

YELLOW CORYDALIS

Corydalis lutea

H 30cm (12in) S 30cm (12in)

Evergreen perennial. This is a low, mound-forming perennial with a hummock of finely cut, filigree foliage. Over this, spikes of lemon-yellow flowers appear over a long period from spring to autumn. These are plants for rock gardens or the fronts of borders, although they have the habit of sowing themselves in just the right kind of odd corners and crevices (including in walls). Although they self-sow they are rarely a nuisance. They grow in any soil, but prefer a well-drained one. A sunny or shady position will be suitable.

Bergenia cordifolia

Catananche caerulea

Convallaria majalis

Delphinium

Dianthus 'Blue Hills'

Diascia cordata

DELPHINIUM

Delphinium

H 2.1m (7ft) S 60cm (24in)

Herbaceous perennial. Although these are quite big herbaceous plants they are not spreading and are suitable for a small garden with small borders. Indeed they are perfect for adding height to the borders. Most produce tall spires of blue flowers, although there are also pink and white cultivars. The flowers appear in summer. They can be grown in separate beds for exhibition or flower arranging purposes. The plants need staking and slugs must be kept at bay. They need a deep rich soil that does not dry out. A sunny position is preferred.

PINKS

Dianthus

H 36cm (14in) S 45cm (18in)

Evergreen perennial. Wonderful old-fashioned plants. The flowers are carried on stiff, arching stems in summer and in modern varieties into autumn. There are a variety of colours from pink to red, and purple and white. Many of the older varieties and some of the modern ones are scented, some highly so. They make good cut flowers. Out of flower they make good foliage plants with their silver leaves. They are ideal for cottage garden borders and for edging paths. They prefer a well-drained soil and live longer on non-acidic soils. They need a sunny position.

DIASCIA

Diascia

H 30cm (12in) S 45cm (18in)

Herbaceous perennial. Perfect plants for the small garden as they are comparatively compact and never get out of control. They are covered with flowers from early summer through to late autumn. Most are in shades of pink but there are some with purple or white flowers. They work well as front-of-border plants but some are good for weaving among low shrubs and other plants, tying the border together. They look as though they need a dry soil, but in fact they need a moist one to perform well. A sunny position is required.

MEXICAN DAISY

Erigeron karvinskianus

H 45cm (18in) S 60cm (2ft)

Herbaceous perennial. A delightful plant that should be in every small garden. The flowers are very similar to lawn daisies except that they are carried on thin stems. They are white and pink. The plants form large airy hummocks which are in flower from late spring through to late autumn. They self sow, often in the most delightful places. They are perfect for growing in cracks in paving or in walls. More conventional places include rock gardens and raised beds. They will grow in any soil and do best in sun.

SPURGE

Euphorbia dulcis 'Chameleon'

H 60cm (24in) S 45cm (18in)

Herbaceous perennial. There are so many good garden spurges, many of them suitable for the small garden. This one is especially good as it does not grow too big and is attractive for most of the growing season, from spring until autumn. Its big attraction is its purple-bronze foliage which is speckled with tiny yellow flowers. It is a very good foliage plant and fits in with many colour schemes. It is not long-lived but supplies enough replacements by gently self-sowing. Any soil and a sunny position is suitable.

HARDY GERANIUM

Geranium 'Patricia'

H 45cm (18in) S 60cm (24in)

Herbaceous perennial. An extremely good plant for the small garden. It is extremely floriferous over a long period and never gets too big. The flowers are magenta but not too harsh a colour. The ground beneath the plant is often also coloured magenta with fallen petals. It mixes well with softer colours or against a green or silver background. The plant forms a neat dome. It will grow in any good garden soil and prefers a sunny position although it will grow in the shade of other nearby plants.

HARDY GERANIUM

Geranium x riversleaianum 'Mavis Simpson'

H 30cm (14in) S 1m (3ft)

Herbaceous perennial. A wonderful geranium with a very long flowering season from midsummer onwards. It has pale pink flowers with a paler, almost white centre. These are set off beautifully by soft, greyish-green leaves. Each year the plant sends out stems in all directions which weave in and out between other plants which unite them all beautifully. It works especially well with silver foliage plants. The stems die back in winter. Plant in any good garden soil and give it a sunny position towards the front of a border.

SNEEZEWEED

Helenium

H 1.5m (5ft) S 1.2m (4ft)

Herbaceous perennial. Attractive, upright-stemmed plants that carry lots of daisy-like flowers in summer and autumn. The flowers vary in colour from golden and yellow single colours to mixtures of yellows, browns and oranges. They have a cheerful disposition and are perfect for the summer border. Some are perhaps too tall for the smallest gardens but there are some shorter varieties. They work well in a variety of settings, but look best with other hot colours: flame reds, oranges and golds. They like a rich moist soil and a sunny position.

HELLEBORE

Helleborus orientalis

H 45cm (18in) S 45cm (18in)

Evergreen perennial. Many of the hellebores make good small garden plants but the Oriental hybrids are some of the most useful. These have the widest range of flower colours varying from white to a deep purple that is almost black. Some have spots others have picotee edging. There is an increasing number of doubles. They flower in the spring and should be planted at the backs of borders where they can be seen in spring but are covered with more interesting plants in summer. Plant in a rich soil in light shade.

DAYLILIES

Hemerocallis

H 1m (3ft) S 1m (3ft)

Herbaceous perennial. These have exotic-looking flowers and make a good contrast to many other herbaceous perennials. Tall, stiff stems of flowers are produced above a fountain of strap-like leaves. The flowers only last a day but there is a sufficient stream of buds to present continuous flowering over quite a long period in the summer. The colour of the flowers varies from yellow to mahogany red. Some may be too big for smaller gardens but there are smaller species and cultivars which would be perfect. Plant daylilies in a moist soil in sun or light shade.

Helenium 'Pumilum Magnificum'

Helleborus orientalis

Hemerocallis 'Pink Damask'

Hosta 'Tall Boy'

Kniphofia 'Little Maid'

Lamium maculatum 'Beacon Silver'

CORAL FLOWER

Heuchera micrantha var *diversifolia* 'Palace Purple'

H 45cm (18in) S 45cm (18in)

Evergreen perennial. There are many heuchera that are suitable for the small garden but this one is particularly noteworthy because of its superb foliage which is a beautiful purple. Tall thin stems of tiny white bells airily float above the foliage in summer. Since this plant is usually grown from seed there is variation in the quality of the foliage so choose one when in growth so you can get a good leaf colour. Many of the modern cultivars have silver markings on the leaves. Give it a rich soil and a sunny position.

HOSTA

Hosta

H 1m (3ft) S 1m (3ft)

Herbaceous perennial. Hostas are some of the best foliage plants for any size of garden; even the smallest courtyard can accommodate them in containers. The plants form clumps with strongly shaped and marked leaves. They come in all shades of green and also include blues and yellows. There are also many variegated forms from which to choose. The flowers, usually pale blue or white, are also attractive and lily-like on tall stems. They make good ground cover. Give them a moist soil in sun or shade; they will tolerate much drier conditions if they are grown in shade.

IRIS

Iris

H 1.5m (5ft) S 45cm (18in)

Semi-evergreen perennial. A very large genus of plants varying from small bulbs to tall herbaceous plants, all with the typical iris-type flower of three drooping petals (falls) and three upright ones (standards). They come in a wide variety of colours either singly or mixed. The foliage is usually stiff and sword-like, making a good contrast to many other herbaceous plants, especially round-leaved ones. Those with thick rhizomes should have these exposed above the soil. Plant in any good garden soil. They should be in a sunny position.

RED-HOT POKER

Kniphofia

H 2.4m (8ft) S 1.5m (5ft)

Semi-evergreen perennial. A genus of plants from very tall to small miniatures that are perfect for the small garden. The flowers are carried on tall stems above the fountain of thin, strap-like leaves. The flowerheads consist of a cylindrical spike varying in colour from yellow to orange-red, and sometimes green. Some flower early in the year others much later. They contrast well with more rounded clumps of herbaceous plants and mix well with other hot colours. They need a rich soil and a sunny position to thrive.

DEADNETTLE

Lamium maculatum

H 30cm (12in) S 1m (3ft)

Evergreen perennial. A valuable ground-covering plant with small nettle-like leaves. These usually have a central silver stripe and sometimes the majority of the leaf is an attractive silver. The flowers vary in colour from pink to dark pink or purple. They flower in late spring and early summer with flushes later in the season. It is a good plant for weaving between others and filling in gaps. It can become straggly and need replanting after two or three years, but this is easy. It will grow on most soils in sun or light shade.

LILYTURF

Liriope muscari

H 30cm (12in) S 45cm (18in)

Evergreen perennial. A valuable perennial for its late flowering. Spikes of tiny round flowers appear in autumn and often continue into winter. They are a rich blue, a valuable colour for that time of year. The spikes of flowers rise out of tufts of grass-like foliage. These tufts are dense and several plants together create a good ground cover. They look good with late pink or red flowers. They will grow in most soils (but prefer acid) and like a shaded position. However, they will grow in a sunny spot if the soil is moist enough.

CATMINT

Nepeta x faassenii

H 45cm (18in) S 60cm (24in)

Herbaceous perennial. An excellent plant for any size of garden. The grey-green leaves and small lavender flowers carried on airy, arching spikes create a wonderful misty effect, ideal for romantic or cottage-style gardens. They mix very well with other soft colours, especially pinks and silvers. Yellow makes a good contrast. The plants begin to look untidy in late summer and are best cut to the ground when they will reshoot for an autumn flowering. Any well-drained soil will be suitable. A sunny position is needed.

MARJORAM

Origanum laevigatum

H 45cm (18in) S 45cm (18in)

Herbaceous perennial. A spreading plant grown for its foliage and flowers. Its leaves are scented when crushed so plant it next to a path if possible. The flowers grow on tall thin stems that appear above the mat of ground-hugging foliage. They are carried in clusters and are generally pink or purple although there is also a dirty white. The flowers create a slightly misty effect and are perfect for the front of a border. Cut off the flowerheads before they seed. These plants mix well with pink and blue flowers. They will grow on any soil and need a sunny position.

PENSTEMON

Penstemon

H 60cm (24in) S 60cm (24in)

Evergreen perennial. Very valuable plants for any size of garden as they are available in a wide range of colours and flower over a long period. The long flowers are tubular and come in a variety of pinks, reds, purples, whites and blues. The larger-flowered ones tend to be less hardy, but many will come through winter, some even flowering in mid-winter. Cut back hard in the spring as growth restarts. They will grow in any type of soil and should be planted in a sunny position

PERSICARIA

Persicaria affinis

H 30cm (12in) S 60cm (24in)

Evergreen perennial. A spreading, mat-forming plant which has something to offer in all seasons. It forms a tight mat of bright green foliage, which turns red in autumn and then brown, maintaining its colour throughout the winter months. The flowers are pink opening from red buds. They are short, cylindrical spikes held well above the foliage. They turn rust red in autumn and are still attractive right throughout the winter months. The dense foliage makes a good ground cover. This handsome plant will grow in any type of soil and is happy in either sun or light shade.

Liriope muscari

Penstemon 'Cherry'

Persicaria affinis 'Superbum'

Primula vulgaris

Pulmonaria rubra 'David Ward'

Sedum 'Ruby Glow'

Polemonium caeruleum

H 1m (3ft) S 30cm (12in) Z 4–9

Herbaceous perennial. This is an attractive plant with tall, upright stems that carry bright blue flowers in spring and early summer. There is also a white form. The leaves are made up from a number of parallel leaflets which give the concept of the ladder in the name. It works well as a clump in an herbaceous or mixed border. It fits in well with a green foliage background or with other bright early flowers such as doronicum. This plant will grow in most garden soils but does best on a moisture-retentive one. Planting can be in either sun or light shade.

PRIMROSE

Primula vulgaris

H 15cm (6in) S 20cm (8in) Z 4–8

Evergreen perennial. One of the best-loved of spring flowers. Soft yellow blooms are carried on thin stems above a rosette of light to medium green leaves. They have the most delicious scent. These are plants of light woodland and in the garden they are best placed under deciduous shrubs or trees, preferably informally mixed with other spring flowers. A lot of their charm is lost if they are planted formally or in serried ranks as a bedding plant. They must have a moisture-retentive soil if they are to do well.

LUNGWORT

Pulmonaria

H 30cm (12in) S 45cm (18in) Z vary

Evergreen perennial. A pretty spring-flowering plant that is useful for the rest of the year as a foliage plant. The flowers are carried in clusters on rising stems. Many have flowers that open from pink buds and then mature to blue of varying shades, giving the plant an unusual mixture of colors. Some remain pink or almost red, others are white. The foliage is rough with bristly hairs, sometimes plain green but often spotted or blotched with shiny silver. Sheer the plant over after flowering to get fresh foliage for the summer. Plant in shade in a moist soil.

SAGE

Salvia x *sylvestris*

H 75cm (30in) S 60cm (24in) Z 5–9

Evergreen perennial. A shrubby plant with spikes of small flowers in the summer. The flowers come in various shades of blue or purple, depending on the cultivar, of which there are a number available. The foliage is a mid-green and softly hairy. This is a plant for well-drained soils and is perfect for use in gravel gardens or Mediterranean beds. These plants mix well with pink, blue and purple-red flowering plants. They must have a sunny position to thrive, but they will grow well in any soil as long as it is free-draining.

STONECROP

Sedum 'Ruby Glow'

H 25cm (10in) S 45cm (18in) Z 5–9

Herbaceous perennial. Many of the sedums would be suitable for the small garden, but this is one of the best. It does not get too tall nor spread too far. It has flat-topped heads of deep red flowers from midsummer onwards. These are well set off against fleshy leaves of a rich reddish-green color. This plant can be used at the front of a border or it can be planted on a rock garden or raised bed. Any free-draining soil will be suitable and a sunny position is required.

HOUSELEEK

Sempervivum

H 10cm (4in) S 30cm (12in)

Evergreen perennial. Although these little plants do produce flowers, they are mainly grown for their foliage. This is fleshy and is produced in whorled rosettes, giving them a very graphic look. Most have a glaucous bloom on the leaves and some are distinctly hairy, as if covered with spider's webs. The colour of the foliage varies from many shades of green to bronze, purple and almost red depending on the variety. Houseleeks are very good for rock gardens and raised beds. They also do well in containers, including bird baths or other shallow receptacles. Try mixing several varieties together. Any soil with sun.

SISYRINCHIUM

Sisyrinchium striatum

H 1m (3ft) S 60cm (24in)

Evergreen perennial. Fans of iris-like foliage are produced by this plant, from which rise tall stems of flowers in summer. These are pale yellow and are only fully open in the sun, when they have a star-like quality. The leaves are pale green and suffer from brown tips that die back in late summer. It is a beautiful plant that mixes well with a wide variety of other plants, especially soft-coloured ones. Remove the flower stems before they set seed as they self-sow prodigiously. Any good garden soil and a sunny position is required.

VERBENA

Verbena bonariensis

H 1.8m (6ft) S 45cm (18in)

Semi-evergreen perennial. An incredible plant in that it is very tall and spindly with thin, wiry stems that carry small clusters of purple flowers for a very long period from summer until the first frosts. The stems are rough to the touch. In spite of the plant's height they appear almost transparent and can easily be seen through, making this one of the few tall plants that can be planted at the front of a border. It is not a long-lived plant, and needs a well-drained soil and a sunny position.

VERONICA

Veronica spicata

H 30cm (12in) S 45cm (18in)

Herbaceous perennial. A very beautiful plant with erect spikes of usually blue flowers set off against green or bluish foliage. There are several cultivars with different shades of blue flowers and some of pink, and others of white. The flowers appear in summer. These veronicas look good with other soft-coloured flowers. They are mat forming and perfect for the front of a mixed border, although they will also work well on rock gardens or raised beds. Remove the flower spikes as the flowers fade. Plant these plants in any well-drained soil in a sunny position.

VIOLA

Viola riviniana 'Purpurea'

H 15cm (6in) S 20cm (8in)

Evergreen perennial. There are many violas that will grow in a small garden, some being easier to grow than others. This is one of the easiest. It has bronze-coloured foliage which sets off the violet-purple flowers that appear in spring and again later in the year. Unfortunately, it is not scented. It is a vigorous self-sower and needs to be kept under control. It makes a wonderful edging to a path, especially round a bed of roses. It will grow in any soil, and although it will survive in shade, it loses its purple coloration.

Sempervivum 'Commander Hay'

Verbena bonariensis

Veronica spicata

Antirrhinum 'Royal Carpet'

Begonia semperflorens 'Venus'

Calendula officinalis

BEDDING PLANTS

SNAPDRAGON
Antirrhinum majus
H 45cm (18in) S 30cm (12in)

Annual or biennial. This is a hardy annual or biennial which is grown for its distinctive tubular
flowers, which when gently pressed, open like a
dragon's mouth. They come in a wide range of
colors, blue being the only one missing. Each plant
can have single-colored flowers or bicoloured
ones. They can be used in borders, bedding displays
or in containers. Antirrhinums can be bought as
plants or grown from seed sown under glass or
directly in the soil. Any good garden soil will be
suitable. Plant in a sunny position.

SEMPERFLORENS BEGONIA
Begonia semperflorens
H 30cm (12in) S 30cm (12in)

Tender perennial. This is a popular plant, both for
its foliage and for its flowers during the summer
and autumn. It has a waxy foliage in various shades
of green and bronze. The flowers are white, pink,
red or orange and often appear in profusion. They
are mainly used as bedding and container plants.
Although perennial, they are usually bought afresh
each year or grown from cuttings, and increasingly
also from seed. They should not be placed outside
until the frosts have passed. Any good soil. Light
shade or moderate sun.

BIDENS
Bidens ferulifolia
H 30cm (12in) S 45cm (18in)

Tender perennial. An attractive, sprawling plant
that can be used as a bedding plant but is more
frequently used as a container and hanging basket

plant. It has daisy-like flowers with yellow petals
and a bronze central disc. The flowers appear all
summer and well into autumn. The foliage is very
finely cut and delicate. It works well with orange
or flame red-flowered plants. It is bought afresh
each year or grown from seed or cuttings. Do not
plant out until frosts have passed. Any good soil
and sun are required.

SWAN RIVER DAISY
Brachycome iberidifolium
H 45cm (18in) S 45cm (18in)

Annual. This is a tender plant that is grown for its
profusion of small blue flowers. These are daisy-
like with vivid blue petals and a yellow central
disc. There are also strains that have white, pink or
purple flowers. They are used as bedding plants or
in containers of various sorts. Swan river daisies
can be purchased as plants or grown from seed
sown in the spring under glass. Do not plant them
out until after the threat of frost is over. They will
grow in any good garden soil and should be given
a sunny position to thrive.

POT MARIGOLD
Calendula officinalis
H 60cm (24in) S 45cm (18in)

Annual or biennial. This has yellow or orange
daisy-like flowers and can be single or double
depending on variety. Pot marigolds are used in
borders and as bedding and can also be grown in
herb gardens. They are usually grown from seed,
but can occasionally be found as plants in nurseries. They will also self-sow, but the resulting
plants tend to have basic single orange flowers.
Being brightly colored, they do well in hot-
colored borders. Plant in any good garden soil and
choose a sunny position.

COSMOS

Cosmos bipinnatus

H 1.5m (5ft) S 45cm (18in)

Annual. An attractive annual that is good for filling gaps at the back of a border. The flowers are flat saucers with white or pink petals and a yellow central disc. The foliage is very finely cut and has a filigree appearance. It is light green. The flowers can be planted in mixed-colour groups, but look more attractive when planted as a single colour. The white forms are superb for white gardens and borders. Grow from seed. They need a good garden soil, preferably moist, and a sunny position.

FOXGLOVE

Digitalis purpurea

H 2.1m (7ft) S 45cm (18in)

Biennial. The wild plant is very elegant with a tall spire of purple 'gloves' arranged up one side of the stem. There are also white forms. These self-sow and rarely need to be replanted. There are also cultivated varieties which have larger flowers that are arranged all around the stem. These come in a wider range of colours including apricot. The cultivated ones are best planted as a group, but the wild species works well when dotted through a border; it adds a romantic, old-fashioned air to the design. Any soil and sun or light shade.

WALLFLOWER

Erysimum cheirii

H 35cm (14in) S 30cm (12in)

Biennial. An old-fashioned bedding plant with erect stems of single- or multicoloured flowers. The colours are mainly in the yellow-orange-red range. Most forms have a wonderful, evocative scent. They are very colourful and can be used as spring bedding plants to be replaced with summer bedding once their flowers fade. They are grown from seed sown in spring and planted out in their flowering position in autumn to flower in the following spring. Avoid planting them in the same soil two years running. Wallflowers need a good garden soil and a sunny position.

CALIFORNIAN POPPY

Eschscholzia californica

H 30cm (12in) S 30cm (12in)

Annual. A beautiful annual with poppy-like, tissue paper flowers. The basic colour is rich golden yellow but there are also orange, red and white forms. These fragile flowers are set off by a mid-green foliage that is very finely cut. They will flower all summer and into autumn. These flowers can be used as a bedding plant or can be mixed into a general border. They look especially good with other hot colours, such as orange and flame reds. They need a well-drained soil and must be sited in a sunny position. Remove the seedheads to prevent invasive self-seeding.

HELICHRYSUM

Helichrysum petiolare

H 50cm (20in) S 1m (3ft)

Tender perennial. This is grown as a foliage plant because of its small, furry leaves that are grey-green. It has no significant flowers. The colour of the foliage is perfect for setting off the colousr of so many other flowering plants, both in a border or containers, including hanging baskets. The silvery foliage weaves its way through and between other plants. It is a perennial, but usually bought fresh each spring, or grown from overwintered cuttings. It is tender, so plant it out after frosts. Grows in any good soil in a sunny position.

Cosmos bipinnatus 'Candy Stripe'

Digitalis purpurea

Eschscholzia 'Harlequin Hybrids'

Lobelia erinus 'Colour Parade'

Matthiola incana

Nicotiana 'Crimson Rock'

BUSY LIZZIE

Impatiens

H 35cm (14in) S 45cm (18in)

Tender perennial. Colourful perennials that when grown outside are treated as annuals. The flat-faced flowers come in a wide range of colours mainly based on red and pink, but including white. As well as single-colour flowers there are also varieties with bicoloured flowers. They are mainly used as bedding and container plants. These plants are valuable as they are among the few really colourful subjects that can be grown in the shade. They look good when grown as a single colour in a large container. Plant in rich, moist soil and partial shade.

POACHED EGG PLANT

Limnanthes douglasii

H 15cm (6in) S 25cm (10in)

Annual. This plant gets its curious name from the fact that the flowers are white with a bright yellow centre, like a poached egg. The plants make very colourful edging to paths as well as drifts between other plants. They can also be used for bedding purposes. Flowering time is early summer or a bit later. Although they are grown from seed sown in spring, they also freely self-sow so once planted they will recur year after year. These plants are very attractive to honey bees. Plant in any soil and give them a sunny position.

LOBELIA

Lobelia erinus

H 15cm (6in) S 25cm (10in)

Annual. A versatile plant that is available in varieties that form hummocks or loose sprawling plants that are useful for hanging baskets or window boxes. The flowers are basically various shades of blue with a white spot, but there are an increasing number of pinks, purples, reds and white. Lobelia can be grown from seed or bought as small plants ready for planting out. It can get rather leggy and so is worth clipping over when this happens to rejuvenate it. It will grow in any moist soil and in either sun or partial shade.

STOCK

Matthiola incana

H 75cm (30in) S 30cm (12in)

Perennial. This perennial is usually treated as an annual. There are several different types of stocks, but they all have closely packed spikes of highly scented flowers. They are double flowers varying in colour depending on cultivar from white through pink to purple, often in soft colours. The leaves are softly hairy and grey-green. These plants are usually grown from seed but can be purchased as young plants. They are mainly used for bedding or in a mixed border. Any good soil will suffice and they should have a sunny position.

TOBACCO PLANT

Nicotiana

H 1.5m (5ft) S 60cm (24in)

Annuals and biennials. There are several different species varying in height from 30cm (12in) to the tall *N. sylvestris* at 1.5m (5ft). The trumpet-shaped flowers are common to all species and varieties as is the range of colours from white to red, including pinks, reds and purples as well as green. Most tobacco plants are deliciously scented. The foliage is softly hairy and sticky. They are used for bedding, the taller ones being suitable for the back of mixed borders. Tobacco plants can be grown from seed or bought as young plants. Any good soil will do and sun or light shade.

LOVE-IN-A-MIST

Nigella damascena

H 45cm (18in) S 45cm (18in)

Annual. These hardy annuals are delightful plants with flowers surrounded by filigree bracts which create the 'mist' in the name. Basically they are a soft creamy blue but there are also white and pink forms. The seed pods are also very beautiful and are worth drying for indoor use. The foliage is very finely cut. Love-in-a-mist can be grown in any border, either in groups or scattered throughout. They are grown from seed but will usually self-sow for the following year. They will grow in any soil and prefer a sunny position.

OSTEOSPERMUM

Osteospermum

H 60cm (24in) S 60cm (24in)

Tender perennial. These plants have daisy-like flowers in a wide range of colours including multicoloured ones. Some have curious, but attractively distorted petals. Most of them only fully open in sunshine. In milder areas they may be hardy but in most it is best to overwinter cuttings and start again in the following year. They can also be bought as young plants, ready to go out. These can be used as bedding plants or planted in groups towards the front of a mixed or herbaceous border. They will grow in any good garden soil and need a sunny position to thrive.

OPIUM POPPY

Papaver somniferum

H 1.5m (5ft) S 45cm (18in)

Annual. Tall, upright plants with beautiful papery poppy flowers in a variety of colours from pink through red to purple as well as white. There are double forms as well as some with cut petal margins. The foliage is a light grey-green. The dried seed pods are attractive and useful for indoor decorations. Opium poppies are grown from seed and will usually self-sow, making it unnecessary to resow the following year. They can be used in any situation in the garden as long as it is sunny. Any garden soil will do.

PELARGONIUM

Pelargonium

H 45cm (18in) S 45cm (18in)

Tender perennial. Often also called geranium. These are colourful plants that are mainly used in containers although they can be used as bedding plants. Some form a bushy plant while others are sprawling and are useful as trailing plants for hanging baskets and window boxes. The flowers are mainly reds, pinks and white. The foliage in some varieties is also very colourful and in others it is glossy. Plants are usually started afresh each year from cuttings. They will grow in any good soil and should be given a sunny position.

PETUNIA

Petunia

H 40cm (16in) S 1m (3ft)

Annual. Very colourful plants that are popular for both containers, especially hanging baskets, and bedding. They have funnel-shaped flowers which are often delightfully scented. The range of colours is extensive, some being a single colour while others are bicoloured, sometimes with stripes or spots. Most have either a deeper or paler central eye. Petunias can be grown from seed or cuttings. They are widely available to buy as plants in nurseries or garden centres. They will grow in any good soil and prefer a sunny position.

Nigella damascena

Osteospermum 'Trewidden Pink'

Pelargonium 'Pink Golden Harry Hieover'

Astilbe x *arendsii* 'Hyazinth'

Caltha palustris 'Flore Plena'

Houttuynia cordata 'Chameleon'

MOISTURE-LOVING PLANTS

ASTILBE

Astilbe x *arendsii*

H 1.2m (4ft) S 60cm (24in)

Perennial. A delightful plant with vertical, feathery plumes of flowers. The colours are mainly creams, pinks, purples and reds. They are held well above the deeply divided foliage, which is attractive in its own right. The flowers appear in summer and the brown, dead flowers look attractive in winter. They can be grown in a bog garden or beside water, preferably in drifts. The soil should be moist but not waterlogged. They grow in light shade but can be grown in sun as long as the soil is moist enough.

MARSH MARIGOLD

Caltha palustris

H 30cm (12in) S 1m (3ft)

Perennial. Also known as kingcups and one of the glories of the spring. They have large buttercup-like flowers that are a shining gold, set off against shiny green leaves. There are double varieties. They will grow in bog gardens or beside water. As long as it is not deep they will also grow in water. They will tolerate shade but shine out best in sunshine. They also grow in ordinary borders as long as the soil is moist enough. Any good garden soil will do.

WATER HYACINTH

Eichhornia crassipes

H 15cm (6in) S infinite

Tender perennial. This can become invasive but in colder areas it is kept in check by the winter. It has handsome spikes of blue flowers which ride above the rosettes of shiny green leaves. It quickly forms a large mat on the water but is cut back by frosts and pieces should be overwintered in a bucket in a greenhouse to be on the safe side. Water hyacinth floats on any depth of water. No soil is required but it should be given a sunny position.

CANADIAN PONDWEED

Elodea canadensis

H submerged S indefinite

Perennial. This pond weed has the potential to become a nuisance in that it spreads rapidly and can choke a pond. On the other hand it is a very good oxygenating plant, essential for a pond with fish in it. In spite of its rapid growth this weed is easy to pull out and areas of the pond should be kept clear of it. The narrow leaves spiral out from the branching stems and form a kind of open cylinder. It has insignificant white flowers. To start it off, tie a bundle of the weed stems with a strip of lead or other weight and drop it into the pond where it will sink to the bottom. It needs a sunny situation to thrive.

WATER VIOLET

Hottonia palustris

H submerged S indefinite

Perennial. A submerged perennial water plant that produces tall (up to 60cm/24in) flower spikes above the surface of the water. These airy spikes carry whorls of pretty small white or lilac flowers and appear during the summer months. The foliage stays below water and is finely divided and bright green in colour. The plant will grow in up to about 60cm (24in) of water, so is suitable for shallow ponds. Plant cuttings in a basket or tie a bundle with a strip of lead or other weight and drop it into the pond. It needs a sunny position.

HOUTTUYNIA
Houttuynia cordata 'Chameleon'
H 30cm (12in) S 1m (3ft)

Perennial. This is an excellent moisture-loving plant for the bog garden or margin of a pond. It will grow in wet conditions, including shallow water. It has a variegated foliage, coloured in dull green, yellow and red. The stems are also red. During the spring it produces greenish-yellow cone-like flowers surrounded by white, petal-like bracts. It tends to sprawl, sending out long trails of colourful foliage between and through other plants. It will grow in any moist soil and in either sun or light shade. There are also green-leaved and double-flowered forms.

ASIATIC WATER IRIS
Iris laevigata
H 1m (3ft) S 30cm (12in)

Perennial. An excellent iris for either growing in a bog garden or in shallow water. It produces typical iris-like flowers with three hanging petals and three erect ones. The basic colour is blue but there are many cultivars to choose from including white and purple ones. Most are bicoloured. The foliage is sword-shaped and upright, making it look good when planted in association with water. It will spread to form a large clump, but is not invasive. It will grow in any good soil as long as it does not dry out too much. It needs a sunny position.

CORKSCREW RUSH
Juncus effusus 'Spiralis'
H 45cm (18in) S 45cm (18in)

Perennial. This is a curious rather than beautiful plant, although it does have some charm. It forms a tufted plant with very thin, needle-like stems and no leaves (the stems act as leaves). These stems are contorted and grow in spirals, producing a rather bizarre curly-headed plant. Its flowers are insignificant. This plant will grow either in a bog garden or beside a pond. It will also grow in shallow water on the margins of the pond. Any soil will do. It will grow best in sun or light shade.

CARDINAL FLOWER
Lobelia cardinalis
H 1m (3ft) S 30cm (12in)

Perennial. This handsome plant is called the cardinal flower because of its bright red flower, reminiscent of a cardinals' robes. The scarlet flowers appear on tall spikes over a long period in summer and well into autumn. The flowers are just like larger versions of the bedding lobelia, with its distinctive trumpet shape. The foliage is green and offsets the flowers beautifully. There excellent cultivars such as 'Queen Victoria' with purple foliage and 'Cherry Ripe'. It will grow well as a bog garden plant or beside water. Any garden soil and a sunny position is required.

PURPLE LOOSESTRIFE
Lythrum salicaria
H 1.2m (4ft) S 45cm (18in)

Perennial. This is a colourful perennial for the bog garden or for planting beside a pond. It is a slowly spreading, clump-forming plant with upright stems carrying spires of purple-red flowers. It flowers in the summer and into autumn. It is a very useful plant for adding strong blocks of purple-red beside a pond. The narrow foliage provides a good background to the flowers. It can be grown in any soil, preferably a moist one, but it should not be waterlogged or actually standing in water. It needs a sunny position to do well.

Iris laevigata

Lobelia cardinalis

Lythrum salicaria 'Feuerkerze'

Mimulus luteus

Nymphaea 'Lotus'

Nymphaea 'Pink Sensation'

WATER MINT

Mentha aquatica

H 1m (3ft) S 1m (3ft)

Perennial. An upright plant with running underground stems that spread to create a large patch. The plant can be invasive but is good for a wildlife or natural pond. It has roundish flower heads of lavender pink flowers in summer. The foliage is very aromatic with a distinct mint fragrance. It can be grown in a bog garden or beside a pond. It will tolerate most soils as long as they are moist and will grow in shallow water. These plants should be given a sunny position. In limited space plant the mint in a sunken container to prevent it spreading into the other plants around it.

YELLOW MONKEY FLOWER

Mimulus luteus

H 30cm (12in) S 60cm (24in)

Perennial. A wonderful perennial for growing round the margins of ponds or through other plants at the front of a bog garden. The flowers look a bit like cheeky faces. They are yellow with red spots. The plant is sprawling, with trailing stems that scramble up through other plants in a rather delightful way. It will grow either in moist soil or in shallow water on the edge of a pond. The questing stems will root, eventually covering a large area but it is not invasive and is easy to remove if you want to. It needs sun to do well.

WATER FORGET-ME-NOT

Myosotis scorpioides

H 30cm (12in) S 30cm (12in)

Perennial. Like the ordinary garden forget-me-not this has small blue flowers that open in a spiral. They appear in early summer and spangle the waterside plants with dots of bright blue. It is a plant for both the bog garden and for the edges of ponds. It will grow in shallow water (up to 15cm/6in deep) at the edge of the pond as well as on the banks beside the pond. Unlike the garden forget-me-not this plant is perennial and continues without replacement. It will grow in any soil as long as it is moist, and needs a sunny position.

WATERLILY

Nymphaea

H floating S indefinite

Perennial. There are hundreds of different waterlilies of varying colours and shapes. The leaves also vary in shape and colour, many having bronze markings. They also vary in their vigour, some spread rapidly across the pond while others are much slower. Some are more hardy than others and they may also grow in different depths of water. So, when buying, check that you are getting one that suits your needs. In a small garden it is best to avoid vigorous waterlilies. They will grow in any aquatic compost and need a sunny position.

BISTORT

Persicaria bistorta 'Superba'

H 1m (3ft) S 1.8m (6ft)

Perennial. A fresh-looking plant for the bog garden or edge of a pond or stream. It has tall stems which carry tight, cylindrical heads of pink flowers. These hover above the dense mat of large leaves that makes an excellent ground cover. The plants come into flower in early summer when they have their main flush and then continue intermittently until autumn. It mixes with many of the other bog plants and works well with contrasting plants such as grasses and hostas. It will grow in any moist soil and in either sun or light shade.

PICKEREL WEED
Pontederia cordata
H 1 m (3ft) S 75cm (30in)

Perennial. This is a rather beautiful plant for growing in the pond. It produces long stems above the surface of the water that carry tight cylindrical heads of pale blue flowers. They flower during the summer and early autumn months. The foliage is a glossy green and lance shaped. This foliage forms a good background to the flowerheads and is decorative in its own right. The plant will grow in moist soil, but it looks best growing in water. It will thrive in any soil, as long as it is moist, and needs to be planted in a sunny position.

JAPANESE PRIMROSE
Primula japonica
H 45cm (18in) S 36cm (14in)

Perennial. Many of the primulas are happy to grow near water but this is one of the easiest and most attractive. The flowers appear in whorls up the stem. They are either reddish-purple or white. The plants are in flower in late spring and early summer. The tall spikes appear from a rosette of typical primula leaves. They are not long lived but they happily self-sow so that they are always present. These attractive plants will grow in any moist soil in a bog garden or beside a pond or stream. Light shade or sun is best.

GREATER SPEARWORT
Ranunculus flammula
H 1.2m (4ft) S 1m (3ft)

Perennial. This is a plant for bog gardens and the margins of ponds. It is especially valuable in natural or wildlife ponds. It is just like a giant buttercup with shiny golden cup-like flowers borne on tall, slender stems. The long, strap-like foliage grows on separate stems to the flowers. The leaves are blue-green. The plant forms a clump and the tall stems often weave through nearby plants. It grows in moist soil or in shallow water, up to 15cm (6in) deep. This plant should be planted in a bright sunny position to do well.

CHINESE RHUBARB
Rheum palmatum
H 2.4m (8ft) S 1.8m (6ft)

Perennial. A spectacular plant for the bog garden or for planting beside water. It has giant rhubarb-like leaves with jagged margins, making a very architectural statement in the garden. The undersides of the leaves are a rich purple. In early summer rheum throws up very tall, bright red flowering stems that are covered with clusters of cream or red flowers in a very eye-catching way. Even when the flowers are dead the brown stems are still a sight to see. This plant will grow in any moist but not waterlogged soil. A sunny position is needed. For the smaller garden, *R*. 'Ace of Hearts' would be better as it is half the size of the species.

GLOBEFLOWER
Trollius europaeus
H 75cm (30in) S 45cm (18in)

Perennial. A colourful plant for the spring in the bog garden or waterside border. As its name suggests the flowers are spherical. They are a rich gold although there are also paler varieties. They are really a larger form of a buttercup flower. These plants flower from late spring into early summer. The foliage is deeply divided, again like the leaves of many buttercups. The plant forms a rounded clump. They grow in any moist soil. Plant in either a sunny or lightly shaded position.

Persicaria bistorta 'Superba'

Pontederia cordata

Primula japonica 'Miller's Crimson'

Agapanthus Headbourne hybrid

Chionodoxa gigantea

Dahlia 'Alva's Doris'

BULBS

AFRICAN BLUE LILY

Agapanthus

H 1m (3ft) S 60cm (24in)

A perennial but often considered a bulb because of its fleshy roots. This is a very attractive plant with round heads of blue or white trumpet flowers carried on a tall stem. They flower in summer. The flower stems arise from a fountain of strap-like leaves. The shape and colour of agapanthus are very useful when designing a border. They go well with so many other plants, especially pinks and reds. They like a moisture-retentive but well-drained soil and should be planted in a sunny position.

ORNAMENTAL ONION

Allium

H 1m (3ft) S 30cm (12in)

There are many ornamental onions for the small garden. The various species and cultivars flower at differing times in spring and summer. The flowers are carried in heads on the top of a leafless stalk. In some species the heads are spherical and make good dried decoration. The colours of the flowers are mainly shades of pink or purple, but also include white, blue and yellow. The foliage is strap-like and comes from the base of the plant. It often looks tatty and the bulbs are best planted between other plants to hide it. Plant in any soil in sun.

GLORY OF THE SNOW

Chionodoxa

H 20cm (8in) S 5cm (2in)

So called because they often flower through the retreating snow. These are small bulbous plants that have star-like flowers with blue petals and a white centre. There are also white and pink varieties. The short leaves are strap like. These delightful plants can be planted in odd places between other plants where they shine out in spring, before much else is in flower. They look particularly effective in drifts and can also be used in containers. Plant in autumn in a free-draining soil in a sunny position.

NAKED LADIES

Colchicum

H 30cm (12in) S 15cm (6in)

The flowers of these bulbs appear in the autumn directly from the soil without any foliage (hence the name 'naked ladies'). They are shaped rather like crocuses. They are mainly shades of pink and purple, but there are also white forms. The shiny foliage appears in the late spring and has disappeared again by the time the flowers arrive. They are usually planted between other plants so that the flowers can be seen in autumn but the leaves are covered up and out of sight. Plant in any good soil in a sunny position.

CROCUS

Crocus

H 15cm (6in) S 2.5cm (1in)

There is a large number of these well-loved bulbs. The majority flower in spring, appearing in a wide range of colours, especially blues, purples, yellows and white. They are goblet shaped and have a ruff of very narrow leaves. The larger crocuses can be naturalized in grass. There are also some species that flower in autumn, when blue predominates. There are also another group of more difficult bulbs which are usually grown in containers. Crocuses will grow in any well-drained soil in a sunny position, which includes under deciduous trees and bushes.

CYCLAMEN

Cyclamen hederifolium

H 10cm (4in) S 30cm (12in)

These delightful bulbs are completely hardy. They flower in late summer and into the autumn, producing pink or white flowers held above the bare soil. As the flowers fade so the leaves appear and remain until the following year. The foliage has decorative markings and is ornamental in its own right. The tuber should be planted with the top above the soil. Eventually these will grow very large. They readily self-sow to eventually produce a colony. Any well-drained soil and light to medium shade. Very good for difficult areas.

DAHLIA

Dahlia

H 1.5m (5ft) S 60cm (24in)

A decorative plant for the border but also for cut flowers for the house and exhibition. They flower in summer and autumn. There is a wide variety of shapes, sizes and colours. It is one of those plants to which people can be addicted and collect many varieties. They can be used in borders or grown in separate beds. They are tender and the tubers are usually lifted each autumn and stored in a cool frost-free place. Plant in a rich soil in a sunny position. Taller varieties need staking.

WINTER ACONITE

Eranthis hyemalis

H 7.5cm (3in) S 7.5cm (3in)

Delightful little plants that act as a harbinger of spring; once seen, warmer days are not far away. These have buttercup-like flowers with shiny golden petals, that are surrounded by a ruff of deeply cut green leaves, making each an individual posy.

Once planted they will naturalize and spread, forming a carpet of gold. They are useful under deciduous trees and shrubs where little else will grow once there is a leaf cover. They will grow in any garden soil and can be planted in a sunny position or light shade.

DOG'S-TOOTH VIOLET

Erythronium dens-canis

H 15cm (6in) S 15cm (6in)

These are so-called because the small bulbs look like a dog's tooth. The flowers are exquisite and it is a plant that ought to be more widely planted. The nodding flowers come in shades of pink with narrow petals bent back. They look very dainty and graceful. The flowers appear on leafless stems floating above the foliage, which is attractively mottled brown over a bluish-green background. Once planted they spread to form a clump. These are woodland plants and need a moist fibrous soil. They should be planted in light shade; under deciduous trees is ideal.

FRITILLARIES

Fritillaria

H 45cm (18in) S 25cm (10in)

There are a number of fritillary species of which a few are suitable for the open garden, and a large number more suited to containers. They vary from low-growing species with solitary bells to taller ones with multiple flowers. The colours vary, with blue being the only one missing. The snake's head fritillary (F. meleagris) is one of the most beautiful and easiest to grow. This needs a moist soil and a sunny position. It can be naturalized in grass if you have a meadow or rough area. Most of the other species are best grown in a well-drained soil on a rock garden or raised bed in a sunny position.

Eranthis hyemalis 'Guinea Gold'

Erythronium dens-canis

Fritillaria imperialis

Galanthus nivalis 'Straffan'

Iris reticulata 'Harmony'

Lilium 'Enchantment'

SNOWDROP

Galanthus

H 20cm (8in) S 5cm (2in)

One of the delights of the winter months. Although they are all alike to the untutored eye, there are over 300 species and varieties, but the common ones are just perfect for most gardeners. The white nodding flowers hang over green, strap-like leaves. The bulbs clump up quickly and should be divided every three years, immediately after flowering. In this way the colony is kept healthy and an attractive drift can be created. Buy growing plants rather than dried bulbs. Plant them in any garden soil, preferably in a lightly shaded position, such as under deciduous shrubs or trees.

GLADIOLUS

Gladiolus

H 1.5m (5ft) S 25cm (10in)

Very distinct plants, these cormous bulbs produce tall, slightly arching stems of funnel-shaped flowers. The flowers appear down one side of the stem. There is a wide range of colours of which soft ones predominate although there are some fiery reds and oranges. The leaves are stiffly erect and sword-like. They can be grown in the open border, but some gardeners get addicted to them and prefer to have a separate bed, growing for cutting and for exhibition. Lift corms in autumn and store until the following spring. Any free-draining soil in sun.

BLUEBELLS

Hyacinthoides non-scripta

H 30cm (12in) S 30cm (12in)

This is one of the glories of the springtime wood-land scene. These blue bells hang from leafless stems surrounded by arching, strap-like leaves.

They spread rapidly by seed and should be planted with caution. *H. hispanica* is very similar, although with paler bells, but has the advantage that it does not spread so rapidly and is a better choice for a more formal garden. This species includes pink varieties. Plant in any good garden soil. They will grow in sun, but are useful for unused spaces under deciduous shrubs or trees.

HYACINTH

Hyacinthus

H 30cm (12in) S 10cm (4in)

This is a wonderful plant for spring, either grown in the open garden or in containers. It produces dense flower spikes of bell-like flowers. There is a very wide range of colours and they are usually heavily scented with a distinctive fragrance. The flower spike rises from stiff strap-like leaves. A good way of using them is to plant a few bulbs in containers for one spring and then plant them out in the garden for subsequent years. They can be forced for indoor use. Plant in any good garden soil in sun or light shade.

RETICULATA IRIS

Iris reticulata

H 15cm (6in) S 10cm (4in)

There a number of other species and several hybrids besides this one of winter bulbous irises. They flower in late winter and early spring. The flowers are typically iris-shaped, with three hang-ing petals and three upright ones, but they are on a much smaller scale than most. The leaves are very narrow and shorter than the flowers, but extend well above them after the blooms have faded. The colours are mainly based on blue or purple with yellow often a secondary colour. Plant in a well drained soil in a sunny position.

LILY
Lilium
H 1.5m (5ft) s 60cm (24in)

Few gardeners can resist growing lilies for the touch of the exotic that they add to the borders. There are hundreds of different species and varieties to choose from, with several different basic flower shapes and colours varying from white to bright red and including yellow and orange. They can be grown in the border with other plants or kept in containers. Plant in a well-drained but moisture-retentive soil. Some prefer an acid to neutral soil, while others tolerate or prefer an alkaline one. The majority prefer a sunny position but some like light shade.

GRAPE HYACINTH
Muscari armeniacum
H 20cm (8in) s 5cm (2in)

These are small plants with conical heads tightly packed with round, bell-like flowers. The bells are blue with a small pale lip. They rise above narrow foliage that is rather lax and floppy. The flowers are very attractive but the foliage can look very untidy, especially after flowering. The bulbs rapidly clump up, producing a carpet of leaves and flowers. There are other similar species, some with white or pink-purple flowers. They should be grown in moisture-retentive, but well-drained soil and given a position in the sun.

DAFFODIL
Narcissus
H 50cm (20in) s 15cm (6in)

One of the best-loved groups of bulbs. There are very many species and cultivars, all with flowers roughly based on the same shape of a trumpet emerging from a flat disc. The colour is basically yellow with a few white and orange variants. The flowers are held singly or in groups on stems above the stiff, strap-like foliage. They flower in spring. Daffodils can be grown in borders or containers or can be naturalized in grass. They can be grown in any good garden soil and can be used in either the sun or dappled shade.

NERINE
Nerine bowdenii
H 36cm (14in) s 7.5cm (3in)

Delightful plants that flower late in the year. The flowers are carried in heads on tall, leafless stems. They are trumpet shaped with a number of turned back, narrow petals. They are pink in colour. The foliage is narrow and strap-like and much smaller than the flower stems and often goes unnoticed. The flowers look particularly good when growing through silver foliage of some kind. Nerine bulbs clump up quite quickly to form a small colony. They should be planted in a free-draining soil in full sun to do really well.

TULIP
Tulipa
H 60cm (24in) s 20cm (8in)

These are favourite plants of the late spring although there are some that flower as early as late winter. They are basically goblet- or cup-shaped flowers in a wide range of colours, some being a single colour, others of two or more. The leaves are quite broad. Some tulips are tall but there are some, especially the species, which are very short and more suited to the rock garden or containers than to the border. They can be used as bedding and should then be lifted after flowering. Plant in any good garden soil in a sunny position.

Muscari armeniacum

Nerine bowdenii

Tulipa praestans

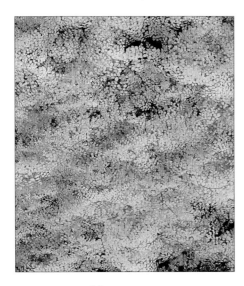

Adiantum venustum

Asplenium scolopendrium

Carex buchananii

FERNS, GRASSES & BAMBOOS

HIMALAYAN MAIDENHAIR FERN

Adiantum venustum

H 15cm (6in) S 60cm (24in)

Fern. This is a delightful fern with triangular fronds that are deeply cut, giving a very delicate, lacy effect. The stems are thin and wiry and black in colour which adds to the fern's charm. It is not a large fern, and is ideal for damp positions such as near a pool or waterspout. It should be grown in a moist, woodland-type soil that is free draining. It should be planted in light shade and not in the sun.

VARIEGATED FOXTAIL GRASS

Alopecurus pratensis 'Aureomarginatus'

H 1.2m (4ft) S 45cm (18in)

Grass. An attractive grass grown for its foliage rather than flowers. The leaves are narrow and relatively stiff. They are green with golden-yellow stripes along their length. The green-purple flowers are carried on tall thin stalks in a cylindrical head. The grass grows in tufts, but spreads in a non-invasive way. It is good for making a contrast with the more rounded clumps of perennial plants. It can be grown in a border or by itself. Plant in a rich, well-drained soil in a sunny position.

HART'S TONGUE FERN

Asplenium scolopendrium

H 60cm (24in) S 60cm (24in)

Fern. A very distinct fern with strap-like fronds. They are slightly wavy along their margins and are shaped like hart's tongues (hence the name) and pointed at their tips. These plants are evergreen and the foliage is a striking bright green in colour. The solid shape of these elegant ferns makes them a good contrast to the more typical, deeply cut ferns. They love shade and should be planted in the shelter of shrubs, trees or other plants. They can also be grown in containers. They need a moist but well-drained soil.

MAIDENHAIR SPLEENWORT

Asplenium trichomanes

H 15cm (6in) S 25cm (10in)

Fern. This is an attractive fern with long fronds made up of stalked, rounded leaflets (pinnae) that are deep green in colour. The stems are a glossy black or brown which adds to the attraction. They make a good contrast to the more typical ferns. These ferns are evergreen or semi-evergreen. Like most ferns, the maidenhair spleenwort should be grown in a shady position, perhaps against a house wall or in a border under lightly-leafed trees or shrubs. These plants need a moisture-retentive but well-drained soil.

JAPANESE PAINTED FERN

Athyrium niponicum var *pictum*

H 25cm (10in) S 60cm (24in)

Fern. This must be one of the prettiest of all ferns. The outline of the fronds is triangular and they are divided twice into smaller leaflets (pinnae). The joy of these fronds is that they are 'painted'. The base colour is silver-grey. Over this is washed purplish markings, making it very attractive indeed. Plant hostas nearby for a good contrast of shape and colour. Like most ferns, it should have a lightly shaded position. It should be planted in a moisture-retentive but free-draining soil.

LEATHERLEAF SEDGE

Carex buchananii

H 60cm (24in) S 75cm (30in) Z 6–9

Sedge. This is one of a number of fine-leaved sedges that are a coppery-brown in color. It forms a fountain of narrow leaves, often creating a "nest" in the center of the plant. It is very useful as there are few foliage plants of this color. It can be used as a low specimen plant by itself or planted in a border with other plants. It makes a good contrast with green foliage plants, especially light green. It is best planted in full sun. This plant will be happy in most types of garden soil.

VARIEGATED SEDGE

Carex oshimensis 'Evergold'

H 30cm (12in) S 36cm (14in) Z 6–9

Sedge. This is an attractive sedge for brightening up a dull spot. It is a clump-forming plant producing a tuft of grass-like foliage. This foliage is dark green in color with a creamy-yellow stripe down the center of each leaf. This eye-catching plant is arching and forms a low fountain of foliage. It is useful to break up an area of plain green foliage or to lighten a shaded spot. Plant in either a sunny or lightly shaded position. It requires a moist but free-draining soil.

DWARF PAMPAS GRASS

Cortaderia selloana 'Pumila'

H 1.5m (5ft) S 1.2m (4ft) Z 7–10

Grass. Pampas grasses are very good garden plants, but many of them are much too big for the small garden. This award-winning variety is just about the right size, big enough to be impressive but small enough not to swamp the garden. It has a fountain of narrow leaves (they have very sharp edges and can cut, so take care) and tall stems which carry large silvery plumes in the summer and autumn months. Grow the dwarf pampas grass as a specimen plant by itself in a lawn or as part of a border amidst shrubs and other plants of contrasting shapes and textures. This plant will happily grow in any reasonable garden soil and needs a sunny position to thrive.

MALE FERN

Dryopteris filix-mas

H 1m (3ft) S 1m (3ft) Z 4–8

Fern. This is a deciduous fern with large, arching fronds that are very delicately cut with fine leaflets (pinnae). As the new fronds open in the spring, they unroll with tops like croziers, the combined fronds forming a shuttlecock. There are several different forms, some with curious crested fronds. They are among the easiest ferns to grow and make a good contrast to many other types of plants. Planting them with hostas, for example, works well. Plant in a lightly shaded position and provide them with a reasonably moist but free-draining soil.

HAKONECHLOA

Hakonechloa macra 'Aureola'

H 45cm (18in) S 40cm (16in) Z 5–9

Grass. This is an attractive grass that is not too big for a small garden. It is a clump-forming plant making a tuft of arching leaves. The leaves are quite broad and colored gold with narrow green stripes down their length. This is a good plant for brightening up a dull spot. It works well in a border devoted to hot colors and also works as a contrast with all-green foliage plants. From late summer onwards it has stems carrying tufts of airy flowers. Plant it in sun or light shade and give it a moist but free-draining soil.

Cortaderia selloana 'Pumila'

Dryopteris filix-mas

Hakonechloa macra 'Aureola'

Hordeum jubatum

Miscanthus sinensis 'Gracillimus'

Phalaris arundinacea var *picta* 'Picta'

SQUIRREL TAIL GRASS
Hordeum jubatum
H 50cm (20in) S 30cm (12in)

Grass. This is an annual or short-lived perennial grass. The foliage is insignificant, it is the flower-heads that are the attractive part. It has a typical barley head with thin whiskers which catch the sun beautifully, making this a very attractive plant. The nodding flowerheads are a soft silvery-purple in colour. Place this plant so that the sun is behind it and shines through the flowerheads. It can be planted as a drift, but looks very good when mixed with a variety of flowering plants, especially eschscholzia. Plant this grass in full sun. It will grow well in any reasonable garden soil.

HARE'S TAIL
Lagurus ovatus
H 50cm (20in) S 30cm (12in)

Grass. This is an attractive and fun annual grass. Children will love it because of the stubby, cylindrical heads which are so nice to touch. These are very soft and look like a rabbit's or hare's tail. The fluffy heads can be cut and dried for indoor decorations. The narrow, arching leaves are of no particular interest. These plants work well at the front of a general border, contrasting with green foliage as well as with colourful flowers. It will grow in any well-drained soil and needs to be planted in a sunny position.

BOWLES' GOLDEN GRASS
Milium effusum 'Aureum'
H 60cm (24in) S 30cm (12in)

Grass. This is one of the nicest of all grasses and one that works well in a small garden. It is not a dense grass but produces an open tuft of arching leaves that are a pale yellowish-green in colour. Above the leaves there is a very airy, open flowerhead of the same colour. The whole thing is very delicate. It works well with a variety of plants. Try planting primroses close to it, for example. Plant in a lightly shaded position or in sun if the soil is kept moist. Any good garden soil will do as long as it is reasonably moist.

MISCANTHUS
Miscanthus sinensis 'Gracillimus'
H 1.2m (4ft) S 1m (3ft)

Grass. Most of the *M. sinensis* are too large for the small garden and this is unfortunate as they are very beautiful plants. However, this one is small enough to be suitable and does not lose any of the elegance and grace of this species. It has arching leaves from which arise tall stems with plumes of very soft silver-purple flowers. It works very well with the sun behind it and also looks perfect when associated with water. Most good garden soils are suitable for this plant, especially if they are reasonably moisture-retentive. A sunny position should be chosen for it to do well.

FEATHERTOP
Pennisetum villosum
H 60cm (24in) S 60cm (24in)

Grass. This is an excellent grass for the small garden. The foliage is of not much interest and indeed it can be mistaken for a weed if you are not careful, but once it has flowered there is no mistaking its beauty. The arching stems carry airy cylinders that look like bottle brushes. They are very soft and ask to be stroked; it works well at the front of most borders. It is not long lived but comes easily from seed. Plant in a well-drained soil and in a warm, sunny position.

GARDENER'S GARTERS

Phalaris arundinacea var *picta* 'Picta'

H 1m (3ft) S indefinite

Grass. This plant can be a thug, spreading invasively through all the plants around it. However, it is so beautiful that it is worth finding a place, perhaps hemmed in with concrete paths, where it can grow. The foliage is pale green, striped silvery white and often with a pink flush. In the summer it has tall flower heads which some gardeners like but others don't and cut them off. Be careful where you plant it, but it will grow in most soils. Plant in sun or light shade.

GOLDEN BAMBOO

Pleioblastus auricomis

H 1.5m (5ft) S 1.5m (5ft)

Bamboo. Unlike many bamboos this is a well-behaved plant that does not become invasive. It has attractive foliage which stands out horizontally from the canes. The leaves are narrow and golden-yellow with green stripes running down their length. It does well when planted as a specimen plant by itself, perhaps in a gravel garden, or as a background to other plants in a mixed border. Hot-coloured flowers, especially oranges and reds, will look good against it. This is a hardy bamboo. Plant it in any reasonable garden soil and make sure it is in full sun. Avoid planting in a windy position as the leaves may scorch.

SOFT SHIELD FERN

Polystichum setiferum

H 1.2m (4ft) S 1m (3ft)

Fern. This is a very delicately cut, evergreen fern. The dark-green fronds are long and pointed and appear like a shuttlecock. There are many varieties, all with some minor variation, from which to choose. They work well with less delicate ferns and with other shade-loving foliage plants such as hostas. They also work well when planted in odd positions, such as against corners of buildings or steps. Like most ferns these need moist woodland-type soil with plenty of humus and yet reasonably free-draining. They need a shady position.

SASA BAMBOO

Sasa veitchii

H 1.8m (6ft) S 1m (3ft)

Bamboo. Bamboos can be difficult in a small garden as they tend to be too invasive. This one spreads but not too quickly and can be kept under control. It has quite broad leaves that stick out horizontally from the purple canes. The leaves are dark green with white margins where the leaf edges are starting to die back. This is a useful plant for filling an odd corner or for using as background planting in a border and it will grow in any reasonably free-draining soil in sun or shade. Choose a moist soil if growing it in sun.

FEATHER GRASS

Stipa calamogrostis

H 1m (3ft) S 1m (3ft)

Grass. Some of the stipas are, unfortunately, too large for a small garden, but this one is smaller and still retains the charm of the genus. It is a deciduous grass with arching foliage and tall stems carrying feathery heads. These are a soft, silver-purple in colour and look particularly beautiful when lit by the sun from behind. It forms a dense clump and fits very well into most borders, creating a contrast in shape to most perennials. It will grow in most garden soils, as long as they are reasonably well drained. Plant it in a sunny position.

Pleioblastus auricomis

Polystichum setiferum

Stipa calamogrostis

INDEX

**Page numbers in italics refer
to illustrations.**

A

Abelia x *grandiflora*, 214
Abutilon, 68, *120*
  A. megapotamicum, 130, 151, 214, *214*
Acaena, 143
  A. buchananii, 46
Acanthus, 19
  A. mollis, 147
  A. spinosus, 136
Acca sellowiana, 131
Acer, 37
  A. capillipes, 136
  A. griseum, 136
  A. palmatum, 151, 210, *210*
    A.p. dissectum, 136, 150
      A.p.d. 'Atropurpureum', 134
  A. pseudoplatanus 'Brilliantissimum',
  210, *210*
Achillea, 142, 143, 151
Aconitum, 147, 162
Acorus calamus 'Variegatus', 163
  A. gramineus 'Ogon', *138*, 139
Actinidia kolomikta, 33, 151
Adiantum venustum, 246, *246*
aeonium, 68
African blue lily, *see Agapanthus*
Agapanthus, 242
  A. africanus, 142, 152
  A. Headbourne Hybrids, *242*
agave, 68, *112, 142*
ailanthus, 136
Ajuga, 72, 147
  A. reptans, 149, 226
Akebia quinata, 130
Alchemilla mollis, 46, 48, 139, 143, 146,
  226, *226*
alleghany moss, *see Robinia kelseyi*
alleyways, 10, *24*, 28–31, *46*, *113*
Allium, 27, 38, 151, 242
  A. christophii, 135, 152
  planting depth, 192
Alopecurus pratensis 'Aureomarginatus',
  246
  A.p. 'Aureovariegatus', *139*
alpines, *121*
alstroemeria, 142
alyssum, 55, 154
Amelanchier lamarkii, 210
Ampelopsis brevipedunculata 'Elegans', 90
anchusa, *142*
Anemone, 147
  A. blanda
    A.b. 'Blue Shade', 157
    planting depth, 192

  A. 'De Caen', planting depth, 192
  A. fulgans, 143
  A. x *hybrida*, 152, 226
    A.h. 'Honorine Jobert', *226*
  A. nemorosa, 226
Angelica archangelica, 135
annuals, *21*, 27, *33*, *36*, *38*, 120, 128,
  129, 140
  for containers, 152
Anthemis punctata cupaniana, 142
Antirrhinum majus, 234
  A. 'Royal Carpet', *234*
Aponogeton distachyos, 163
Aralia elata 'Variegata', 136, *137*
arbours, *14, 15*, 18, 82, *96*
Arbutus x *andrachnoides*, 132
  A. menziesii, 132, 136
arches, 14, 82, 84, *85*, 86, *87*, 134
architectural plants, 14, 16, 21, 22, *35,
41*, 134, 136, *137*
argyranthemum, 140
Aristolochia macrophylla, 132
Armeria, 143, 226
  A. juniperifolia 'Bevan's Variety', *226*
Artemisia, 9, 30, 142
  A. lactiflora, 163
arum lily, *see Zantedeschia aethiopica*
Arundo donax, 135, 136, 163
Asplenium scolopendrium, 147, 246, *246*
  A. trichomanes, 246
asters, *153*
Astilbe, 162, 166
  A. x *arendsii*, 163, 238
    A.a. 'Hyazinth', *238*
Astilboides tabularis, 105, 135, 163
Athyrium niponicum var *pictum*, 246
aubrieta, 143
Aucuba japonica, 148, 214
  A.j. 'Crotonifolia', 128
  A.j. 'Marmorata', *214*
awnings, 116, *116*
azaleas, Yakushimanum, 35
azolla, *165*

B

baby's tears, *see Soleirolia*
balconies, 10, 36–9, 77, 97, 142, 150
bamboos, *9*, 14, *16, 17, 31*, 35, *49*, 131,
  136, 138, 139, *147*
banana, *see Ensete* and *Musa*
barbecues, *14, 15, 16*, 18, 99
barberry, *see Berberis*
bark chippings, *31*, 72, *72*, 186, *187*
bark, coloured, 136
barrel water feature, 164
basements, 24–7, *25, 26, 27*, 113
basil, 38, 174, 176

bay, 33, 38, 158, 177, 212
  see also Laurus nobilis
beans, *174*
bedding plants, 140
beech, 80
beetroot, 172
Begonia, 141, 152, 153
  B. semperflorens, 140, 234
    B.s. 'Venus', *234*
bellflower, *see Campanula*
benches, *16, 17, 19*, 43, *74*, 86, 96, *96,
97*
  building, 100
  stone, 101, *101*
berberis, 214
Bergenia, 139, 147, 149
  B. cordifolia, 135, 227, *227*
Betula albosinensis, 136
  B. pendula 'Youngii', 136, 210
  B. utilis jacquemontii, 136
Bidens ferulifolia, 234
birch, 79
bird cherry, *see Prunus padua*
bistort, *see Persicaria bistorta* 'Superba'
black-eyed susan, *see Thunbergia alata*
blackberry, *175*
blue cupidone, *see Catananche caerulea*
bluebells, 149
  see also Hyacinthoides non-scripta
bog gardens, 107, 162, 165
  in containers, 166
  making, 167, *167*
bog plants, 166
bonsai, 68
bougainvillea, 160
boundaries, living, 80, 130
Bouteloua gracilis, 139
Bowles' golden grass,
  see Milium effusum 'Aureum'
Bowles' golden sedge,
  see Carex elata 'Variegata'
box, *9*, 20, 21, *21*, 28, 30, 35, *38, 46*, 48,
  56, *74*, 79, *112*, 114, 128, *128, 129*,
  151, 158, 176
  topiary, 160
  see also Buxus
Brachycome, 121, 140
  B. iberidifolium, 152, 234
Brachyglottis laxifolia, 143
  B. 'Sunshine', 47
Brassica oleracea 'Sekito', 150
bricks, 19, *25*, 44, 47, *49*, 56–7, *57, 61,
62*, 65, *105*
  cutting, 60
  laying, 57
bridges, 105, *107*
Briza media, 138

Broussonetia papyrifera, 136
Brugmansia, 134, 169
  B. x *candida*, 151
Buddleja, 144, 169, 214
  B. alternifolia 'Argentea', 143
  B. davidii, 205
    pruning, 205
  cuttings, 196
  pruning, 202, *205*
bugle, *see Ajuga*
bulbs, 27, 38, 128
  for containers, 151, 152, 156
  large, 135
  planting, 192, 193
busy lizzy, 27, *27*, 28, 36, *153*, 154
  see also Impatiens
Butomus umbellatus, 164, 165
butterfly bush, *see Buddleja*
Buxus sempervirens, 21, 30, 134, 150, 215
  B.s. 'Aureovariegata', *177*
  B.s. 'Suffruticosa', 161
  see also box

C

Calendula, 134, 141, 173
  C. officinalis, 234
Californian lilac, *see Ceanothus*
Californian poppy, *see Eschscholzia*
Caltha palustris, 105, 163, 238
  C.p. alba, 167
  C.p. 'Flore Plena', *238*
Camassia leichtlinii, 135
Camellia, 35, 68, 134, 215
  C. japonica, 151
    C.j. 'Tricolor', *214*
  deadheading, *191*
Campanula, 28, 135, 227
  C. latifolia, 135
  C. portenschlagiana, 48
Campsis x *tagliabuana*, 130
  C.t. 'Madame Galen', 134
Canadian pondweed, *see Elodea*
Canna, 135, 140
  C. indica, 152
Caragana arborescens 'Lorbergii', 136
  C.a. 'Pendula', 136
cardinal flower, *see Lobelia cardinalis*
Cardiocrinum giganteum, 135
Carex alata 'Aurea', *138*, 162, 163
  C. buchananii, 246, 247
  C. comans, 139
  C. 'Evergold', 139, *139*
  C. grayi, 138
  C. hachijoensis, 139
  C. ornithopoda 'Variegata', *139*
  C. oshimensis 'Evergold', 247
  C. pendula, 138

Carpenteria californica, 76, 136
Catalpa, 136
   C. speciosa, 134
Catananche caerulea, 227, *227*
cathedral bells, *see Cobaea scandens*
catmint, *142*
   see also Nepeta
Ceanothus, 215
   C. arboreus, 132
   C. 'Blue Cushion', *144*
   C. burkwoodii, 131
   C. 'Pin Cushion', *215*
   pruning, 205
centaurea, 142
Cercis siliquastrum, 132, 210
   C.s. 'Rubra', *210*
chairs,
   deckchair, *98*, 99
   steamer, *98*
Chaenomeles, 215
   C. 'Fire Dance', *215*
   C. speciosa, 131
   C.s. 'Tortuosa', 136
Chamaecyparis, 38
   C. lawsoniana, 132
   C.l. 'Elwoodii', 79
   C. nootkatensis 'Pendula', 150
Chamaemelum 'Treneague', *177*
chamomile, 176
   lawns, *16*, 17
   see also Chamaemelum
chicory, *178*
chilean glory flower,
   see Eccremocarpus scaber
Chimonanthus praecox, 169, 170
Chinese cabbage, 178, *178*, *179*
Chinese dogwood,
   see Cornus kousa var *chinensis*
Chinese rhubarb, *see Rheum palmatum*
Chinese witch hazel,
   see Hamamelis mollis
Chionodoxa, 242
   C. gigantea, *242*
   planting depth, 192
chives, *173*, *175*
Choisya ternata, 35, 128, 131, 134, 148,
   215, *215*
Christmas box, *see Sarcococca*
chrysanthemums, 30, 48, 129, 151, 152
cineraria, 154
cinquefoil, *see Potentilla*
Cistus, 144, *144*, 216
   C. 'Paladin', *216*
   C. purpureus, *205*
   pruning, 205
city gardens, 22, 24, *74*, *87*, *116*
classical style, 19, *22*, 82, 113, 130

Clematis, 19, 25, 31, 33, 41, 48, 76, *85*,
   90, 92, *113*, *130*
   C. alpina, 91, 148
   C. 'Arctic Queen', *91*
   C. armandii, 38, 87, 130, 134
   C. 'Jackmanii', *90*
   C. macropetala, 130
   C. 'Madame Julia Correvon', *84*, 220
   C. montana, 25, 38, 130, 148, 220
   C. 'Nellie Moser', *220*
   C. 'Silver Moon', 84
   C. tangutica, 130
   C. texensis, 90
      C.t. 'Etoile Rose', *91*
   C. 'Ville de Lyon', *88*
   C. viticella, 90, 220
      C.v. 'Etoile Violette', *91*
      C.v. 'Polish Spirit', *91*
   large-flowered forms, 220
   layering, *199*
   planting, 90, 192
Clerodendron, 144
   C. trichotomum var *fargesii*, 15
climbers, *21*, 24, *25*, 27, *27*, 33, *35*, 80,
   86, 87, 90, 128, 130, 131
   annual, *85*
   for containers, 152
   scented, 168, 169
   supports for, *82*
Clivia miniata, 150, 152
Cobaea scandens, 151, 220, *220*
cobblestones, 14, *14*, 16, *17*, 62, 73, 145
   laying, 62
coco shell, *187*
coir, 186
colchicum, 242
cold frames, making, 102
Colletia armata, 136
   C. cruciana, 136
coloured stems, pruning for, 201, *202*
comfrey, as compost, 189
conifers, 38
   hedges, *80*
   pruning, 201
containers, 18, 19, 22, *25*, 27, *28*, 30, *31*,
   34, 112, 120–5, *129*, 135, 140, *151*, *152*
   bog garden, 166
   bulbs in, 156
   decorating, 122–3
   flowering plants for, 151
   herbs in, *175*
   plants for, 150
   self-watering, 120
   strawberries in, 182
   tomatoes in, 180
   vegetables in, 178
Convallaria majalis, 171

Convolvulus cneorum, 142, 216, *216*, 227,
   227
coral flower, *see Heuchera*
Cordyline, *112*, 128
   C. australis, 135, 136
coriander, 174
corkscrew rush, *see Juncus effusus* 'Spiralis'
corn salad, 172
Cornus, *37*
   C. controversa, 132
      C.c. 'Variegata', 136
   C. kousa var *chinensis*, 211, *211*
   pruning, 202
Corokia cotoneaster, 136
Cortaderia selloana 'Pumila', 247, *247*
Corydalis, 28, 149, 153
   C. lutea, 146, 150, 227
Corylus avellana 'Contorta', 136
Cosmos, 151
   C. bipinnatus, 135, 235
      C.b. 'Candy Stripe', *235*
Cotoneaster, 38, 48
   C. horizontalis, 131, 148, 216, *216*
   cuttings, 197
   C. x *watereri*, 132
cotton lavender,
   see Santolina chamaecyparissus
courgettes, 173
courtyards, 24–7, *25*, *57*, *105*, 120
crab apple, *see Malus*
Crambe cordifolia, 135, 142
Crataegus laevigata, 132, 211
   C.l. 'Rosea Flore Plena', *211*
creeping Jenny, *see Lysimachia nummularia*
Crinodendron hookerianum, 15, 131, 148
Crocosmia, 142
   C. 'Lucifer', 135
crocus, 37, 38, 242
   planting depth, 192
cryptomeria, 15
curled pondweed, *see Potamogeton*
cuttings,
   buddleja, 196
   cotoneaster, 197
   hardwood, 196
   leaf bud, 197
   potting up, 197
   semi-ripe, 21, 196
   softwood, 196
   stem, 197
Cyclamen, 129, 147, 149, 151
   C. hederifolium, 243
Cynara cardunculus, 135, 142
   C. scolymus, 173
Cyperus alternifolius, 163

D

daffodils, *125*, 156
   planting depth, 192
   see also Narcissus
Dahlia, *141*, 152, 243
   D. 'Alva's Doris', *242*
Daphne bohlua, 169, 170
   D. odora, 169
   D. tangutica, 216
Darmera peltata, 135
datura, 140
daylilies, *see Hemerocallis*
deadheading, 191
deadnettle, *see Lamium*
decking, *9*, 28, *32*, *33*, 34, *38*, *41*, *43*,
   44, *49*, 66–71, *71*, 104, 105, *105*, *107*
   designs, 70
   tiles, 69
delphiniums, 19, 135, 228, *228*
Dendromecon rigida, 136
Deschampsia flexuosa 'Tatra Gold', *139*
deutzia, pruning, 205
Dianthus, 30, 143, 228
   D. 'Blue Hills', *228*
   D. 'Mrs Sinkins', 142, 171
Diascia, 27, 37, 143, 153, 228
   D. cordata, *228*
Dicentra spectabilis, 152
Dicksonia antarctica, 134, 150
Digitalis, 147
   D. purpurea, 135, 147, 235, *235*
dill, 174
diseases, 207
dividing plants, 198
dog's-tooth violet,
   see Erythronium dens-canis
Drypoteris filix-mas, 147, 247, *247*
Dutchman's pipe, *see Aristolochia*
dwarf pampas grass,
   see Cortaderia selloana 'Pumila'

E

eating al fresco, 99
Eccremocarpus scaber, 130, 220, *221*
echeverias, *142*
edging, 114
   laying, 63
   rope twist, 59
Eichhornia crassipes, 163, 238
Elaeagnus, 79
   E. x *ebbingei*, 79, 132
   E. pungens, 148, 169
      E.p. 'Maculata', 216
elephant's ears, *see Bergenia cordifolia*
Elodea canadensis, 163, 238
Elymus arenarius, 139
Ensete ventricosum, *41*, 134, 150

entertaining, 19, 99, 118, 119
entrances, 30–1, *129*
Epimedium, 135, 147, 149
    E. grandiflorum, 146
Eranthis hyemalis, 243
    E. hyemalis 'Guinea Gold', 243, *243*
Erica, 217
    E. carnea, *217*
Erigeron karvinskianus, 46, 143, 228
Eryngium giganteum, 135
Erysimum cheirii, 171, 235
Erythronium dens-canis, 243, *243*
Escallonia, 217
    E. 'Apple Blossom', 131
    pruning, *201*, 205
Eschscholzia californica, 235
    E. 'Harlequin Hybrids', *235*
Eucalyptus, 136
    E. gunnii, 132
Euonymus, *37*, *85*, 149, 158
    E. fortunei, 131, 148, 160, 217
        E.f. 'Blondy', 160
        E.f. 'Emerald 'n' Gold', 160
Eupatorium purpureum, 163
Euphorbia, *142*, 147, 149
    E. characias wulfenii, 47, 135, 150
    E. dulcis 'Chameleon', 228

F
fairy moss, *see Azolla*
Fallopia baldschuanica, 132
x *Fatshedera lizei*, 134, 148
Fatsia japonica, 28, 35, *128*, 134, 136, 148
feather grass, *see Stipa calamogrostis*
feathertop, *see Pennisetum villosum*
feeding, 191
fences, 76, *76*, 80, 84
ferns, *26*, 28, *28*, *31*, 49, 68, 105, *147*, 149, 153
Festuca, 138, 139
    F. glauca 'Blue Fox', 139
        F.g. 'Golden Toupée', 139
Ficus carica, 136
fig tree, *126*
Filipendula palmata, 163
fish, 107
flowering rush, *see Butomus umbellatus*
focal points, 14, *14*, 18, *19*, 22, *25*, *113*, 120
foliage plants, *25*, *35*, *37*, *49*, 113, *126*, *132*, 136, 147, *150*
    for containers, 150
    perennials, 135
formal gardens, *12*, 14, 18–9, 20–3, *25*, 35, 104, 159
Forsythia,
    F. suspensa, 131
    pruning, *202*
fountains, *17*, *21*, *74*, 104, *104*, 110, 111
foxgloves, *28*

see also Digitalis
freesia, 171
Fremontodendron 'Californian Glory', 131
    F. californicum, 76, 136, 144, *144*
French marigolds, 181
Fritillaria, 243
    F. imperialis, *243*
fritillaries, *see Fritillaria*
fruit, 175
    pruning, 200
Fuchsia, *121*, *123*, 129, *129*, 134, 140, 217
    F. 'Dorothy', *205*
    F. 'Leonora', 151
    F. 'Thalia', 151, *217*
    cuttings, 196
    hardy, *205*
    pruning, 205
furniture, 9, *15*, 16, 18, 19, *25*, *33*, 35, 43, *46*, 96–9

G
Galanthus, 244
    G. nivalis 'Saffran', *244*
    see also snowdrops
garden compost, 186, *187*
    making, 188
garden rooms, 40–3, 119
gardener's garters, *see Phalaris arundinacea* var *picta* 'Picta'
garlic, 174
Garrya elliptica, 131, 148
gates, 31
gazanias, *141*
gazebo, living, *88*
Genista,
    G. aetnensis, 15, 136
    G. lydia, 144, *145*
    pruning, 205
geometric gardens, 14
Geranium, 135, 143
    G. macrorrhizum, 105, 146
    G. palmatum, 162
    G. phaeum, 146, 149
    G. 'Patricia', 229
    G. x *riversleaianum* 'Mavis Simpson', 229
ginger lily, *see Hedychium*
Ginko biloba 'Fastigiata', 136
gladiolus, *142*, 244
Gleditsia triacanthos 'Sunburst', 211
globe artichoke, *174*
    see also Cynara scolymus
globeflower, *see Trollius europaeus*
glory of the snow, *see Chionodoxa*
golden bamboo, *see Pleioblastus auricomis*
golden hop, *see Humulus lupulus* 'Aureus'
golden rain, *see Laburnum*
gooseberries, 173
grape hyacinth, *see Muscari armeniacum*
grape vines, 19
grasses, 16, *16*, *17*, 138–9

for bog gardens, 162, 163
gravel, 14, *14*, *15*, *20*, 22, 35, *40*, *43*, 47, 49, *62*, *66*, 67, *142*
    as a mulch, 186, *187*
    laying, 64–5
greater spearwort, *see Ranunculus flammula*
grisellinia, 79
ground cover for shade, 149
ground elder, *150*
growbags, 180
Gunnera manicata, 107, 135

H
Hakonechloa macra 'Alboaurea', 139
    H.m. 'Aureola', 247, *247*
Hamamelis, 136
    H. mollis, 132, 169, 170
        H.m. 'Pallida', 170
hanging baskets, 37, *82*, *87*, *121*, 140, 153
    planting, 154
    tomatoes in, 180
hare's tail, *see Lagurus ovatus*
hart's tongue fern,
    see Asplenium scolopendrium
hawthorn, *see Crataegus*
heathers, 129
    deadheading, *191*
    pruning, 200, *202*
    see also Erica
Hebe, 35, 144
    H. amplexicaulis 'Amy', *145*
    H. corstophinensis 'Cranleighensis', *145*
    H. x *franciscana* 'Variegata', *145*
    H. gracillima 'Great Orme', *145*
    H. matthewsii 'Midsummer Beauty', *145*
    pruning, 205
Hedera, 130, 221
    H. canariensis 'Gloire de Marengo', *130*
    H. helix, 132, 146, 149, 150, *155*
        H.h. 'Chrysophylla', *81*
        H.h. 'Goldheart', 25
        H.h. 'Saggitifolia', 160
hedges, 18, 19, *21*, 30, 80
hedychium, 140
Helenium, 229
    H. 'Pumilum Magnificum', *229*
Helianthemum, 143, 144, 151, 217
    H. cupreum, *217*
    H. 'Rosa Königin', *145*
Helichrysum, *120*, 153
    H. petiolare, *128*, 235
Helictotrichon sempervirens, 139
hellebore, 147, 152
    see also Helleborus
Helleborus argutifolius, 135, 147, 149
    H. orientalis, 229, *229*
    see also hellebore
helxine, *see Soleirolia*
Hemerocallis, 135, 147 , 229
    H. 'Pink Damask', *229*

hepatica, 146, 149
Heracleum mantegazzianum, 135
herb gardens, *173*, 174
    formal, 176
    making, 176
    maintaining, 177
herbs, 7, 20, *21*, 38, *129*, *142*, *151*, 168, 173
    in containers, *175*
Heuchera micrantha var *diversifolia* 'Palace Purple', 150, 230
Hibiscus, 144
    H. rosa-sinensis, 151
    H. syriacus 'Woodbridge', *145*
    pruning, 205
Himalayan maidenhair fern,
    see Adiantum venustum
holly, 19, 79, 130
    see also Ilex
honey locust, *see Gleditsia*
honeysuckle, 33, 38, 41, 76, *82*, *87*, 92, *93*, *130*, *168*, 169
    grown on a pole, 92
    see also Lonicera
Hordeum jubatum, 248, *248*
hornbeam, 80
hosepipe, perforated, *167*
Hosta, *26*, 28, *49*, 68, 72, 107, *128*, 139, *147*, *147*, 150, *150*, *163*, 166, 230
    H. fortunei, 150, 163
    H. sieboldiana, 150, 163
        H.s. elegans, 135
    H. 'Tall Boy', *230*
    dividing, 198
hot tubs, 78
Hottonia palustris, 163, 238
houseleek, *see Sempervivum*
Houttuynia, 166
    H. cordata 'Chameleon', *238*, 239
        H.c. 'Variegata', *167*
Humulus lupulus 'Aureus', 35, 48, 87, 130, 132, 148, 221
hurdles, *81*, *93*, *115*
hyacinth bean, *see Lablab purpureus*
Hyacinthoides non-scripta, 244
hyacinths, 151, 156, *156*, 171
    planting depth, 192
    potting, 156
    see also Hyacinthus
Hyacinthus, 244
    see also hyacinths
Hydrangea, *24*, 35, 41, 56, 134, 135, *208*
    H. anomala petiolaris, 25, 79, 130, 134, 221
    H. macrophylla, 151, 218, *218*
    H. quercifolia, 148
    cuttings, 196
    pruning, 205
Hydrocharis morsus-ranae, 163
hypericum, pruning, 205

I

Ilex x *altaclarensis* 'Golden King', 211, *211*
    I. aquifolium, 132
    see also holly
Impatiens, 141, 152, *155*, 236
    I. New Guinea Hybrids, 146, 152
Imperata cylindrica, 139
informal gardens, *13*, 14, 16, *16*, 17
Ipomoea, 85
    I. tricolor, 130, 221, *221*
Iris, 34, 107, 164, 230
    I. ensata, 163
    I. japonica, layering, 199
    I. laevigata, 163, 239, *239*
        I.l. 'Atropurpurea', *162*
    I. reticulata, 244
        I.r. 'Harmony', *244*
        planting depth, 192
    I. sibirica, 163
    I. unguicularis, 171
    dividing, 198
ivy, 25, *26*, 28, 37, *37*, 48, 73, 79, 80, *81*, 113, 129, 146, 148, 151, 161
    cuttings, 197
    topiary, 160
    see also *Hedera*

J

jacob's ladder, see *Polemonium caeruleum*
Japanese anemones, 149
    see also *Anemone* x *hybrida*
Japanese blood grass,
    see *Imperata cylindrica*
Japanese cherry, see *Prunus* 'Anamogawa'
Japanese gardens, 22, 35, 105
Japanese iris, see *Iris ensata*
Japanese maple, see *Acer*
Japanese painted fern,
    see *Athyrium niponicum* var *pictum*
jasmine, 33, 41, 76
    see also *Jasminum*
Jasminum nudiflorum, 160
    J. offficinale, 130, 169, 221, *221*
    see also jasmine
Judas tree, see *Cercis siliquastrum*
Juncus effusus 'Spiralis', 138, 239
Juniperus scopulorum, 150
    J.s. 'Skyrocket', 211

K

kashmir mountain ash,
    see *Sorbus cashmiriana*
kiwi fruit, see *Actinidia*
kniphofia, 16, 142, 230, *230*
Koeleria glauca, 139

L

Lablab purpureus, 140
Laburnum, 132
    L. x *watereri* 'Vossii', 212, *212*
lady's mantle, *142*
    see also *Alchemilla mollis*
Lagurus ovatus, 248
Lamium maculatum, 147, 149, 230
    L.m. 'Beacon Silver', *230*
Lanata camara, 152
land cress, 178
Lathyrus latifolius, 130, 148
    L. odoratus, 140, 171, 222, *222*
    see also sweet pea
Laurus nobilis, 132, *151*, 212
    see also bay
Lavandula, 142, 169
    L. angustifolia, 218
        L.a. 'Twickel Purple', *218*
    L. 'Munstead'*, 177*
    L. spicata, 204
    see also lavender
Lavatera olbia 'Rosea', 144, 218
lavender, 9, *9*, *21*, 30, 38, 56, 79, 114, 143, 177
    cuttings, 196
    pruning, *204*, 205
    see also *Lavandula*
lawn care, 206
lawns, *9*, 72, 73, *74*
    feeding, 206
    raking, 206
    weeds in, 206
layering, 199
le Nôtre, André, 20
leatherleaf sedge, see *Carex buchananii*
lemon balm, *173*
Leonotis leonurus, 140
lettuces, 172, 173, *173*
    'Blush', *179*
    'Salad Bowl', 178
    sowing, 179
Leucanthemum vulgare, 31
lewisia, *121*, 143, 152
lighting, 41, 118–9
Ligularia, 41, *49*, 107, 135, *148*, 162
    L. dentata 'Desdemona', 135, *146*
    L. tungutica 'The Rocket', *146*
Ligustrum japonicum, 132, 148
    L. lucindum, 132
lilac, 170
    see also *Syringa*
lilies, 19, *31*, 38, 43, 68, 151, 171
    see also *Lilium*
Lilium, 135, 245
    L. 'Enchantment', *244*
    L. regale, 30, 152, 171, *171*
    L. 'Stargazer', *24*, *171*
    see also lilies

lily-of-the-valley, 149
    see also *Convallaria*
lilyturf, see *Liriope muscari*
Limnanthes douglasii, 236
linum, 142
liquid manure, 189
Liriope muscari, 231, *231*
Lobelia, 27, *27*, 37, 140, 152, 153
    L. cardinalis, *120*, 135, 239, *239*
        L.c. 'Queen Victoria', *166*, *167*
    L. erinus, 236
        L.e. 'Colour Parade', *236*
    L. syphylitica, 167
Lobularia maritima 'Snow Crystals', *155*
Lonicera, 134, 158
    L. fragrantissima, 169
    L. japonica 'Aureoreticulata', 160
    L. periclymenum, 130, 222
        L.p. 'Serotina', 169
    L. x *purpusii*, 38
    L. x *tellmanniana*, 130
    pruning, 205
    see also honeysuckle
Lotus berthelotti, *121*, 154, *155*
love-in-a-mist, see *Nigella*
lungwort, see *Pulmonaria*
lupins, *16*, *134*
Lychnis coronaria, 30
Lysimachia nummularia, 163
    L.n. 'Aurea'*, 166*, *167*
Lythrum, 166
    L. salicaria, 163, 239
        L.s. 'Feuerkerze', 239

M

mace sedge, see *Carex grayi*
Macleaya cordata, 135
Magnolia, 170
    M. grandiflora, 131, 132, 169
    M. salicifolia, 132
    M. x *soulangeana*, 132, 134, 151, 170
    M. stellata, 136, 151, 170, 212, *212*
        M.s. 'Royal Star', 170
        M.s. 'Rosea', 170
Mahonia, 136
    M. x *media* 'Charity', *134*, 136, *137*, 148
maidenhair spleenwort,
    see *Asplenium trichomanes*
Malcomia, 171
    M. maritima, 140
male fern, see *Dryopteris filix-mas*
Malus 'Golden Hornet', 136
    M. 'Profusion', 212
    M. 'Red Jade', 136
    M. x *schiedeckeri*, 132
manure, composted, 186
    liquid, 189
maples, *147*
marginal plants, 162, 164
    repotting, 165

marguerites, *24*, *129*
marjoram, *142*, 174, 177, *177*
    see also *Origanum*
marsh marigold, 107, 164
    see also *Caltha palustris*
Matthiola, 171
    M. bicornis, 140
    M. incana, 236, *236*
Mediterranean style, 9, 24, *38*, *101*, 120, 142
Melianthus major, 136
Mentha aquatica, 240
Mexican daisy, see *Erigeron karvinskianus*
Mexican orange blossom,
    see *Choisya ternata*
Michaelmas daisy, dividing, 198
Milium effusum, 150
    M.e 'Aureum', 139, *167*, 248
Mimulus luteus, 240, *240*
Mina lobata, 140
miniature bulrush, see *Typha minima*
mint, 38, 168, 174, 176
mirrors, 112, 113
Miscanthus, 136, 139
    M. sinensis 'Gracillimus', 248, *248*
        M.s. 'Morning Light', 138
        M.s. 'Zebrinus', 135, 138, 162, 163
mock orange blossom, see *Philadelphus*
moisture-loving plants, 162–3
monkshood, see *Aconitum*
morning glory, see *Ipomoea*
mortar, mixing, 53
mosaic, *63*
mosquito grass, see *Bouteloua gracilis*
mulch, 177, 186, 187
Musa basjoo, 136, *137*
Muscari armeniacum, 152, 245, *245*
    planting depth, 192
mutisia, 140
Myosotis scorpioides, 240
myrtle, 128
Myrtus communis, 131, 150, 169

N

naked ladies, see *Colchicum*
Narcissus, 27, 149, 152, 171, 245
    N. 'Golden Harvest', 157
    N. 'Paperwhite', 28
    N. 'Tête-à-Tête', *125*
nasturtium, 27, 37, 93, 153
    see also *Tropaeolum*
Nemesia fruticans, 154, *155*
Nepeta, 153
    N. x *faassenii*, 231
Nerine bowdenii, 245, *245*
Nerium oleander, 151
Nicotiana, 171, *171*, 236
    N. 'Crimson Rock', *236*
    N. 'Fragrant Cloud', 140
    N. sylvestris, 135

Nigella damascena, 237
night-scented stock, *see Matthiola bicornis*
night stock, *see Zaluzianskya capensis*
Nothofagus menziesii, 132
Nuphar lutea, 163
Nymphaea, 240
   N. alba, 163
   N. 'Escarboule', 163
   N. 'Lotus', *240*
   N. 'Pink Sensation', *240*
   N. tetragona, 163

O

obelisks, 19, 84, *84,* 90–1
olearia, 144
Ophiopogon planiscapus 'Nigrescens', *138*
opium poppy, *see Papaver somniferum*
Oriental gardens, *9*
Origanum, 143
   O. laevigatum, 231
ornamental cabbages, *153*
ornamental cherry, *see Prunus*
ornamental oats, *see Stipa gigantea*
ornamental quince, *see Chaenomeles*
ornamental rhubarb, *see Rheum palmatum*
ornaments, *22*, 114, *115*
ornithogalum, planting depth, 192
Orontium aquaticum, 163
Osteospermum, 152, 237
   O. 'Sunny Lady', 154, *155*
   O. 'Trewidden Pink', *237*
   O. 'Whirlygig', 151
oxalis, 143
ox-eye daisy, 31
oxygenating plants, 163

P

Pachysandra terminalis, 149
Paliurus spina-christi, 136
palms, *25*, *31*, 68
pansies, 36, *152*, 153
Papaver, 142
   P. somniferum, 237
Parrotia persica 'Pendula', 19
parsley, *173*, *174*, 175
parterres, 20
Parthenocissus, 28, 80, 131, 222
   P. tricuspidata 'Vietchii', *222*
Passiflora caerulea, 33, 35, 130, 148, 151, 222, *222*
   see also passion flower
passion flower, 87, 160
   see also Passiflora
paths, 20, 30–1, 48–9, *51*, *62*, 65, *66*
patios, *20*, *22*, 40, *80*, 120, 142
paulownia, 136
pavers, 56–7, 59, 61, *61*, 65
   cutting, 60
   patterns with, 60

paving, *14*, *15*, 16, *16*, *17*, 18, 19, *31*, 46–7, *51*, *52*, 61, 62
   laying, 58
   laying on mortar, 52
   laying on sand, 50–1
   planting in, 54–5, 143
peat, 186
Pelargonium, 9, *10*, *24*, 27, *27*, 37, 38, 48, *48*, *121*, *126*, 129, 140, *141*, 152, 171, 237
   P. 'Aphrodite', *155*
   P. graveolens, 152
   P. 'Pink Golden Harry Hieover', *237*
   cuttings, 197
Pennisetum alopecuroides, 139
   P. villosum, 248
Penstemon, 142, 231
   P. 'Andenken an Friedrich Hahn', 152
   P. 'Cherry', *231*
peony, tree, 136
perennials, 16, *16*, *17*, *21*, 27, *31*, 128
   architectural, 135
   foliage, 135
   for containers, 152
   tender, 141
pergolas, 14, 35, 41, 82, 84, 86–8, *86*, *87*, *88*, *113*, *130*
   erecting, 88–9
Perovskia, 142
   P. atriplicifolia 'Blue Spire', *144*
Persian ironwood, *see Parrotia*
Persicaria affinis, 231
   P.a. 'Superbum', *231*
   P. bistorta 'Superba', 163, 240, *241*
pests, 207
Petasites japonicus giganteus, 135
Petunia, *24*, *123*, 140, 152, 154, 237
   P. 'Celebrity White', *155*
Phalaris arundinacea, 163
   P.a. var picta 'Picta', *248*, 249
Philadelphus, 170
   P. 'Beauclerk', 169
   P. 'Manteau d'Hermine', 218, *218*
phlomis, 142
phlox, dividing, 198
phormium, 68, *134*, 136
Phygelius, 142
   P. 'Moonraker', 16
pickerel weed, 163, *164*
   see also Pontederia cordata
pinks, 142
   see also Dianthus
Pittosporum tenuifolium, 131
planting, 192
Pleioblastus, 132
   P. auricomis, 138, 249, *249*
   P. variegatus, 138, *138*
plumbago, 160
plumbago egg plant,

see Limnanthes douglasii
pointing, 53
Polemonium caeruleum, 232
polygonatum, 147
Polypodium vulgare, 147
Polystichum setiferum, 147, 249, *249*
Poncirus trifoliata, 136, 144
pond liner, 108
ponds, 19, *25*
   edgings, 105, 109
   filters, 111
   flexible liner, 108
   installing, 108
   plants, 164, 165
   pumps, 110
   rigid, 108
   see also water features
Pontederia, 107
   P. cordata, 34, *165*, 241, *241*
pot marigold, *see Calendula*
Potamogeton crispus, 163
potato vine, *see Solanum*
Potentilla, 142, 143
   P. fruticosa, 218
   pruning, *201*
primroses, *125*
   see also Primula
Primula, 152, 171
   P. florindae, 163
   P. japonica, 163, 241
      P.j. 'Miller's Crimson', *241*
   P. vulgaris, 232, *232*
   candelabra, 105, *163*
   drumstick, 162
privet, 79, 80
pruning, 200–5
   buddleja, 202, *205*
   conifers, 201
   early-flowering shrubs, 200, 202
   escallonia, *201*
   for coloured stems, 201, *202*
   forsythia, *202*
   fruit, 200
   hardy fuchsias, *205*
   heathers, 200, *202*
   hydrangeas, *204*
   late-flowering shrubs, 201, 204–5
   lavender, *204*
   potentilla, *201*
   roses, 200, *203*
   spiraea, 202
Prunus 'Amanogawa', 171
   P. padua, 171
   P. serrula, 212, *212*
   P. serrulata, 132
   P. 'Shirotae', 171
   P. subhirtella, 132
      P.s. 'Autumnalis', 132
      P.s. 'Pendula Rosea', 136

P. x *yedoensis*, 171
   P.y. 'Shidare Yoshino', 213
Pseudopanax crassifolia, 136
Pulmonaria, *28*, 149, 232
   P. longifolia, 146
   P. rubra 'David Ward', *232*
purple loosestrife, *see Lythrum salicaria*
purslane, 178, *179*
pushkinia, planting depth, 192
pyracantha, 38, 132
Pyrus salicifolia 'Pendula', 136, 213, *213*

Q

Quercus coccifera, 132

R

radicchio 'Pallo Rossa Bello', *179*
radishes, 172, 173
railway sleepers, 14, *14*, *15*, 49, 67, 96
raised beds, 14, *14*, 114
Ranunculus aquatilus, 163
   R. flammula, 241
raoulia, 143
red-hot poker, *see Kniphofia*
reed screens, *9*, 35
Rhamnus frangula 'Aspleniifolia', 136
Rheum palmatum, 107, 135, 162, 163, 241
Rhododendron, 68, 148
   R. luteum, 170
   R. yakushimanum, 134, 135, 151, 219, *219*
Rhus glabra 'Laciniata', 136
Robinia kelseyi, 132, 213
   R. pseudoacacia 'Lace Lady', 136
rock mountain juniper,
   see Juniperus scopulorum 'Skyrocket'
rock rose, *see Helianthemum* and *Cistus*
rocket, 173, 178, *179*
rodgersia, 107, 135, 147, 162
Romneya coulteri, 136, 144
roof gardens, *9*, 10, 32–5, *43*, *44*, 49, 67, *67*, 77, 97, 142, 150, 172
Rosa, 130, 151, 169
   R. Abraham Darby, 224, *224*
   R. 'Albertine, 87, 132
   R. Aloha, 224
   R. 'Bobby James', 169
   R. Cécile Brunner, 224, *224*
   R. China Doll, 224
   R. Dublin Bay, 224
   R. filipes 'Kiftsgate', 132, 169
   R. Gertrude Jeckyll, 224, *225*
   R. glauca, 84
   R. Graham Thomas, 225, *225*
   R. Iceberg, 225, *225*
   R. Little White Pet, 225
   R. 'Madame Alfred Carrière', 169
   R. 'Marigold', 169
   R. moyesii 'Geranium', 203